For Ann

John Unterecker * A reader's guide to

William Butler Yeats

OCTAGON BOOKS

A DIVISION OF FARRAR, STRAUS AND GIROUX

New York   1980

Reprinted 1971
Second Octagon printing 1977
Third Octagon printing 1980

OCTAGON BOOKS
A DIVISION OF FARRAR, STRAUS & GIROUX, INC.
19 Union Square West
New York, N.Y. 10003

LIBRARY OF CONGRESS CATALOG CARD NUMBER: 75-154661
ISBN 0-374-98048-9

Manufactured by Braun-Brumfield, Inc.
Ann Arbor, Michigan
Printed in the United States of America

Acknowledgments

Though my indebtedness extends to all Yeats scholars, I am particularly grateful for information and suggestions provided by Russell K. Alspach, William York Tindall, Frederick W. Dupee, and Vivian Mercier. Their insight in conversation or in correspondence has been of far greater value to me than these public thanks can indicate.

I wish also to thank my students who, in discussing Yeats, taught me what to look for, and particularly I wish to thank Judith Eisenstein, John S. Mann, Donald Miller, George Stade, and George Whiteside for bringing to my attention their perceptive readings of difficult texts.

Yeats scholars who are familiar with Hugh Kenner's article "The Sacred Book of the Arts" (*Irish Writing*, 1955) will realize that this study parallels and expands his notion that Yeats's work is best studied in context. My approach to Yeats's symbols is, as I have indicated in the text, similar to that developed by Donald Stauffer in *The Golden Nightingale* (Macmillan, 1949).

My debt to friends—particularly Margery Anderson, Roderick Craib, Bernard Heringman, Granville Hicks, Pearley C. Perkins, and George Weinheimer, all of whom have had to listen to me work out my ideas in conversation—is, though more elusive, no less real than my debt to Robert Parker who helped me search galleys for inconsistencies or Cecil Hemley whose cheerful encouragement has extended far beyond the call of editorial duty Least definable but most deeply felt of all is my debt to my mother, my aunt, and my wife, to whom this book is with much love dedicated.

Yeats, who valued personality, would have been sympathetic

to thanks of this sort. Since he was as well a good businessman, he would have understood my gratitude to the following persons and firms, each of whom has kindly allowed me to quote from copyrighted material: The Macmillan Company, for quotations from *The Autobiography of William Butler Yeats* (copyright 1916 and 1936; combined edition of August, 1938), W. B. Yeats's *Essays* (copyright, 1924), *The Collected Plays of W. B. Yeats* (copyright, 1934, 1952; new edition, 1953), W. B. Yeats's *A Vision* (copyright, 1938; "with the author's final revisions," 1956), *The Variorum Edition of the Poems of W. B. Yeats* (edited by Peter Allt and Russell K. Alspach, copyright 1903, 1906, 1907, 1912, 1916, 1918, 1919, 1924, 1928, 1931, 1933, 1934, 1935, 1940, 1944, 1945, 1946, 1950, 1956, 1957 by The Macmillan Company; copyright, 1940, by Georgie Yeats), Richard Ellmann's *Yeats, The Man and the Masks* (copyright, 1948), Virginia Moore's *The Unicorn* (copyright, 1954) and *The Letters of W. B. Yeats* (edited by Allan Wade and copyrighted 1953, 1954 by Anne Butler Yeats); Harcourt, Brace and Company for quotations from T. S. Eliot's *Essays Ancient and Modern*; Yale University Press for quotations from A. Norman Jeffares' *W. B. Yeats, Man and Poet*; Rupert Hart-Davis Limited, for most gracious permission to quote from *The Letters of W. B. Yeats*; and Routledge and Kegan Paul Limited for permission to quote from *W. B. Yeats and T. Sturge Moore: Their Correspondence* (edited by Ursula Bridge).

I am also grateful to be able to quote brief passages from T. S. Eliot's essay "The Music of Poetry," which appears in his *On Poetry and Poets* (Farrar, Straus & Cudahy); Yeats's *Letters on Poetry to Dorothy Wellesley* (Oxford University Press); Joseph Hone's *W. B. Yeats* (Macmillan); Joseph Hone's edition of J. B. Yeats's *Letters to His Son W. B. Yeats and Others* (Faber & Faber); and Richard Ellmann's *The Identity of Yeats* (Oxford University Press).

A note on the use and abuse of this book

A *Reader's Guide to William Butler Yeats* is intended to supplement Yeats's *Collected Poems* by providing for the reader some of the basic information he will need in order to come to an intelligent evaluation of those poems.

Perhaps the best way to use this book is to read through the first part, in which basic biographical information is given and Yeats's principal themes are examined, and then to turn to the poems themselves. Ideally, one should read Yeats's *Collected Poems* in much the same way one reads a novel, beginning at the beginning and going through the text in the order in which the author set it down. That is how Yeats wanted his poems read. Because poem is almost always linked to poem, a hit-or-miss sampling of Yeats frequently creates artificial difficulties. Similarly, a hit-or-miss sampling of the *Guide* is likely to be of little value.

An efficient way to use this *Guide* is, therefore, to attack the

Collected Poems section by section, postponing a reading of my comments on each section until *after* the poems in it have been read. An even more efficient way is to read a section of poems, then the corresponding section of the *Guide*, and then once again the same section of poems. The reader's object is, after all, familiarity with the poems, and this sort of an approach should give him that familiarity.

At the end of the *Guide* is a brief list of books about Yeats which I have found particularly valuable and a year-by-year chronology of some of the most significant events in Yeats's life.

I have followed the order of poems in Allt and Alspach's fine *Variorum Edition of the Poems of W. B. Yeats* which is itself based on the two-volume English Definitive Edition. The most recent American edition of the *Collected Poems* (that marked "Definitive Edition" and published by Macmillan) is also based on this text and is considerably more accurate than earlier editions.

Contents

I * THE MAJOR THEMES

II * THE POEMS

I * THE MAJOR THEMES

Very early in his career Yeats made up his mind to be a great poet and with a remarkable single-mindedness dedicated his life to that end. Like Shakespeare, who in the sonnets anticipates a posterity examining his works, or Whitman, who in "Crossing Brooklyn Ferry" still jolts readers by telling them that, dead and gone though he is, he had precisely them in mind when he wrote the revelatory words about his private living self that constitute the poem, Yeats set his main sights not only on that immediate future in which we read his words but as well on the distant future whose citizens will read them when we are dust.

In order to construct for that future a coherent body of work, Yeats wrote and rewrote poems, essays, and—when he had the chance—letters. (". . . if you are going to publish any more letters of mine," he once wrote Katharine Tynan, "please let me see them first. I may even, in defiance of all right conduct, improve them.")

His project, always, was to give his work organic unity. Everything, he felt, should fit into a whole.

For Yeats, part of the great writer's normal task was therefore revision, rearrangement, and deletion. In preparing for Bullen's 1908 edition of the eight-volume *Collected Works*, he reworked many of his poems and plays, rearranging the sequence of the poems so that they would construct harmonious units, dropping those that did not fit into the grand scheme. "It is of no use your going ahead with the poems till you have a list of the proper order of them from me," he wrote his publisher, ". . . I am not arranging any of these books on a chronological system." And later, shortly before the Collected Edition finally appeared, he explained to Bullen, "Why I have been so insistent upon my revisions etc. in this expensive edition is that I know I must get my general personality and the total weight of my work into people's minds, as a preliminary to new work. I know that I have just reached a time when I can give up constant revisions but not till the old is right." He did not, as a matter of fact, ever give up those revisions. In 1930, anticipating a projected "Edition de Luxe" of all his work, he wrote a joyous letter to his old friend Mrs. Shakespear, the mother of Ezra Pound's wife, "Months of re-writing! What happiness!"

If we bear in mind Yeats's own consciousness of his work as an architectural structure, section fitting into section to clarify and strengthen the total design, a great deal that—piecemeal—seems arbitrary or illogical ultimately makes sense. Political, occult, autobiographical, historical material was all carefully organized and reorganized as Yeats's master plan for his work evolved. Recurring mythological, imaginary, and living figures—often paired as opposites (Oisin and St. Patrick, Michael Robartes and Owen Aherne, Maud Gonne and Yeats himself)—lace together a poetry and prose further unified by sets of interrelated images and symbols, themes and plots.

But what was that elaborate structure, the ideal Collected Works Yeats was always striving to put together, intended to represent? Yeats was never quite explicit, and my answer is therefore only one man's—I think good—guess. The Collected Works were, I believe, to be what T. S. Eliot would call an objective correlative for the entirety of Yeats's life and thought, a kind of literary equivalent for the total experience of a man, a total experience shaped, through art, into a form less perishable than flesh, a form freed from accident. (The golden bird singing at the end of "Sailing to Byzantium" was an image for such art.) By hedging in his poetry and plays with revelatory essays, autobiographical statements, and a theory of history (A Vision), Yeats helped make that central design clear. "I have finished a little philosophical book," Yeats wrote his father in 1917. ". . . I shall publish it in a new book of verse, side by side, I think. Reviewers find it easier to write if they have ideas to write about—ideas or a narrative like that in my Reveries." Using his prose, therefore, to construct frameworks of ideas and facts which would help make his poetry meaningful, Yeats struggled—as publicly as possible—to integrate his life and work, to construct a kind of vast Gestalt in which his experience, his prose statements, and his art would unite in one complex but vivid thing.

As he prepared for death, his letters were filled with talk of "completion." He wanted to write one more essay, this one explaining his "private" philosophy, a kind of personal counterpart to the "public" theory of history and metaphysics which he regarded A Vision to be. In writing that last essay, he felt, he could make clear the indivisible pattern of his life and work, "explain" his studies, bring his life to its "completion":

> . . . I know for certain that my time will not be long. I have put away everything that can be put away that I may speak what I have to speak, and I find 'expression' is a part of 'study.' In two or three weeks—I am now idle that I may rest after writing much verse— I will begin to write my most fundamental thoughts and the arrangement of thought which I am convinced will complete my studies. I am happy, and I think full of an energy, of an energy I had despaired of. It seems to me that I have found what I wanted.

When I try to put all into a phrase I say, 'Man can embody truth but he cannot know it.' I must embody it in the completion of my life.

Yeats did not live to write down that "arrangement of thought." Four weeks after he had written the letter to Lady Elizabeth Pelham which I have in part quoted, Yeats died, his projected essay unfinished, the final Collected Edition still unpublished. Yeats had, however, completed his work on a last revision of the poems, and his final texts have been used for the 1949 English *Definitive Edition*, the great *Variorum Edition* of Allt and Alspach, and the most recent American editions of the *Collected Poems*; and surviving prefaces and letters let us reconstruct with a good deal of accuracy an approximation of what he wanted the final body of his work to resemble.

Because he did see his work as one organic whole and because particular poems and plays are most easily understood in terms of that whole, Yeats is best approached not in terms of this poem or that but rather as if his entire output constituted (as it almost does) a single work of art. Our project, as we read him, is synthesis; and though we should know the poems, plays, and essays as separate entities, though we should see clearly the internal structure of each—the thing that makes it a work of art—we should also look for relationships between poem and poem, the hundreds of carefully engineered elements in the great design he attempted to construct. "Talent," as twenty-one year old Yeats noted in a manuscript book, "perceives differences, Genius unity." When we withdraw far enough from individual works to see Yeats's entire production as that unified thing, one comprehensive work of art, then we begin to realize that it is the thematic and imagistic links —bits of information, ideas, and images that echo and reecho from work to work—which give it its final shape.

THE USE OF BIOGRAPHY

Perhaps the most obvious of these organizational devices is that set of very personal references which, especially toward the end of his life, Yeats drew on in building for himself a public personality. "You that would judge me," he pointed out in "The Municipal Gallery Revisited,"

> do not judge alone
> This book or that, come to this hallowed place
> Where my friends' portraits hang and look thereon;
> Ireland's history in their lineaments trace;
> Think where man's glory most begins and ends,
> And say my glory was I had such friends.

In that part of his diary written in 1909 and published as "Estrangement" in *Dramatis Personae*, Yeats stated the same theme in cold prose: "Friendship is all the house I have."

His friends, as Yeats notes in the Preface to *The Trembling of the Veil*, another one of the autobiographies written, in part at least, as a kind of companion volume to the personal poetry, "were artists and writers and certain among them men of genius, and the life of a man of genius, because of his greater sincerity, is often an experiment that needs analysis and record. At least my generation so valued personality that it thought so." But even earlier, almost from the beginning of his career, Yeats had worked out a theory of the personal as a crucial element in poetry. Early in his twenties, he felt "we should write out our thoughts in as nearly as possible the language we thought them in, as though in a letter to an intimate friend. We should not disguise them in any way; for our lives give them force as the lives of people in plays give force to their words." The great poets, Yeats argued, employed always "personal utterance," dramatizing—sometimes overtly—their own lives. "If I can be sincere," he used to think to himself, "and make my language natural, and without becoming discursive, like a novelist, and so indiscreet and prosaic . . . I shall, if good luck or bad luck make my life interesting, be a great poet; for it will be no longer a matter of literature at all."

His effort to capitalize on a life made interesting not only by luck but by good management gives us such great work as the poems written about Augusta Gregory's son, Robert Gregory; all those involving Maud Gonne; the poems celebrating those men— among them Maud Gonne's husband—who were executed as a result of the Easter, 1916 rising; and all that rich late autobiographical poetry, "The Circus Animals' Desertion," for instance, and "Under Ben Bulben." These poems, saved from sentimentality by a tone of impersonal evaluation, demand that the reader know at least a few facts concerning the figures they celebrate. Yeats's own stitching-together of the lives of his friends can be found in the autobiographical volumes which—in effect—provide necessary footnotes to the poems. Joseph Hone's biography fills in some of the details Yeats neglected. Yeats's *Letters*, brilliantly edited by Allan Wade, provide unofficial backstage views of the public man Yeats was constructing.

I do not mean to suggest that Yeats chose his friends with an eye to their ultimate utility as figures in a designed world which had as its central element his own figure. He loved and admired his friends and valued them not as literary material but as persons. Yet he recognized that if he were to make his art great and his life meaningful through "personal utterance," the persons he celebrated had to have or to be given enough fame to make their names household words for his readers. Dante, who stuck enemies in Hell and Beatrice in Heaven and who, in so doing, transformed biography to art, was very much in Yeats's mind as his poetry became both increasingly personal and at the same time increasingly objective.

Though Yeats linked poem to poem through reference to a great many relatives and friends, the most crucial figures form a relatively small group.

Of his relatives, an astrologer uncle, George Pollexfen, and

Yeats's father, the painter John Butler Yeats, are probably most important.

Yeats's father, a meticulously careful portrait painter who, according to his son, spoiled his paintings by working far too long at them and who was never able to charge the high prices he felt his art deserved, was, though unsuccessful financially, an eloquent, stimulating conversationalist. Words, though casually spoken, were as much his medium as his son's; and Yeats's published memories of childhood are dominated by his father's fluent, sometimes overbearing, talk. John Butler Yeats preached—sometimes hours on end—a gospel of beauty and atheism, read aloud (at breakfast) all the most passionate scenes from Shakespeare, and saw to it that his son accompanied him on visits to a very wide circle of friends, almost all writers and painters. No wonder that years after his father died Yeats found himself still dreaming of him—sometimes as a stool and sometimes as the eyepiece of a telescope.

Believing firmly, as his son later, that the artist's subject matter is inextricably knotted to his life ("A man can only paint the life he has lived!") and that the greatest artist is a man passionately devoted to his friends (Shakespeare, he once wrote Yeats, must have been "very lovable and fond of his friends," and then, underlining the words, added, ". . . *he couldn't have been otherwise. How else could he have written his dramas?*"), Yeats's father drummed into his young son aesthetic principles which, at first rejecting, Yeats eventually modified into some of the most basic structural elements in his own system of aesthetics.

As late as 1921, self-exiled in New York, an old man of eighty-two, Yeats's father was still trying to shape the career of his admiring but recalcitrant son:

. . . When is your poetry at its best? I challenge all the critics if it is not when its wild spirit of your imagination is wedded to concrete fact. Had you stayed with me and not left me for Lady Gregory, and her friends and associations, you would have loved and adored concrete life for which as I know you have a real affection. . . . The moment you touch however lightly on concrete fact, how alert you are! and how attentive we your readers become!

. . . .

Am I talking wildly? Am I senile? I don't think so, for I would have said the same any time these 20 or 30 years. The best thing in life is the game of life, and some day a poet will find this out. I hope you will be that poet. It is easier to write poetry that is far away from life, but it is *infinitely more exciting* to write the poetry of life—and it is what the whole world is crying out for as pants the hart for the water brook. I bet it is what your wife wants—ask her. She will know what I mean and drive it home. I have great confidence in her. Does she lack the courage to say it?

Ultimately, of course, Yeats's work did become concrete and was used, though not perhaps as his father had intended, to fit John Butler Yeats, along with John O'Leary, Standish O'Grady, Augusta Gregory, and Maud Gonne into that splendid catalogue of "Olympians," his poem "Beautiful Lofty Things."

In spite of the fact that Yeats showed little public affection for his father (who complained to his daughter Lily "I wish Willie . . . did not sometimes treat me as if I was a black beetle"), their debates over the artist's function shaped his mind, gave precision to his ideas.

One subject, however, he could not discuss with his father: that was the occult. When the old Fenian leader John O'Leary, knowing that Yeats's family was concerned about his investigations in mysticism, suggested that Yeats might profitably give up those investigations, Yeats's answer was unequivocal: magic was the business of his life.

. . . Now as to Magic. It is surely absurd to hold me 'weak' or otherwise because I chose to persist in a study which I decided deliberately four or five years ago to make, next to my poetry, the most important pursuit of my life. Whether it be, or be not, bad for my health can only be decided by one who knows what magic is and not at all by any amateur. The probable explanation however of your somewhat testy postcard is that you were out at Bedford

Park and heard my father discoursing about my magical pursuits out of the immense depths of his ignorance as to everything that I am doing and thinking. If I had not made magic my constant study I could not have written a single word of my Blake book, nor would *The Countess Kathleen* have ever come to exist. The mystical life is the centre of all that I do and all that I think and all that I write.

If Yeats's father could not help him in this interest, his astrologer uncle George Pollexfen could. Together they performed cabalistic experiments at Rosses Point where George had a little house in which he spent his summers. Yeats, manipulating cards on which were drawn colored symbols, was delighted to discover that he could evoke parallel visions in himself, in George, and in George's second-sighted servant, Mary Battle. Introverted, melancholy, in every respect the opposite of Yeats's father who had once noted that even as a boy he had been attracted to George as an opposite, George Pollexfen became for Yeats an unforgettable figure. Linking him to his father, Yeats may have formed from their antithetical personalities one of his images of the impossible whole man he wanted to be: an intellectual of feeling, an isolated man whose intense friendships suggest to him patterns of order for his artistic achievement.

Most of the men Yeats came to know well were writers and politicians, and almost all of them—because of the nature of the world in which they were born, Yeats later came to feel—after much promise, failed to achieve what had seemed in their youths certain greatness. The writers Lionel Johnson and Ernest Dowson whose dissipations destroyed them, Oscar Wilde who was trapped by his own vanity into public disgrace, the mystic George Russell (AE) who wrote no great book, Yeats felt, because he had become a visionary saint entangled in mundane and practical affairs, the occultist MacGregor Mathers whom fanaticism drove half-mad, and John O'Leary (who, reduced to three Fenian disciples, cast out one) were all, in Yeats's eyes, men whom circumstances had defeated before their talent could perfect itself.

Only one of his friends, Yeats felt, had managed, though dying young and hounded by a public that could not value his work, to accomplish great art. That man, John Synge, Yeats recognized as an authentic genius, the only writer he could speak to freely as an equal. "We should unite stoicism, asceticism and ecstasy," Synge told Yeats in Paris. "Two of them have often come together, but the three never." Yeats, who took Synge's words to heart, could also give good advice: "I urged him to go to the Aran Islands and find a life that had never been expressed in literature, instead of a life where all had been expressed."

Yeats gathered images from which to construct his soul. And if, as he studied the men he knew, those men sometimes became transformed to images—his father to gregarious aesthetician, George Pollexfen to introverted mystic, John Synge to proud literary genius—the images of all those warring personalities were all, Yeats realized, aspects of himself. So too were the images—from which he also constructed patterns of order—of those women who are celebrated in his poetry.

Maud Gonne is, of course, the most famous of those necessary ladies. An intense, passionate nationalist; beautiful, eloquent, and domineering, she swept him off his feet when on January 30, 1889, ostensibly visiting his father with an introduction from O'Leary but actually, as Elizabeth, Yeats's younger sister noted, calling "on Willie, of course," she praised his poetry and became for him from that moment on the prototype of feminine beauty, "A Helen," a "Pallas Athene." "Her complexion was luminous, like that of apple blossom through which the light falls, and I remember her standing that first day by a great heap of such blossoms in the window." Four days after that meeting, in a letter to Ellen O'Leary, Yeats celebrated her conquest: "Did I tell you how much I admire Miss Gonne? She will make many converts to her political belief. If she said the world was flat or the moon an old caubeen tossed up into the sky I would be proud to be of her party."

Though Yeats tried hard to make himself enough of a nationalist to satisfy her thirst for revolution, though he focused his poetry on Irish themes and joined her in public meetings where "her beauty, backed by her great stature, could instantly affect an assembly," though he wrote as a vehicle for her politics and her acting *Cathleen ni Houlihan,* and though for more than thirteen years he courted her unsuccessfully (a courtship that ended only when she married Major John MacBride in 1903), his devotion, as he pointed out in *Dramatis Personae,* "might as well have been offered to an image in a milliner's window, or to a statue in a museum." And it is as a statue, in "A Bronze Head," that he finally commemorated her who, in bronze reduced to a "dark tombhaunter," had once been a person of supernatural intensity, of gentleness, and of "wildness": ". . . who can tell/ Which of her forms has shown her substance right?"

Yeats saw her as destroyed by a kind of Irish nationalism, revolutionary and hysterical, a nationalism in his mind both modern and vulgar but which, in spite of all its shoddy trappings, created an opportunity for herosim. Because he felt she was fated by personality and her times to act out a role of tragic, unnecessary violence, he watched fascinated as she chose one of the two possible parts he felt she was doomed to play: "She had to choose (perhaps all women must) between broomstick and distaff and she has chosen the broomstick—I mean the witches' hats."

If Maud Gonne became ideal beauty wrecked in service of an unworthy cause, Olivia Shakespear, to whom Yeats had been writing when he set his heroine on that metaphorical broomstick, was woman as confidant. Yeats had first met her through her cousin Lionel Johnson in the spring of 1894. The young wife of an elderly solicitor, she found in Yeats, as he in her, a person who could discuss literature and ideas. Of his close friends the one least publicly celebrated in his poetry and in his autobiographical prose, yet the woman perhaps most intimately known, she was one of the few persons with whom he could be completely relaxed. Though he destroyed many of his letters when they were returned to him after her death by her son-in-law, Ezra Pound, those casual gentle notes that survive show Yeats in a very different character from the aggressive figure he was laboring to make of himself. Temperamentally precisely opposed to Maud Gonne's flamboyant brilliance, Olivia Shakespear was a lovely generous woman of great human warmth. She too fit into Yeats's pattern, helped complete his personality through the affection, sympathy and comradeship that Maud Gonne was never able to provide. When three and a half months before his own death he heard she had died, a part of his world died. "Yesterday morning I had tragic news," he wrote Dorothy Wellesley:

> Olivia Shakespear has died suddenly. For more than forty years she has been the centre of my life in London and during all that time we have never had a quarrel, sadness sometimes but never a difference. When I first met her she was in her late twenties but in looks a lovely young girl. When she died she was a lovely old woman. You would have approved her. She came of a long line of soldiers and during the last war thought it her duty to stay in London through all the air raids. She was not more lovely than distinguished—no matter what happened she never lost her solitude. . . . For the moment I cannot bear the thought of London. I will find her memory everywhere.

Maud Gonne offered Yeats subject matter for poetry, the "interesting" life he had hoped for, and Olivia Shakespear offered him repose. But Augusta Gregory gave him a time and place to work. For twenty summers, from 1897 until he rebuilt his tower at Ballylee, Yeats was her guest at Coole Park where, under her sometimes strict supervision, he ate and wrote well. She served, however, as more than patron. "John Synge, I and Augusta Gregory," he wrote in "The Municipal Gallery Revisited," "thought/All that we did, all that we said or sang/ Must come from contact with the soil. . . . We three alone in modern times had brought/ Everything down to that sole test again,/ Dream of the noble and the beggar-man." Gathering folklore with Yeats in the peasant cottages on her estate and in the Galway neighborhood, she became for him an image of aristocratic courtesy, too well-bred not to

be humble, too assured not to be simple and direct in speech. Together they planned and organized the theatre societies which
eventually became the Abbey Theatre; they collaborated on plays;
they worked together in furthering her nephew Hugh Lane's ill-
fated Dublin picture gallery. Yeats came, especially after the death
of her son Robert in the first World War, to think of himself as
a kind of son adopted by her not from necessity but from choice.
"She has been to me mother, friend, sister and brother. I cannot realize the world without her—she brought to my wavering
thoughts steadfast nobility." He praised her extravagantly: "Her
literary style became in my ears the best written by woman." "I
doubt if I should have done much with my life but for her firm-
ness and her care." Both her estate and her person seemed to
Yeats a survival of an aristocratic past richer than our present,
and when she died, he wrote Olivia Shakespear a letter describing
"a queer Dublin sculptor" who, coming "to pay his respects," had
walked through the house until he came to the family portraits:
". . . and after standing silent said 'All the nobility of earth.' I
felt he did not mean it for that room alone but for lost tradition.
How much of my own verse has not been but the repetition of
those words."

When in the poem "Friends" Yeats honored the "Three women
that have wrought/ What joy is in my days" he was trying to assign Lady Gregory, Mrs. Shakespear, and Maud Gonne precise
places in that design of personality which, made public, would let
him survive himself. By defining and redefining himself in terms
of these people and those other men and women closest to him,
Yeats felt he could reveal to his perceptive reader that "Unity of
Being" at the core of his many-faceted self.

THE DOCTRINE OF THE MASK

Though Yeats was of course right in believing that his genius
lay in "personal utterance" he recognized that personal utterance

alone could not organize a body of lyric poetry and drama into the organic structure he hoped to build. For one thing, personal utterance, as he had discovered in his earliest experiments in verse, is beset always by the danger of sentimentality which leads poetry away from that reality the poetry would deal with to various kinds of self-pity and self-deception.

His problem, therefore, was to discover a technique by which the personal could somehow be objectified, be given the appearance of impersonal "truth" and yet retain the emotive force of privately felt belief. A partial solution was the theory of the Mask which, perhaps compounded from popular psychology on one hand and occult material on the other, was used by Yeats to make public his secret selves.

We are all familiar enough with the false faces we wear in the ordinary business of life, the unreal and different persons we present to parents, teachers, employers, lovers, and tax collectors. Most of us, little concerned with truth, present still another false face to ourselves, "the real me," and live and die happy in our deception. The writer interested in reality, however, must make a more difficult decision: he must choose one as genuinely real or, if he is like Yeats, find ultimate reality not in any one of them but in their interaction.

"Reality," for Yeats, is neither to be found in that buried self which directs and orders a man's life or in its Mask, the anti-self, but in the product born of their struggle. Extroverts, Yeats felt, must flee their Masks. Introverts—painters, writers, musicians; all creative men—must recognize their own proper Masks, ideal opposites, and in trying to become those nearly impossible other selves create the dramatic tensions from which art arises.

The doctrine of the Mask erects, therefore, on the artist's personality a kind of private mythology in which the individual struggles to become that which is most unlike himself: the introvert artist puts on an extrovert Mask; the subjective man assumes the Mask of the man of action. And because mythology and history, reducing men to types, mere images, simpler figures than flesh and blood men, does offer us patterns, we can, if we will, choose our Mask from those stored up by the past. A modern introvert's Mask —say Yeats's—might in many ways resemble one of the great stone faces of myth—say Cuchulain's face, a hero striding out of the remote legendary Irish past, a man of action, great fighter and great lover.

Convinced that "every passionate man . . . is, as it were, linked with another age, historical or imaginary, where alone he finds images that rouse his energy," Yeats speculated that perhaps his doctrine of the Mask might be extended from person to country and so give direction not only to an individual but a people. "I, that my native scenery might find imaginary inhabitants, half-planned a new method and a new culture." A modern country's Mask, he felt—say Ireland's—might resemble that which is most unlike modern Ireland, the Ireland of priest, merchant, and politician, might resemble "an Ireland/ The poets have imagined, terrible and gay," might, in fact, resemble Cuchulain's Ireland, a land of reckless heroes:

> Have not all races had their first unity from a mythology, that marries them to rock and hill? We had in Ireland imaginative stories, which the uneducated classes knew and even sang, and might we not make those stories current among the educated classes, rediscovering for the work's sake what I have called "the applied arts of literature," the association of literature, that is, with music, speech, and dance; and at last, it might be, so deepen the political passion of the nation that all, artist and poet, craftsman and day-labourer would accept a common design?

This common design—this great image—was the myth-founded Mask of Ireland which, being opposite to the modern world, was the Mask for the modern world, "of all states of mind not impossible, the most difficult to that man, race, or nation." Yet if the modern Yeats, the modern Irishman, or modern Ireland chose to put it on, from that Hegelian tension of opposites a greatness might be synthesized, in the union of opposites a new kind of nation might be born:

> Nations, races, and individual men are unified by an image, or bundle of images, symbolical or evocative of the state of mind, which is of all states of mind not impossible, the most difficult to that man, race or nation; because only the greatest obstacle that can be contemplated without despair, rouses the will to full intensity. . . . I had seen Ireland in my own time turn from the bragging rhetoric and gregarious humour of O'Connell's generation and school, and offer herself to the solitary and proud Parnell as to her anti-self, buskin following hard on sock, and I had begun to hope, or to half-hope, that we might be the first in Europe to seek unity as deliberately as it had been sought by theologian, poet, sculptor, architect, from the eleventh to the thirteenth century.

In spite of the fact that his hope for an Ireland united in the contemplation of a heroic mask has not been realized, the doctrine of the Mask helped Yeats write a poetry firmer, far more intense than his early verse. Seeking to be what he was not, Yeats disciplined himself and his art to form: "I take pleasure alone in those verses where it seems to me I have found something hard and cold, some articulation of the Image, which is the opposite of all that I am in my daily life, and all that my country is." "Style, personality—deliberately adopted and therefore a mask—," Yeats decided finally, "is the only escape from the hot-faced bargainers and the money-changers."

SYSTEMS: OCCULT AND VISIONARY

Though his doctrine of the Mask offered Yeats a technique by which he could strengthen his own personality and shape his art, and though, for a while, it seemed to him possible that through Irish literary societies, the Abbey Theatre, and a revived interest both in Irish mythology and in the great historical figures of eighteenth-century Ireland, particularly Swift and Berkeley, Modern Ireland itself might put on a heroic Mask and so rise to greatness, the doctrine of the Mask alone could not make sense for him of what seemed essentially a senseless world. Through the Mask great things might be accomplished, but to what avail in a disordered universe? If those unities he fought for—Unity of Being, Unity of Image (the Mask), and Unity of Culture—were to be meaningful they had to be achieved in a coherent cosmos. For him to become the great poet he hoped to be, the man who had integrated all things to himself and, through the catalytic triumph of his art, expressed them in imperishable form, it was imperative that he discover the secret pattern of those things.

With the aid of magic, in defense of which he had denounced his father in that angry letter to O'Leary, Yeats hoped to locate that secret pattern. By "magic," Yeats meant the whole area of occult knowledge. That and the equally secret patterns of his art were Yeats's lifelong obsessions. "I am an artist's son and must take some work as the whole end of life," he had thought as a boy. But he had thought, too, that art would be of little value if it did not represent an order greater than itself: "My father's unbelief had set me thinking about the evidence of religion and I weighed the matter perpetually with great anxiety, for I did not think I could live without religion."

Since his father's convincing arguments made formal religions impossible for Yeats, he spent a lifetime investigating informal and exotic ones. Everywhere, he felt, was incontrovertible evidence of an invisible but eminently active spiritual world. He had only to chart its geography.

His "secret fanaticism" blossomed first into boyhood investigations of folk belief in Sligo where, out of his father's reach on summer holidays, he could wander about raths and fairy hills. By the time he was ready to celebrate his twentieth birthday, he had —with his schoolfellow George Russell—become a founding member of the "Dublin Hermetic Society" which, on June 16, 1885, met for the first time. Yeats was chairman of that meeting From that point his interest in the occult never wavered.

In 1887 his family moved to London. As soon as they were settled, Yeats, armed with a letter of introduction from his friend the young Dublin Theosophist leader Charles Johnston, went to call on the founder of the movement, Madame Blavatsky, who, herself newly arrived in London, was in the process of organizing a London Blavatsky Lodge of the Theosophical Society. He had already read deeply in Theosophical literature but had been made skeptical by Richard Hodgson's denunciation of Madame Blavatsky's activities in India. Hodgson, sent to India by The Society for Psychical Research, had been confidently expected to return singing her praises. Instead he had come back with reports from her servants of secret panels and had labeled her a fraud. Yeats was, nevertheless, more than half-persuaded of the validity of her claims and was anxious to meet her. She proved to be everything he had anticipated: "A great passionate nature, a sort of female Dr. Johnson, impressive I think to every man or woman who had themselves any richness," she was "almost always full of gaiety that, unlike the occasional joking of those about her, was illogical and incalculable and yet always kindly and tolerant." Yeats immediately joined the society.

Very soon afterwards he met MacGregor Mathers, the translator of *The Kabbala Unveiled*, and through his invitation became a member of the Hermetic Students of the Golden Dawn, another secret organization similar in structure to the Blavatsky Lodge but one which, unlike the Theosophical Society, encouraged its members to practice "magic" through alchemical and psychic experiments.

In both societies and others like them that Yeats later investigated, the students attempted to purify themselves through meditation on the secret wisdom revealed in such books as Madame Blavatsky's *Isis Unveiled*, A. P. Sinnett's *Esoteric Buddhism*, and Eliphas Lévi's *The History of Magic*. Their labors were, partly because of the nearly impenetrable prose in which some of the books were written, Herculean. These texts tried, through a system of interlocking symbolism derived in part from Eastern religions and in part from the Jewish and Christian Apocrypha, to present to their students the primary patterns through which everything can be apprehended. Such patterns, linking—in the famous formula of Hermes—that which is above to that which is below, gave those who contemplated them peace.

Because Yeats does draw consistently on cabalistic, neo-Platonist, and—late in his career—oriental material, an example of the kind of work he studied is perhaps in order. My example, drawn from the Cabala, will not please Platonists who find their systems more coherent. Yeats, on the other hand, interested in reconciliation, took what he could from every discipline he investigated.

A good illustration of the sort of thing Yeats found both poetically useful and emotionally satisfying is one of the basic images of the Cabala, the ten Sephiroth, emanations of that which is above, which through various letter and number relationships can be combined into an almost infinite series of designs. Usually they are arranged in the pattern of the "tree of life," itself familiar enough through the Bible. But the Hermetic Students—as other occultists—struggled to penetrate its secret nature. Mathers, who wrote what well may be the most tortured prose of modern times, presents it in this fashion:

> In their totality and unity the ten Sephiroth represent the archetypal man, ADM QDMVN, *Adam Qadmon*, the Protogonos. In looking at the Sephiroth constituting the first triad, it is evident that they represent the intellect; and hence this triad is called the intellectual world, OVLM MVShKL, *Olahm Mevshekal*. The second triad corresponds to the moral world, OVLM MVRGSh, *Olahm Vorgash*. The third represents power and stability, and is therefore called the material world, OVLM HMVTBO, *Olahm Ha-Mevetbau*. These three aspects are called the faces, ANPIN, *Anpin*. Thus is the tree of life, OTz ChIIM, *Otz Chaiim*, formed: the first triad being placed above, the second and third below, in such a manner that the three masculine Sephiroth are on the right,

the three feminine on the left, whilst the four uniting Sephiroth occupy the centre. This is the qabalistical "tree of life," on which all things depend. There is considerable analogy between this and the tree Yggdrasil of the Scandinavians.

This great tree, paralleling the body of Adam, united the Tree of Knowledge and the Tree of Life into one image: "The tree of life is the united body, and the tree of knowledge of good and evil the separated." Filling the branches of this multiform, ever-branching image are a host of birds. At this point Mathers' prose almost completely disintegrates, but Yeats, who refers to the passage obliquely in his poetry and explicitly in his prose, was in pursuit of dominant imagery that could make meaningful a confusing world and so found it useful. From such unpromising material as the following passage from *The Kabbalah Unveiled* came "The Two Trees," frequent bird and tree references in Yeats's later poetry and plays, and at least hints for the structure of *A Vision:*

> The tree which is mitigated (that is, the path of the kingdom or Schechinah, which is the tree of the knowledge of good and evil, which in itself existeth from the judgments, but is mitigated by the bridegroom through the influx of mercies) resideth within (within the shells; because the kingdom hath its dominion over all things, and its feet descend into death). In its branches (in the inferior worlds) the birds lodge and build their nests (the souls and the angels have their place). . . . This is the tree which hath two paths (for thus is this passage restored in the corrected Codex) for the same end (namely, good and evil, because it is the tree of the knowledge of good and evil) . . .

Mathers goes on to point out that the Cabala gathers up the by-now-enormous symbol into a hymn to procreation in which all relationships are resolved in generation. But here, torn between the phallus and the censor's blue pencil, his nerve gives out. He translates what he dares and encourages the curious to study Latin. Suffice to say that the tree's double aspect continues but it now symbolizes man, God, and "all things" joined "face to face" with all that is female. From this union, "in the excellence of the Sabbath, all things become one body."

Like Éliphas Lévi, whose work he also studied, Yeats felt that it is needless even to consider "the views, or rather the simplicity of those who take everything literally and believe that knowledge and life were once manifested under the form of trees; let us confess rather and only to the deep meaning of sacred symbols. The Tree of Knowledge does actually inflict death when its fruit is eaten; that fruit is the adornment of this world; those golden apples are the glitter of the earth."

What was the value of such study for Yeats? It gave him, first of all, a supply of imagery that he drew on for the rest of his life. Stocked with multiple, antithetical, and secret meanings for trees, birds, roses, stars, and wells, Yeats delighted in constructing puzzles which had not only clear overt "meanings" but which could as well be rightly interpreted in an almost unlimited number of ways. Because all occult symbols linked ultimately to a universal harmony, any consistent interpretation of one of them was "right" since it in turn led to that harmony. The only danger, as Yeats frequently pointed out, is that the reader is likely to limit the symbol's meaning and so throw it into the area of allegory.

Yeats's cabalistic studies, as later his investigations of Platonism, spiritualism, and oriental philosophy, were as well an effort on his part to map out the "as above" part of Hermes' formula. Only, Yeats believed, if he could discover the design of the world of spirit would the pattern of the world of matter in which he felt himself to be trapped make sense. The occult, imprecise yet furiously logical, offered systems of order which brought those two worlds close to each other, so close as a matter of fact that great adepts could penetrate the veil and discover from the spirits beyond clues to the essential nature of things.

Frustrated by studies which teased his intellect, which hovered always on the brink of that great insight he desired, Yeats was startled to find what seemed success where he had least anticipated it. After the execution of her husband following the Easter rising of 1916, Yeats had again proposed to Maud Gonne, again been rejected, had proposed to her adopted daughter Iseult and had been rejected, and, baffled and lonely, had very suddenly proposed to and married Georgie Hyde-Lees. Four days after their marriage, in an effort to lighten her husband's depression, Mrs. Yeats undertook automatic writing. Yeats, intrigued, was convinced she was in touch with the world of spirits and urged her to daily efforts. For over a year she labored at her work, filling notebook after notebook. Yeats codified and arranged them. By 1919 Mrs. Yeats was exhausted; but Yeats, at last in touch with supersensual reality, pleaded with her to go on. Luckily for both of them, her spirit communicator suggested that a method less fatiguing might be discovered; several months later, Mrs. Yeats began to talk in her sleep, and Yeats, who was now able to ask questions and so direct the area of exploration, took over the work of writing.

From the hundreds of notebooks, *A Vision* evolved. Yeats worked on the first version of the book for seven years, finally publishing it in 1925. In the thirties, dissatisfied with that first draft, he rewrote the book from beginning to end, publishing it in its final form in 1937.

That final book represents Yeats's effort to construct a metaphor for the correlation of all things. Ultimately it became for Yeats not reality but the pattern of reality. It was "my lunar parable," "a vision," "an arrangement." "Some will ask whether I believe in the actual existence of my circuits of sun and moon." Anticipating his critics, Yeats answered carefully, "To such a question I can but answer that if sometimes, overwhelmed by miracle as all men must be when in the midst of it, I have taken such periods literally, my reason has soon recovered; and now that the system stands out clearly in my imagination I regard them as stylistic arrangements of experience comparable to the cubes in the drawings of Wyndham Lewis and to the ovoids in the sculpture of Brancusi. They have helped me to hold in a single thought reality and justice."

The 305 page explication of that single thought relies very heavily on two crucial diagrams. Both diagrams are expansions of the fundamental idea Yeats had worked out years before in the theory of the Mask.

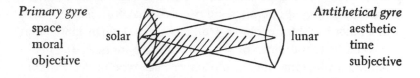

Primary gyre
   space   solar   lunar   aesthetic

Antithetical gyre

space   aesthetic
moral   time
objective   subjective

The first, and simpler, diagram is that of a pair of interpenetrating cones which Yeats called "gyres." These represent the antithetical elements in every man's, nation's, and era's nature. Each of them contains always, in cross-section, some element of the other, though in no two cross-sections will the proportions be identical. Thus every man is to some extent objective, though he may be predominantly subjective. All events are determined by space and time, though one or the other may be more crucial. (The invention of the atomic bomb could have taken place anywhere but not at any time—too many historical events were involved in making it possible precisely when it took place.) By grouping those characteristics which were essentially physical in his Primary gyre and those which he regarded as essentially spiritual in his Antithetical gyre, Yeats had a convenient diagrammatic structure to measure personality, the temper of the times, or almost anything else. In terms of his doctrine of the Mask, Antithetical gyre is Primary gyre's Mask and vice versa; lunar artist's Mask is that of solar moral man; a world of facts is opposed to a world of emotion, etc. As long as one is predominantly on one side of the diagram or the other, all is well; but the man whose nature intersects the diagram midway is torn by opposing forces greater than himself and is consequently incapable either of action or of resolute mind.

A refinement of the interpenetrating cones is Yeats's diagram of The Great Wheel which, equipped with twenty-eight spokes in commemoration of the lunar month, corresponds to all things. These twenty-eight spokes constitute the phases of the moon and represent to Yeats twenty-eight basic types of personality, each arranged on the wheel opposite its Mask, that personality of all possible types most different from it. Because Yeats saw all human life as a mingling of opposites, he declared that for phase 1 (dark of the moon) and for phase 15 (full moon) no human representative could be found, since these, constituting pure types (at phase 1 the impossibly pure moral, objective, solar type of the Primary gyre with no coloration of its opposite; at phase 15 the impossibly pure aesthetic, subjective, lunar type of the Antithetical gyre) could not exist in fact. All the objective types on the solar side of the diagram—scientists, businessmen, and athletes; saints, scholars, and fools—can be happy only by clinging to the physical and so rejecting their Masks. If they recklessly put on those Masks, they will be destroyed or come to nothing. Those on the lunar side, however—artists and men of passion—have a more complicated problem. Each must choose a mask to wear, but two choices are offered every man, a True Mask and a False, and he must choose rightly.

Yeats, for instance, almost certainly assigned himself to phase 17, where he placed explicitly Dante, Shelley and Landor. In this phase (that of the *Daimonic* Man), the True Mask is "Simplification through intensity" and the False "Dispersal." Men of this phase are those capable of Unity of Being and, if they select the right Mask, must use their "synthetic power" to achieve "simplicity." This Mask, Yeats pointed out, "may represent intellectual or sexual passion," and the work of the artist who assumes it will be "never dramatic but always lyrical and personal." Such men, Yeats felt, are "almost always partisans, propagandists and gregarious; yet because of the *Mask* of simplification, which holds up before them the solitary life of hunters and of fishers, . . . they hate parties, crowds, propaganda." Their object of desire, "some woman perhaps," is always snatched away, and they must turn that object of desire into the material of art. The passage becomes, of course, a footnote to "Under Ben Bulben" and a comment on Yeats's relationship to Maud Gonne. Maud Gonne, incidentally, was probably from phase 16 whose women "walk like queens, and seem to carry upon their backs a quiver of arrows, but they are gentle only to those whom they have chosen or subdued, or to the dogs that follow at their heels. Boundless in generosity, and in illusion, they will give themselves to a beggar because he resembles a religious picture and be faithful all their lives." If they choose the False Mask, they devote themselves to "preposterous purpose after purpose till there is nothing left but the fixed idea and some hysterical hatred."

But the Great Wheel, representing everything, represented as well as the twenty-eight basic personalities the twenty-eight incarnations a man must live through, the twenty-eight phases of any single life, and the twenty-eight basic phases of each cycle of world history. It is this latter aspect of the wheel which complicates everything, for a lunar man of phase 17, a subjective artist such as Yeats, finds himself hard-put to get along in solar phase 23 which began, Yeats calculated, in 1927, and which is characterized by the need to "kill all thought that would systematize the world."

One historical revolution of the wheel, Yeats says, should take about two thousand years and should end in a chaos which begets the entire wheel's Mask; then the whole process should begin again. Since Yeats dates phase 1 as the birth of Christ, the "rough beast" of "The Second Coming" that "Slouches towards Bethlehem to be born" and so begin another cycle antithetical to that of the last two thousand years is already in motion, "its hour come round at last."

How much of all of this can be believed? The answer depends, of course, on what is reasonable to the individual. For many men in our time, that time which is dominated, Yeats felt, by the need to "kill all thought that would systematize the world," the only accurate image for the cosmos, for history, and for the life of the individual is chaos itself, essential and random disorder.

Yet as we approach that image an irony begins to manifest

itself, for when we map out the structure of chaos, when we struggle accurately to define it, when we grasp—ultimately—all the
little convolutions of its essential and random disorder, chaos itself
may become a pattern of consummate order. This irony is central
to Yeats. If we construct an image for chaos—say, a mess of black
dots on a blank page—we can always superimpose form on it,
connect some of the dots with lines and have a diagram or, stretching our minds, see an infinity of patterns in them. One might ask:
Is the pattern in the dots or is it in the mind of the man who
regards them? The answer, in this situation, is: It is in both. A
pattern must be there if it can be imposed successfully. To be
imposed successfully it must be apprehended. Yeats recognized
that we can visualize all religious, philosophical, and historical
patterns and that enough material can be assembled from our
imaginations and the records of the past to make each possible
if we choose to believe in it. And though those systems might oppose each other, each one will be reasonable to itself, will be both
possible and "right." If I draw this pattern $\triangle$ on my dots,
that does not mean that this pattern ∇ is not there too. One
is there ∇ ; the other is there $\triangle$; both are there
$\bowtie$ And a great many others are there, too.

The pattern of overlapping gyres which constitutes Yeats's Great
Wheel could only be accepted by the man of phase 17 because
only that man would be concerned with that sort of synthesis. For
men of other phases, other religious, historical or psychological
systems would be not only necessary but the only possibly true
ones. "Truth" itself is ultimately therefore in Yeats's system only
that which the individual can believe. The poet cannot accept the
statesman's truth any more than the priest can accept the witch-
doctor's; but one is no more right than the other. The only true
view of the world is the individual's: *my* religion, *my* moral code,
my political belief. Yeats's system gave him what he needed: a

technique by which he could "hold in a single thought reality and justice."

It gave him as well, as the automatic script promised, "metaphors for poetry." Though almost everything Yeats wrote after 1922 and a good deal that he wrote before that date is linked to A Vision, one can read the poems without knowing the system. "Leda and the Swan" makes a different kind of sense if one sees it as a poem that examines the beginnings of the cycle that preceded ours. Seen in this light it becomes a neat companion poem to "The Second Coming" which examines the genesis of the cycle that will follow ours. But both it and "The Second Coming" can stand by themselves.

THE STRUCTURE OF A POEM

A Vision gave Yeats a philosophical framework on which he could hang such poems as "Phases of the Moon," "Shepherd and Goatherd," the Byzantium poems, and "All Souls' Night." He used it, as he used his Autobiography, to unify his work and his life, to construct for the sake of both a system coherent and simple. But understanding the thought of his poems is only the first step in experiencing them as poems. To accomplish that difficult, simple act we must be prepared to value poetry not as thought but as art, to see thought as only one element in one of the world's most complex compounds.

Yeats himself was painfully aware that most readers approach a poem as if it were bad prose or, worse, prettified prose. To point out the dangers of this approach, and to suggest a better one, he wrote a great many essays which were intended to make clear that the poem is best seen as an organic whole, an "architectural" structure.

In 1898, for instance, long before his own poetic technique crystallized, Yeats, in his essay "The Autumn of the Body," recognized in Mallarmé a craftsman building poems in much the way he wanted to build them:

> Mr. Symons has written lately on M. Mallarmé's method, and has quoted him as saying that we should 'abolish the pretension, aesthetically an error, despite its dominion over almost all the masterpieces, to enclose within the subtle pages other than—for example —the horror of the forest or the silent thunder in the leaves, not the intense dense wood of the trees.' . . . I think that we will learn again how to describe at great length an old man wandering among enchanted islands, his return home at last, his slow-gathering vengeance, a flitting shape of a goddess, and a flight of arrows, and yet to make all of these so different things . . . become 'an entire word,' the signature or symbol of a mood of the divine imagination as imponderable as 'the horror of the forest or the silent thunder in the leaves.'

Though Yeats later questioned a great many techniques of the French symbolists, and though certainly he abandoned everywhere but in his plays the sort of subject matter he outlines here, from first to last he seems to have accepted the basic symbolist proposition: the great symbol is not contained in the poem but is the poem itself: ultimately any work of art is "an entire word." The finished work of art stands for a feeling (Yeats's word is "mood") that can find expression in no other way. This notion of the work of art itself as non-discursive symbol was, of course, not original with the French symbolists; but they popularized it and helped suggest the area of "utility" of the arts in an increasingly pragmatic world. Yeats, elaborating their ideas, sees the poem as a complex relationship of images, rhythms, and sounds which, in conjunction, become a symbol for emotional experiences otherwise inexpressible in words. This poem-as-symbol concept uses the poem itself in almost exactly the same way that the cabalists used the geometric design of the Tree of Life or that Yeats used his Great Wheel. From the poem we are able to glimpse visions of order. And the poet, in assembling the components of that vision, accomplishes a supreme creative act:

> There are no lines with more melancholy beauty than these by Burns—
>> The white moon is setting behind the white wave,
>> And Time is setting with me, O!
> and these lines are perfectly symbolical. Take from them the whiteness of the moon and of the wave, whose relation to the setting of Time is too subtle for the intellect, and you take from them their beauty. But, when all are together, moon and wave and whiteness and setting Time and the last melancholy cry, they evoke an emotion which cannot be evoked by any other arrangement of colours and sounds and forms. We may call this metaphorical writing, but it is better to call it symbolic writing . . .

Art itself, then, in Yeats's system is a formal arrangement of materials which because of the excellent order of their arrangement evoke a unique emotion in the art-spectator. The job of the artist is not philosophical communication; his job is construction, arrangement itself. Consequently each change in a work changes the work, not just part of it. In one of Yeats's last essays this idea is as important as in these early ones: "A modern painter, who thinks, like Whistler, that a picture must be perfect from the first sketch, growing in richness of detail but not in unity, knows that a work of art must remain fluid to the finish, that an alteration in some minor character or in some detail of color compels alteration everywhere."

Without unity the artist can construct no symbol. But achieving unity involves genuine labor, "learnt in disappointment and fatigue." Only once in a while does art result from the anguish of composition, that anguish of painstakingly trying out in all possible combinations phrase after phrase, that struggle for the impossible balance in a medium so slippery as language. When it is achieved, however, "one emotion" is produced in the spectator—

and it is not an emotion determined exclusively by the prose sense he, of course, apprehends. That "one emotion" can only be the experience of art itself. Yeats's essay, "The Symbolism of Poetry," concerned itself with this concept of the organic structure of art:

> All sounds, all colours, all forms, either because of their pre-ordained energies or because of long association, evoke indefinable and yet precise emotions . . . and when sound, and colour, and form are in a musical relation, a beautiful relation to one another, they become as it were one sound, one colour, one form, and evoke an emotion that is made out of their distinct evocations and yet is one emotion. The same relation exists between all portions of every work of art, whether it be an epic or a song, and the more perfect it is, and the more various and numerous the elements that have flowed into its perfection, the more powerful will be the emotion, the power, the god it calls among us . . .

This "musical relation" of the elements of art produces the artistic symbol, the successful work. "If people were to accept the theory that poetry moves us because of its symbolism," Yeats wrote in summary, it would no longer be possible "for anybody to deny the importance of form . . ."

The achieved form, the symbol which the poem itself is, useful to the reader, but not useful as a motive for action, gives him a "vision of reality which satisfies the whole being."

IMAGES, METAPHORS, AND LITERARY SYMBOLS

How is that total symbol, the poem, put together? How does a poet choose the elements that are to be assembled in a "musical relation"? Some of them, such as rhythm and rhyme, have obvious organizational functions. Ideas, for Yeats particularly the ideas that led up to and culminated in A *Vision*, provide the basic propositions and themes—the underlying framework—of the poem. But it is the imagery itself and its expansion into metaphor and symbol which, grounded in the theme, give the poem its final shape.

At this point, definition is in order. "Image," "metaphor," and "symbol" are terms which must be used so often in any discussion of Yeats's work that their meanings had better be pinned down in the very beginning as precisely as possible. All three words are of course intimately related.

"Image" can be defined in terms of metaphor itself—perhaps some such definition: "The substantive from which a metaphor can be constructed." This definition, though in my eyes accurate, does not communicate very much. It does offer, however, one clue to the nature of an image. It must, in grammatical terms, be a substantive—a noun, pronoun, verbal noun, or other part of speech used as a noun equivalent. To be effective, it must also be a substantive which in some way or another involves the reader in the recollection of concrete sensual experience. Though in this broadest sense image almost becomes synonymous with "sign" (the denotative level of a word), unlike "sign" it is capable of annexing metaphorical and symbolical values. (Another possible definition of "image" might run something like this: a sign which has the potential of becoming metaphor or symbol.) An illustration will, I hope, make this abstract discussion slightly clearer. Take the title of Yeats's poem "A Coat." Both words, a and coat, are by definition (since they are words) signs. But only one of them, coat, is or can be an image. It can be as well, as I hope to demonstrate in a moment, metaphor and/or symbol. Its value as an image is not changed by the addition of metaphorical and symbolic values. Its value as a sign, on the other hand, is either destroyed or isolated the moment we recognize it as metaphor or symbol. In other words, its sign value cannot be extended without vanishing while its image, metaphor and symbol values are interrelated. (No symbol cannot involve metaphor; no metaphor can escape involving image.) To create a metaphor for image: an image is a sign stretching toward symbol.

The first line of "A Coat" enriches the image by adding to it a metaphorical value: "I made my song a coat." The metaphor, as a matter of fact, is actually complicated in that it involves an ambiguity ("I made a coat out of my song"/"I made a coat for my song") which the reader, if acute, is bound to struggle with. But no matter how the reader chooses to translate the line (if he's a poet he may accept both versions and look for others), he recognizes that songs can neither wear nor be coats. A metaphor—"a word or phrase literally denoting one kind of object or idea used in place of another by way of suggesting a likeness or analogy between them" (*Webster's New Collegiate Dictionary*)—has been achieved.

The rest of the poem might create a literary symbol for the word coat. I must say *might*, since I feel an effective symbol must almost always have repeated incidence either within a long work or in at least several short ones. Taken by itself, the whole poem probably adds up to little more than an extended metaphor.

The distinction between metaphor and symbol is one between assigned and unassigned meaning. A metaphor always has at least two assigned meanings (its own sign value and the sign value of the object or idea it stands for). But symbol stands on one leg only; the other kicks at the stars. It exists with only its sign value as a fixed meaning. Its other meaning or meanings are unassigned. Any analogy we can construct for the symbol, any meaning we assign to it, is legitimate so long as we recognize that that meaning is *not* its meaning. (Its meaning must always be more elusive than any value we can—with words—fix to it.) All that the meaning we assign to a symbol can ever be is either part of its meaning or one of its possible meanings. No symbol has *a* meaning.

One last metaphor and then farewell definition: Let us assume an empty stage in an empty theatre. On that stage we will paint a small black circle. This we shall call *sign*. On the small black circle, let us place a dancer's foot. This we shall call *image*. Near the foot which rests on the black circle we shall place, solidly, the dancer's other foot. The relationship between these two fixed feet we shall call *metaphor*. Now let us set our dancer whirling into a pirouette, one foot still on the black circle but the other extended up, down, near the body, far from it. The relation between these feet, constantly shifting, constantly new, we shall call *symbol*. Both metaphor and symbol involve a relationship to image, the fixed foot; are in one sense extensions of it; are—I had promised no metaphors but the comparison is apt—precisely second and third dimensions of it. As dimensions of image—our hypothetical first dimension—they must involve it (no second dimension is possible without a first, no third without a first and second). In the same way that metaphor involves image, so does symbol. Sign, on the other hand, is independent. We cannot, in fact, recognize a metaphor at all if we do not keep the sign value of the word in question clearly in mind. There is no metaphor in "I made my song a coat" unless "coat" retains, unaltered, its normal "garment" value. "Coat" as image, however, is half the metaphor and can eventually extend to symbol if its "meaning" grows sufficiently complex.

Yeats uses his imagery both to give form to particular poems and, as well, to link poem to poem into one of the most complex structures in modern lyric poetry. The first function of imagery, the internal organization of a poem through carefully handled dominant images, is fairly obvious. The dominant image knits the work together, gives it coherence and order; it supplements the theme of the work, sometimes takes precedence over it. Take, for example, the candle image in Yeats's short poem "The Moods":

Time drops in decay,
Like a candle burnt out,
And the mountains and woods
Have their day, have their day;
What one in the rout
Of the fire-born moods
Has fallen away?

The imagery of the entire poem is divided between "changing" physical realities (the mountains and woods) and temporal abstractions (time and day). But holding them together is the burnt-out candle that is "like" the decay of time itself and that echoes in physical shape the mountain and tree. The poem itself supports Hermes' great dogma: as above, so below. The first four lines, the "below" section, are paralleled by the last three; but there all the images are extended. The dropping in decay of time in the "below" section is matched by the rout of the fire-born moods. The integrating image of the candle is paralleled by the "fire-born" moods themselves, one of which has fallen away, exactly as the candle has burned out. The candle, an image of quick destruction, dominates the subsidiary images, links the two halves of the poem, and, though burned out in context, provides inextinguishable illumination for the careful reader.

Yet candles never assume any great importance in the total development of Yeats's imagery in spite of the fact that a candle is the integrating image of one poem. Other images, however, do. By sheer bulk—and by Yeats's insistence that they are his chief symbols—tree, bird, tower, sea, house, Mask, and rose eventually strike Yeats's persistent reader as of crucial importance. Tree and bird, particularly, are with Yeats from the beginning of his career to the end. Roses threaten to disappear by the turn of the century, though they are never completely absent from his verse. At about the same time that they fade, Masks begin to assume importance. Images of the sea make a steadily diminishing progression through Yeats's work. Well and house make sporadic appearances, bulking at times very large and then almost vanishing, while tower, at least after Yeats had one, persists strongly to the end.

All of these images may, it seems to me, properly be identified as obsessive. They are not always dominant images in particular works (though frequently they are), but they are remarkably tenacious. Like Shelley's "primary" symbols (cave, river, fountain, well, tower, and star), symbols which Yeats carefully analyzed in his essay on Shelley, these seem often to be almost involuntarily used.

All of his critics have noticed the omnipresence of Yeats's birds. Literally hundreds of them range through his poetry and plays. What is the value of such a world of obsessive imagery to the poet? How does he use it? How, from it, does he construct poetry?

Its first use, and I think its simplest one, is as a kind of catalyst to composition. No poem, alas, writes itself. Poets work, and work hard, at their trade. Yeats felt he had accomplished a full day's work when he had produced six lines, and that was at the height of his career. As a young poet, he would struggle with his six lines for upwards of a week. Even as an old man, Yeats found the labor of writing a stanza a physically exhausting ordeal. His method of composition—the versification of a prose sketch—invariably involved multiple drafts of the work, and an elaborate process of testing out all the possible variants. These "mutterings," as Lady Gregory testifies, would go on for hours though only a line or two of final draft might result from them. In this struggle to get the words down in fairly satisfactory patterns, the obsessive images can be a valuable crutch for the poet. They offer him trustworthy material. Even more important, they are ready. For whatever psychological reason they lie in wait at the very surface of the unconscious, they are certainly there, valuable and dangerous aids to composition. They may well later be altered beyond recognition, but by then they will have served their purpose. By then the labor of organization will have begun; words and lines will have enough shape to bear revision, and the poet will be able to hammer his construction into something like final form. He may ultimately abandon them, use them as part of the subordinate imagistic structure of the poem, or elevate them to symbols that will integrate elements in the particular poem and link it to others.

This linking function of sets of dominant or obsessive images which pull together short, otherwise unrelated, works into larger forms is particularly important in Yeats. To document this takes a book, and luckily a good one has been written. That is Donald A. Stauffer's *The Golden Nightingale*. Stauffer's thesis is that some poets, Yeats included, either consciously or unconsciously organize the imagery of their lyrics in such coherent patterns that the total effect of the lyrics has an epic quality. (Yeats had himself worked out a similar theory to explain the function of obsessive imagery in Shelley and in Blake.) Stauffer uses, for purposes of demonstration, the interrelated imagery of swan and nightingale; but any of Yeats's obsessive images could have been used as well. Such images, enriching the meaning of each poem in which they figure while simultaneously binding together whole areas of poetry, help make "the works" of a poet—particularly a lyric poet—a cohesive whole. And that whole, organized through consistent imagery, almost always succeeds in giving the reader the illusion that it is greater than any of its parts.

Another use to which the careful poet can put obsessive imagery has already been anticipated in much of what I have said so far: the poet can construct from it a symbol for his readers. (It probably has symbolic value to the poet in the first place or it would not be obsessive.) The very frequency of its incidence will give it some importance; the variety of contexts will give it more. Its evolution into a literary symbol will be complete as the author assigns it importance in a work, hints that it holds meanings more complex than those of its sign value.

Yeats himself liked to make lists of his symbols; and though the lists, from time to time, varied, the following catalogue is typical. This one is drawn from a letter to his friend T. Sturge Moore. The letter is dated September 6, 1921: "My main symbols are Sun and Moon (in all phases), Tower, Mask, Tree (Tree with Mask hanging on the trunk), Well . . ." Bird, perhaps Yeats's favorite symbol, is missing from the list because it was the subject of the letter itself, a letter about a cover-design in which a hawk conspicuously figured. Roses, by 1921, had withered and died.

Yet not all obsessive images become symbols. Some, by a peculiar potency of context or a richness forced into them by the poet, seem intricate enough to hold a world of meaning. Others are merely frequently-repeated words. Still others carry a kind of private importance, an importance that drives the poet to use them over and over though their meaning never varies. Several examples of this sort of obsessive imagery—perhaps compulsive imagery would more accurately describe it—can be found in Yeats.

Take, for example, an image—almost a scene—that has its roots in an incident that took place in Yeats's childhood. Son of a family that divided its residence between England and Ireland, Yeats used to sail back and forth between the two countries on his grandfather's ships, the s.s. *Sligo* and s.s. *Liverpool*. Another frequent passenger was an old woman. Yeats described her in *Reveries over Childhood and Youth*. "When I was a little boy, an old woman who had come to Liverpool with crates of fowl, made me miserable by throwing her arms around me, the moment I had alighted from my cab, and telling the sailor who carried my luggage that she had held me in her arms when I was a baby." In *Reveries*, Yeats assigns no conversation to her; but in *John Sherman*, his autobiographical novel, she reappears, this time with a significant sentence. John Sherman, Yeats's hero, is crossing to London on "the cattle boat." He is alone on deck, except for "a very dirty old woman sitting by a crate of geese . . . The old woman made the journey monthly with geese for the Liverpool market." He thinks she is asleep, but suddenly she wakes up: "Why are ye goin' among them savages in London, Misther John? Why don't ye stay among your own people—for what have we in this life but a mouthful of air?" *John Sherman* was published in 1891. In *The King's Threshold*, which Yeats dates 1904, the dying poet, Seanchan, commands the guard to leave him: "You must needs keep your patience yet awhile,/ For I have some few mouthfuls of sweet air/ To swallow before I have grown to be as civil/ As any other dust." The second stanza of the magnificent closing song of *At the Hawk's Well* (1917) uses the image again: "Folly alone I cherish,/ I choose it for my share;/ Being but a mouthful of air,/ I am content to perish;/ I am but a mouthful of sweet air.

In 1935, Yeats ends another play with the same phrase. In the midst of the song for closing the curtain in *The King of the Great Clock Tower*, the First Attendant brings the curtain half-closed as he sings, "O, what is life but a mouthful of air?" And in one of Yeats's last poems, the line, this time slightly varied, is again introduced. This time it ends the second stanza of "A Bronze Head." Remembering Maud Gonne, Yeats has asked, "which of her forms has shown her substance right?" and answers in terms of his by-now-familiar phrase: "Or maybe substance can be composite,/ Profound McTaggart thought so, and in a breath/ A mouthful held the extreme of life and death." There are other examples, but these will do to show its hold over Yeats. Yet it never gains in richness. Such strength as it has, it had in its first startling appearance in *John Sherman*. Perhaps its very power is the reason it can never be extended beyond a compulsive image. A symbol could not be constructed from such vividness.

An effective symbol, as a matter of fact, must almost always be based on something as dry, and as familiar, as dust. In the long run, the symbolist celebrates the importance of the obvious—by making the obvious important. The great literary symbols have almost all been common things. Yeats draws his from the world of nature, that same natural world glorified by the romantics. Because Yeats thinks of himself as "the last of the romantics," a man born out of his time, he assigns his symbols other values than the romantics did. Made "strange" by those values, his "masked" romantic images jolt us into a recognition of their symbolical function.

That function is ultimately one of offering us not "meaning"— no symbol gives us that; it's the worst vehicle in the world for "meaning"—but instead the feeling of meaning, a far different thing, for the feeling of meaning is an undefined sense of order, of rightness, of congruence at the heart of things. For that reason, the symbol can have almost any "meaning" that an audience chooses to read into it in its context in the work which it organizes. A symbolist poet is likely, in fact, to go further, to argue that the symbol may ultimately contain *all* meaning. T. S. Eliot's heroes, for instance, include such men as Lancelot Andrewes who "takes a word and derives the world from it; squeezing and squeezing the word until it yields a full juice of meaning which we should never have supposed any word to possess." Eliot, supremely conscious that no effective symbol can be translated into ordinary discourse, tries in another essay, *The Music of Poetry*, to account for our feeling of mystery and richness in the successful symbol:

> The music of a word is, so to speak, at a point of intersection: it arises from its relation first to the words immediately preceding and following it, and indefinitely to the rest of the context; and from another relation, that of its immediate meaning in that context to all the other meanings which it has had in other contexts, to its greater or less wealth of association. . . . at certain moments . . . a word can be made to insinuate the whole history of a language and a civilization.

Like Eliot, Yeats tries to extend the meaning of the symbol to its furthest reaches. Speaking of Shelley's imagery of caves, Yeats first offers possible "meanings" but then immediately insists that those meanings expand infinitely:

> Again and again one finds some passing allusion to the cave of man's mind, or to the caves of his youth, or to the cave of mysteries we enter at death, for to Shelley as to Porphyry it is more than an image of life in the world. It may mean any enclosed life, as when it is the dwelling-place of Asia and Prometheus, or when it is 'the still cave of poetry,' and it may have all meanings at once, or it may have as little meaning as some ancient religious symbol enwoven from the habit of centuries with the patterns of a carpet or a tapestry. . . .

Though Yeats was more dogmatic about "meaning" in his own poetry, the older he grew the less likely he was to let himself be pinned down to simple equivalents for his symbols. Thus, in 1889 he can write Katharine Tynan, ". . . 'Oisin' needs an interpreter.

There are three incompatible things which man is always seeking —infinite feeling, infinite battle, infinite repose—hence the three islands." By 1906, however, he is careful not to interpret. In a letter to Florence Farr he speaks of a symbolical unicorn: ". . . but I shall not trouble to make the meaning clear—a clear vivid story of a strange sort is enough. The meaning may be different with everyone." And by the end of his career this refusal to limit his work has become a set policy. In 1935, when Maurice Wollman, editor of the anthology *Modern Poetry, 1922-1934*, asked Yeats to comment on one of his poems, Yeats was perfectly willing to make such a comment—but only so long as it did not appear over his name: "I don't want to interpret *The Death of the Hare*. I can help you write a note, if that note is to be over your own name, but you must not give me as your authority. If an author interprets a poem of his own he limits its suggestibility." Shortly before he died, Yeats, amused by the whole game of "meaning" in art, wrote to his friend Ethel Mannin, "I am sending you a copy of my very Rabelasian play *The Herne's Egg*, but do not ask what it means. It disturbed the Abbey board until I withdrew it. An admiring member had decided that the seven ravishers of the heroine are the seven sacraments."

Ultimately meaning in art—both meaning of literary symbol and of that greater symbol the work of art itself—is a joint achievement of artist and audience. As the artist pounds into his symbol all the richness he can summon, as he "takes a word and derives the world from it," so to the symbol the intelligent reader brings all of the past he has been able to gather into himself. "A poetical passage cannot be understood," Yeats says, "without a rich memory, and like the older school of painting appeals to a tradition, and that not merely when it speaks of 'Lethe's Wharf,' or 'Dido on the wild sea-banks' but in rhythm, in vocabulary; for the ear must notice slight variations upon old cadences and customary words . . ." Somewhere between the great writer and the intelligent reader poetry is born; the symbols—drawing all together into harmony—make poems, the achieved symbolic things themselves.

more eloquent than the mere words from which they are compounded.

THE GREAT DESIGN

Though Yeats fails, as every man must who attempts so impossible a synthesis, his effort to unify life and art into one immense achieved form—a complex, organic interconnected whole which, real microcosm, could contain in image all the universe—comes breathtakingly close to success. The framework of autobiography, letters, essays, philosophical speculation, and cosmology on which he suspended a body of delicately engineered poetry, itself carefully interlinked by a tissue of echoing images and strategic proliferating symbols, becomes almost what he says A *Vision* was intended to be "a last act of defense against the chaos of the world." A great poet, Yeats allows us to experience in the totality of his art the necessary if momentary illusions of order which give us courage to live.

II * THE POEMS

1 * The Wanderings of Oisin

In preparing the text for what became the *Definitive Edition* of his poetry, Yeats, dying, moved *The Wanderings of Oisin* from its conventional place in the "Narrative and Dramatic" section at the end of his poems to the very beginning of his book. His purpose may have been in the interest of accurate chronology, but he undoubtedly had better reasons for making the change.

The poem, in the first place, involves the Irish subject matter which, more accurately than the Indian songs of *Crossways*, sets the tone for the bulk of his work.

Perhaps more important, the poem is a firm statement of what he came in his old age to feel was the major theme of his entire work: the horror of old age that brings wisdom only at the price of bodily decrepitude and death. "I spend my days correcting proofs," he wrote Olivia Shakespear on June 30, 1932. "I have just finished the first volume, all my lyric poetry, and am greatly astonished at myself. As it is all speech rather than writing, I keep saying what man is this who . . . says the same thing in so many different ways. My first denunciation of old age I made in *The Wanderings of Usheen* (end of part 1) before I was twenty and the same denunciation comes in the last pages of the book."

Though Yeats may have set *Oisin* first for either of these reasons, it is certainly true that he saw it as the poem most appropriate to introduce his poetry to his new reader. By the end of his life, also, he saw it as the successful product of a long struggle to solve, through diligent revisions, the innumerable technical problems of a long poem. For in spite of the fact that the poem Yeats felt he had "completed" in the fall of 1887 resembles the poem we read, a series of cuts and rephrasings that represented the work of years was needed to bring the work to its firm final form.

Metrically, *Oisin* is carefully designed, expanding from the steady iambic tetrameter of Book I, through the slightly looser iambic pentameter of Book II, to the extremely free mixture of iambs and anapests that constitute the hexameters of Book III.

As meter grows more free, rhyme scheme grows increasingly strict. Book I, though it begins in couplets, opens up almost immediately to a long complex pattern held together by recurring *air* rhymes, internal assonance, and an elaborate structure of various kinds of half-rhymes. (For example consider all the kinds of partial rhymes, particularly those ending in terminal *d* and *n*, that hold together lines 32-45; sai*d*, hea*d*, sa*d*, ha*d*, mouse, house, fer*n*, gla*d*, Fin*n*, ur*n*, slai*n*, plai*n*, ki*n*, ride. Add to these the internal echoes of accented syllables ending in *nd* and *n*—wind, horn, hornless, many, any, granary, hunting, answered, country, pencilled—and add as well the unaccented syllables with the same *nd* and *n* ending—and, than, in, own, woman, and, on, raven, and—and one can see, in these 14 lines at least, how very carefully Yeats builds up an intricate and beautiful structure of sound.) The very free rhyme scheme of Book I gives way in Book II to a dominant pattern of couplets (though Yeats still allows himself great flexibility). By the time he reaches Book III, however, not only has he eliminated the interpolated lyrics which characterize Books I and II, but he follows as well a rigid unvarying a b a b quatrain pattern.

Just as the gross structure of the poem is carefully planned, so too is an internal structure of interrelated images. "The whole poem is full of symbols," Yeats wrote Katharine Tynan in the summer of 1888, and ever since then people have been busily explicating them. Yeats himself was probably indirectly the instigator of their investigations, for in the same letter he announced that the poem contained secrets: "In the second part of 'Oisin' under disguise of symbolism I have said several things to which I only have the key. The romance is for my readers. They must not even know there is a symbol anywhere. They will not find out. If they did it would spoil the art." Better Freudians than I—Morton Seiden, for instance—have risked spoiling the art to pin down those elusive symbols. Seiden finds that the "dusky demon" of Book II who goes through a series of remarkable changes from "great eel" to "fir-tree roaring in its leafless top" to "a drowned dripping body" bears—granted certain unconscious transformations—a family likeness to Yeats's father whom Yeats certainly did battle frequently (though more politely) and who was inevitably reborn to battle again. Though Seiden's interpretation has a kind of ingenuity, one can sympathize with George Brandon Saul's reaction to it ("nauseating"). It is a little hard to visualize John B. Yeats "dropping sea-foam on the wide stair,/ And hung with slime." But then it is hard to visualize him as the eye-piece of a telescope, and Yeats admits to that. Perhaps those amateur psychologists who see the demon as orgasm incarnate are hitting closer to the mark. Or perhaps both are right. The battle was against both father and sex; each reared its ugly head every four days or so and each, somehow, had to be subdued. And since Yeats insisted in his letter that he had said "several things" under disguise of symbolism, I see no reason to rule out other readings of the passage. (Richard Ellmann, for instance, sees the second island as England and the beautiful enchained lady as Ireland. Seiden, in his doctoral dissertation, modifies his earlier identification of demon as father to present him instead as "a personification of the revolving seasons: at regular intervals he is slain and at regular intervals he is reborn.")

But *what the symbols mean* is a lure that can lead us spectacularly astray. *What the symbols do* is, it seems to me, closer to our purpose. The whole poem is held together by a tissue of interlocked images, particularly images of bird and tree which are in turn supplemented by images of water and moon. Frequently these images are combined. ("The dove-grey edge of the sea," for example, manages to associate in one phrase bird and water imagery.) Involved, entangled, interwoven, these images give the poem its shape and, if we follow their convolutions, its "meaning," a meaning larger than any contained in any single theme or symbol. For it is in the interaction of parts, not in the isolation of them, that Yeats's sort of poetry rises to art.

Some notion of the structure of the poem can be gained if we trace through it the framework of significant bird and tree imagery. It would be pointless (and exhausting) to itemize every reference to birds and trees. Most references to them, as a matter of fact, are probably only decorative. (The "dove-grey edge of the sea," the "hundred ladies, merry as birds," and the "dewy forest alleys," for instance, reinforce the dominant imagery of the poem but can hardly be said to participate directly in its imagistic structure.) But some bird and tree references are crucial.

Very early in the poem Niamh, the "pearl-pale, high-born" lady from the land of the Immortals, is associated with birds. Finn, the Irish mythological hero whose exploits are commemorated in the "Fenian Cycle" of Irish folklore, asks her if she came to the land of the living because some Immortal companion had wandered away "From where the birds of Aengus wing." (Aengus, whose kisses were supposed to have been transformed to birds which flew constantly about his head, is Niamh's father, the god of youth, beauty and poetry who rules the first island Oisin visits, the country of the young.) She tells Finn that she is innocent of men but

that she has fallen in love with the heroism and eloquence of his
son Oisin, and Yeats makes her instinctively choose bird imagery
to describe that eloquence. Oisin's stories, she feels, are " 'like coloured Asian birds/ At evening in their rainless lands.' "

Perhaps because art is phoenix-like, immortal, the "coloured
Asian birds" also populate the first island visited by Niamh and
Oisin. As the lovers leave that island, the Immortals who have
entertained them burst into song: "And, as they sang the painted
birds/ Kept time with their bright wings and feet." Not only do
the "painted birds" dance to the tune of the Immortals, they are
themselves subject of the tune which contrasts that mortality
Yeats spoke of in his letter to Olivia Shakespear—the softness of
youth which must wear into age, the tenderness of love which
must die—with the immortal birds: " 'A storm of birds in the
Asian trees/ Like tulips in the air a-winging/ . . . Must murmur
at last, "Unjust, unjust." ' " (Yeats had already begun to work out
in these sketchy images of immortal "painted birds" not only the
pattern of that significant parrot of "The Indian to His Love"
which rages "at his own image in the enamelled sea" but as well
the outline of the great, symbolic golden bird of "Sailing to Byzantium" who, free from sensual music and the limits of flesh, sings
undying song.)

Even before Niamh's horse had brought the lovers to the first
island, Oisin had heard the fabulous birds: "A wandering land
breeze came/ And a far sound of feathery quires." The song had
been overpowering: "The horse towards the music raced,/ Neigh-
ing along the lifeless waste." The tree image, introduced in the
next line, is graphic to the point of being pornographic: trees "like
sooty fingers" rose out of warm water "and they were trembling
ceaselessly." Birds covered them, clung to every branch "like
swarming bees."

This sensual music is only part of a throbbing world. The trees
"were throbbing ceaselessly/ As though they all were beating time"
to the "low laughing woodland rhyme" of the immortal birds. Not
only do these remarkable birds appeal to our sense of hearing and

touch, they also present themselves to us visually: "Round the shore a million stood/ Like drops of frozen rainbow light." Bird-forms are also copied in the boats of the Immortals which have "carven figures on their prows/ Of bitterns, and fish-eating stoats,/ And swans with their exultant throats." The Immortals themselves, decked out in cloaks "trimmed with many a crimson feather," (this, Yeats noted in *Irish Fairy and Folk Tales*, is the conventional identifying mark of fairies) spend their time surrounded by birds in the trees. They rush "from the woods" when Niamh, after tying her horse "where the wood and waters meet," blows "over the bare and woody land" three merry notes.

This is Aengus' island and these are "the birds of Aengus," his companions, and his woods. Just as the poet Oisin is one projection of Yeats, Aengus, the god of poetry, is another. And as Niamh, whose name means both *beauty* and *brightness*, is linked to the shimmering birds, Aengus is linked to trees. Niamh leads Oisin to him through a luxurious forest where "tangled creepers every hour/ Blossom in some new crimson flower." Aengus himself, "A beautiful young man," lives, it turns out, in a house made of "wattles, clay, and skin" in much the way that Yeats had hoped to live in his own ideal island, Innisfree, in a house of "clay and wattles made." Aengus, however—unlike Yeats who, when he wrote the poem, was feeling most isolated—is surrounded by an adoring crowd of men and ladies who, weeping, offer up prayers to him and kiss his remarkable sceptre "with red lips" and touch it "with their finger-tips." Holding "that flashing sceptre up," he sings a hymn to joy that literally knocks him out. The admiring Immortals, who had set the "dark woods" ringing with their song as they approached him, race out of the "wattled hall" toward the seashore in a voluptuous hymn to youth: " 'God is joy and joy is God,/ And things that have grown sad are wicked,/ And things that fear the dawn of the morrow/ Or the grey wandering osprey Sorrow.' " The osprey, one of the largest hawks, a violent, destructive bird of prey, is set up in opposition to the immortal crimson island birds and carefully associated with both sadness and an even greater destroyer than itself, the moving hands of the clock: time. The osprey phrase becomes a refrain to the song of the Immortals, ending the three stanzas of their song.

As they sing, they lead Oisin through an alliterative, punning forest. From "the winding thicket" to "the windless woods" they weave and wander to arrive, winded, on "the woody central hill." Here the "panting band" pauses for breath before plunging into the last stanza of their diatribe against the "grey wandering osprey Sorrow."

Oisin stays "upon that woody shore" for a hundred years, fishing from the bird-carved prows of the boats. But one day "a staff of wood," part of some dead warrior's broken lance, floats ashore at his feet. This, for Oisin, is a symbol—as is the beech-bough of the second part and the dead starling of the third—that his visit to the island is over. Niamh, seeing it in his hands, "spake no word/ Save only many times my name,/ In murmurs, like a frightened bird." And with this return of the central bird-image, the lovers walk through the woods of the island to the waiting horse, saddle him, and pass out onto the water. Behind them they see the Immortals in "the woods' old night" dancing like shadows on the hills and singing. "And, as they sang, the painted birds/ Kept time with their bright wings and feet." Their song is that condemnation of old age which Yeats regarded as the central theme of the poem; the undying "birds in the Asian trees" stare sadly at all mortal life—at man, hare, mouse and mortal bird ("the kingfisher turns to a ball of dust")—and "murmur at last, 'Unjust, unjust.' "

The central imagery of this section of the poem certainly pits the immortal "birds in the Asian trees" against time, "the grey wandering osprey Sorrow." Integrating these bird images, "like sooty fingers," are the trees of the wooded island; and freeing Oisin from the island is "a staff of wood."

Though most of these images, as far as I can determine, are invented by Yeats, fabulous birds and trees did fill the books he had been reading just before he wrote the poem. When he does use allusive bird and tree imagery, frequently it is drawn not from his immediate sources but from analogous ones. Take, for example, the "painted birds." Yeats had based the plot of his poem on Bryan O'Looney's adaptation of Michael Comyn's Gaelic poem, "The Lay of Oisin on the Land of Youth." It is certain that he had read O'Looney's version, but it is almost equally certain that he had read P. W. Joyce's "Oisin in Tirnanoge," a popularization of O'Looney's draft of the poem, partly in prose and partly in verse. But in neither O'Looney nor in Joyce did he find detailed descriptions of those "painted birds." In another tale in Joyce's collection *Old Celtic Romances*, however, an "isle of birds" is described in detail, an isle which corresponds closely to Aengus' island. This island figures in the tale "The Voyage of Maildun," a work Yeats draws on not only for "Oisin" but as well for details in his novel *John Sherman*. The island in "The Voyage of Maildun" is terraced. "On the terraces grew rows of tall trees, on which were perched great numbers of large, bright-coloured birds." Maildun volunteers to see if the birds are tame, discovers that they are, and returns to his ship with them. Joyce summarizes the adventure in awkward verse: "A shield-shaped island, with terraces crowned,/ And great trees circling round and round:/ From the summit down to the wave washed rocks,/ There are bright-coloured birds in myriad flocks—/ Their plumes are radiant . . ." Though Yeats can hardly have found Joyce's poetry exciting, he found the bright-coloured birds memorable. Reasonably, he combined the scenery of Maildun's voyage with the plot of Oisin's.

Some of the bird-imagery of Oisin's second island is also drawn from "The Voyage of Maildun." In his novel *John Sherman* Yeats had referred to "the old and dishevelled eagles that Maeldune saw hurrying toward the waters of life." "Dishevelled" eagles are also central characters of Oisin's second island. Both sets first appeared in Joyce's version of this same "Voyage of Maildun." Maildun's voyage, like that of Saint Brendan on which it is modelled, included visits to numerous islands, many of which were inhabited by remarkable birds. But toward the end of his journey Maildun

reached an island more fascinating than the others and the narra-
tor goes into considerable detail about its scenery. On one side of
the island is a wood of yew trees and great oaks and on the other
a small lake. This lake contains "the waters of life." Maildun discovers its special properties one day when he sees an "immense
bird" slowly and heavily flying in toward the island. Maildun and
his sailors are frightened for the bird is gigantic. Nevertheless,
they determine to spy on its actions. The bird "appeared very old,
and he held in one claw a branch of a tree, which he had brought
with him over the sea." The branch is larger than a full-grown
oak, is covered with fresh green leaves and is "heavily laden with
clusters of fruit, red and rich-looking like grapes, but much larger."
Maildun and his sailors inch toward the bird, but he ignores them
and they eventually manage to steal some of the fruit from him.
He seems not to see them. That evening two other birds, quite
as large but apparently younger, arrive. After they rest a long time
they begin "picking the old bird all over, body, wings, and head,
plucking out the old feathers and the decayed quill points and
smoothing down his plumage with their great beaks." Then all
three birds eat from the red-fruited branch. On the next morning
the two younger birds again preen the older bird. When they
finish grooming him, they again eat the fruit, but this time they
throw the pits and part of the pulp in the lake until the water
becomes "red like wine." The oldest bird then plunges in the lake,
remaining there till evening when he flies up to a different part
of the island "to avoid touching and defiling himself with the old
feathers and the other traces of age and decay." On the third day,
the younger birds again groom him, but this time much more
carefully. At noon they fly away and the old bird, left alone, continues the grooming process. At nightfall he shakes his wings,
soars into the air, and circles the island three times. "And now
the men observed that he had lost all the appearances of old age:
his feathers were thick and glossy, his head was erect and his eye
bright, and he flew with quite as much power and swiftness as the
others." The sailors discuss the remarkable sight they have seen

and conclude that "this bird had undergone a renewal of youth from old age, according to the word of the prophet, which says, 'Thy youth shall be renewed as the eagle.'"

In many ways this incident is useful to the reader interested in the functioning of Yeats's imagery. Not only does it help explain the nature of the pair of eagles in the second part of *The Wanderings of Oisin*, it also sheds light on Yeats's obsessive interest in eagles, hawks, ravens and other birds of prey. For if we associate them with rejuvenation, as this passage does, we can see how effectively they support Yeats's recurring central theme: the horror of old age. They wither into youth; only men wither into death. In tree and bird Yeats locates an imagery of renewal. The immortal Asian birds of Book I who pitied the destructive horror of mortality ("Unjust, unjust") parallel the eagles of *John Sherman* who, hurrying to the waters of life, slough off old age to emerge young once more, potent, and vital.

In the second book of *The Wanderings of Oisin* these eagles appear before their renewal. Dishevelled still, they are "two old eagles." They contemplate the moments of rebirth—both past and to come. "Few feathers were on their dishevelled wings,/ For their dim minds were with the ancient things." These eagles, their minds centered on themselves and "ancient pride," are, like the eagles of Maildun, impervious to human act. Just as Maildun's sailor can steal the life-giving fruit from the old eagle and be ignored ("But the bird went on plucking and eating his fruit, and never took the least notice."), so Oisin can approach the girl chained to the dishevelled eagles and escape unharmed: "I burst the chain: still earless, nerveless, blind/ Wrapped in the things of the unhuman mind,/ In some dim memory or ancient mood,/ Still earless, nerveless, blind, the eagles stood."

The chained girl "with soft eyes like funeral tapers" is the heroine of Oisin's second adventure. He locates her in much the same way that he located the Immortals of the first island. Even his approach to the second island is similar. Instead of trees sticking out of warm water "like sooty fingers," he finds as he approaches the second island that phallic "dark towers/ Rose in the darkness, and the white surf gleamed/ About them." Just as Niamh and Oisin rode between "throbbing trees" when their horse left the water of the first island, here they ride between "seaweed-covered pillars." Halfway up a long moonlit stair, Oisin hears a singing voice (parallel to the singing birds of the first island) which "Fanned the delighted air like wings of birds." The song is that of the mysterious lady whom they are yet to meet. It tells of her brothers who spring out of bed "like young partridge" to hunt with "an ashen hunting spear." In an invocation to "the saddest of all men," obviously Oisin-Yeats, she sends her bird song out on the waters: "O sigh, O fluttering sigh, be kind to me;/ Flutter along the froth lips of the sea/ . . . Flutter along the froth lips of the sea/ And home to me again/ . . . And tell me that you found a man unbid,/ The saddest of all men." Oisin follows the fluttering sigh to its source, sees her, and offers aid. She warns that the demon who guards her is all-powerful: "He is strong and crafty as the seas/ That spring under the Seven Hazel Trees." These trees, Yeats points out in a note, are supposed in Irish mythology to have guarded a sacred well from which sprang seven rivers. The seven rivers Yeats expands for the purpose of his poem to "all the waters of the world." Oisin ignores the sad lady's warning, releases her from the chains which bind her to the eagles, and leads her and Niamh up the stairs to the great central hall of the castle, a hall so vast sound cannot reach its ceiling:

> I saw a foam-white seagull drift and float
> Under the roof, and with a straining throat
> Shouted, and hailed him; he hung there a star,
> For no man's cry shall ever mount so far . . .

The "foam-white seagull" is almost certainly, like other of Yeats's gulls and birds of prey, "an image of fulfillment," but here an image of a fulfillment which man cannot obtain. Oisin, though he shouted "with a straining throat," could not hail the bird: "he hung there a star,/ For no man's cry shall ever mount so far."

That cry of Oisin's, that desperate shout toward the white bird—
so distant as to be almost invisible, "a star"—is a cry which echoes
and reechoes through the bulk of Yeats's work. Could it, the symbolic link between that which is above—the invisible world of
spirit—and that which is below—the mundane perishable world of
flesh and blood, hear man's cry and so effect communication between the two worlds, miracle might take place, fulfillment be
achieved.

After Oisin's shout toward the white bird fails, the three spend
the night in the cavernous hall of the demon. At dawn, Oisin
leaves the ladies to look for the demon himself. The dawn,
a "passionate" one, is characterized by green clouds that seem like
"drifts of leaves."

Though the green clouds hint of life, the demon turns out to
be "dry as a withered sedge." This demon—variously identified by
Yeats's commentators as father, fatherland and phallus, the bark-
ing symbol of the sun itself—is at once enemy and beloved: his
song, combining opposites, is sung in "a sad revelry"; he is both
"bacchant and mournful"; he caresses the runnel's rim "as though/
The flowers still grew there."

Even his eyes contribute to his double nature, for they are the
color of halcyon's wings: "He slowly turned:/ A demon's leisure:
eyes, first white, now burned/ Like wings of kingfishers." These
flashing, lovely, angry eyes catch up all the halcyon references of
the early poetry to support the ambivalent nature of the demon.
The halcyon (kingfisher) is both bird of prey and, on its floating
nest, traditional image for peace. Yeats, loving paradox, ties the intricate bird to the ambiguous demon.

But the battle must be fought, and Oisin—wielding the sword
of Manannan, the Irish sea-god—frightens the demon into his
significant transformations from great eel to fir-tree to drowned
dripping body. When night falls, Oisin kills his thrilling enemy.
For three days Oisin and the ladies celebrate, but then the demon
is reborn. For a hundred years, the cycle repeats itself, a battle
every fourth day.

The sign which indicates to Oisin the end of the second island adventure parallels the staff of wood which had signalled the end of his visit to the first island. When the hundred years have ended, "a beech-bough" floats in to Oisin who stands by the edge of the sea: "the surges bore/ A beech bough to me, and my heart grew sore,/ Remembering how I had stood by white-haired Finn/ Under a beech at Almhuin and heard the thin/ Outcry of bats." The remembered bats, like the immortal birds of the first section which had lamented the whole of mortal life, combine with the tree sym· bol to return Oisin to his wanderings, and he leaves with Niamb for the Island of Forgetfulness.

One other bird image, of no great importance in "Oisin" but very important in Yeats's later work, is touched on twice in Book II and once in Book I. That is the image of the raven. It appears in Book I when Finn explains the reason for the heroes' sadness. They are remembering their slain comrades "On Gabhra's raven-covered plain." In the second section of the poem, Oisin contrasts his heroic deeds on the Island of Victories with "now," the time of Christian conquest. He is talking to St. Patrick: "But now the lying clerics murder song/ With barren words and flatteries of the weak./ In what land do the powerless turn the beak/ Of ravening Sorrow, or the hand of Wrath?" Intentional or acciden-tal, Yeats's pun on the adjective "ravening" makes for effective poetry. That Yeats did not realize that the verb *raven*, from the Old French *raviner*, to take by force, to ravish, is not intimately related to the noun *raven*, from Anglo-Saxon *hraefn*, is probably true. But giving rapacious Sorrow a beak, transforming ravenous Sorrow to a bird similar enough in size and shape to remind the reader of the osprey Sorrow from Book I, and then contrasting the screaming, violent bird he has created with the "barren words" of the clerics—in the process setting up a sterile-prose-of-clerics v. passionate-as-rape-poetry-of-Fenians antithesis—is typical of Yeats's condensation in his poetry. Not only does he make an effective image and link it structurally to other important images, he also defines two sources of art: ravening Sorrow and Wrath. That these

are the primary sources of his own art, the entire bulk of his poetry will testify.

Later in the same conversation with Patrick, Oisin calls up the raven image again. Patrick had spoken of God's thunder, symbol of Christian triumph. Oisin answers that he hears in the midst of the Christian thunder the sound of the trampling of Fenian horses, the tearing of armour, laughter, and cries. "The armies clash and shock,/ And now the daylight-darkening ravens flock." Here, as in the "raven-covered plain" of Book I, ravens are classed among the victorious birds of prey. When laughter and cries are done, the slaughter over, the two great civilizations destroyed in each other, "the daylight-darkening ravens" will flock to herald another turn of the wheel, a new time.

If Book I was introduced with the immortal birds in the sensuous trees and Book II with a bird-voice in Freudian towers, Book III, the Isle of Forgetfulness, is introduced by birdlessness—"no live creatures lived there"—in an immense dripping forest of hazel and oak trees. The relationship of these opening images is, of course, obvious and need hardly be stressed. The trees of the first part that rose out of warm water "like sooty fingers" had been throbbing with birds. The towers of the second part, rising in the darkness from a green slime, had enclosed a lost lady whose "fluttering" bird voice had called Oisin to her: the phallic image had grown; the bird image had diminished. The wet trees of the third part are "immense." The birds are gone. The only sound is made by the "dripping trees": "Dropping; a murmurous dropping; old silence and that one sound." And if at first these trees seem symbolic of the impotence of old age, "Dripping and doubling landward, as though they would hasten away,/ Like an army of old men longing for rest from the moan of the seas," they are soon discovered—in the night that descends just before Oisin and Niamh penetrate their wet darkness—to contain a remarkable potency: "The trees grew taller and closer, immense in their wrinkling bark." As Niamh and Oisin work their way deeper and deeper into this thick virile forest, "cumbrous with stems of the hazel and oak," they discover a sudden valley spreading out before them. Here, at last, the trees grow more openly, though they extend infinitely upward: "The wood was so spacious . . . that He who had stars for His flocks/ Could fondle the leaves with His fingers, nor go from His dew-cumbered skies."

It is in this valley, finally, that the bird imagery of Book III is established. For sleeping in this vast forest are naked giants, handsome except for one peculiarity: "The tops of their ears were feathered, their hands were the claws of birds." Though Yeats never identifies these sleeping giants, his source for them, as Russell K. Alspach has pointed out, is almost certainly one of the Seven Sleepers' legends which he had read in preparing his book of Folk Tales. He was also familiar with Katharine Tynan's "Waiting," a poem in which the sleeping giants are Finn and his warriors who wait for the day of Ireland's need. But Yeats alters his sources significantly. For one thing he suppresses the fact that the sleepers are Finn's warriors, since Oisin would immediately recognize his chief. For another, more to our purpose, he assigns to his giants bird-characteristics, thereby fitting them into the general scheme of his bird-tree imagery. In neither the Seven Sleepers' legend he had used in his Folk Tale book nor in Katharine Tynan's poem is there any justification for this treatment of the sleeping heroes. Yet Yeats goes out of his way to make them bird-like. "Golden the nails of his bird-claws," says Yeats of the leader of the giants.

Not only are the giants bird-like, they are surrounded by birds. "Over the limbs and the valley the slow owls wandered and came." These owls, like the feathered heroes, are "slow" and "white," an ironical parody of the swift, white, distant gull of Book II which had circled impossibly high above Oisin, so high his call could not reach it. These owls are close: "The owls had builded their nests in their locks,/ Filling the fibrous dimness with long generations of eyes"; "Owls ruffling and pacing around/ Sidled their bodies against him [the leader of the giants], filling the shade with their eyes."

These owls, intimate companions of the sleeping giants, parallel the birds of Aengus, the immortal painted birds of Book I. But by this stage of the poem, birds sing no more. Their song had been reduced to a flutter in the second book, and here it is gone completely. The only sound of the owls is their "ruffling."

This disappearance of bird-song is integral to the scheme of the poem. The first island had been filled with sweet noises. The painted birds never stopped their song. The Immortals, Aengus himself, burst into song at the least provocation. But as the great towers of the second part replaced the trees like sooty fingers of the first part and were in turn replaced by the gigantic trees of Book III, "immense in their wrinkled bark," the shouting and singing of Book I dwindled to a "fluttering" song in Book II and at last in Book III to a mere rumble of noise: "dripping," "dropping; old silence and that one sound," "Long sighs arose," "bubbled the ground," "owls ruffling and pacing around/ Sidled their bodies," "Came sound from those monstrous sleepers, a sound like the stirring of flies."

But though the immortal birds no longer sing in the trees, there is a music on the third island, this time a music which emanates directly from tree itself. For a sleeping bird-man waves a musical, magical, supernatural branch: "Golden the nails of his bird-claws, flung loosely along the dim ground;/ In one was a branch soft-shining with bells more many than sighs/ In midst of an old man's bosom . . ." This remarkable branch is "sleep's forebear," the ancestor, the very source of sleep itself. "I saw how those slumberers . . . Laid hands on the bell-branch and swayed it, and fed of unhuman sleep." Oisin himself is put under its spell when, trying to wake the sleepers with Niamh's horn, he shouts, " 'Come out of the shadow, king of the nails of gold!' " The king's lips move but "no answer out of them came;/ Then he swayed in his fingers the bell-branch, slow dropping a sound in faint streams/ Softer than snow-flakes in April and piercing the marrow like flame." Oisin immediately falls asleep, forgets the birds and trees of the real world: "How the falconer follows the falcon in the weeds of the heron's plot"; "a century there I forgot/ That the spear-shaft is made out of ashwood." The bell-branch causes him to dream of the heroes he had known, the kings of the Red Branch. Occasionally he is stirred almost to consciousness "When brushed with the wings of the owls, in the dimness they love going by." It is at such a moment that the sign ending the hundred years arrives. Unlike the staff of wood of Book I or the beech-bough of Book II, the sign in Book III is a living representative from the real world and, as a living representative, it has power the beech-bough and the staff of wood did not have to pull him back to the land he had come from. This sign, of course, is the starling, an un-magical "real" bird, a bird with absolutely no supernatural associations. Because of its reality it can break the spell both of the third island and of Niamh. Oisin first sees it from his "half waking" sleep: "So watched I when . . . fell,/ Weak, in the midst of the meadow, from his miles in the midst of the air,/ A starling like them that forgathered 'neath a moon waking white as a shell/ When the Fenians made foray at morning." He mounts Niamh's horse, leaving her on the island: "The bird in my fingers, I mounted, remembering alone that delight/ Of twilight and slumber were gone, and that hoofs impatiently stept."

As he leaves, Niamh realizes Oisin has broken the double spell of her power and that of the bell-branch: " 'O wandering Oisin, the strength of the bell-branch is naught,/ For there moves alive in your fingers the fluttering sadness of earth.' " This passage, perhaps the most quoted passage in the poem, is deservedly famous; for it beautifully integrates the central theme of the poem and its dominant images. The starling, the mortal bird, becomes "the fluttering sadness of earth." It echoes the theme of the immortal birds of Book I which, looking on life that must die, "murmur at last, 'Unjust, unjust.' " Oisin, finally identified as "wandering" in this passage, gains a new dimension as half-consciously we identify "wandering Oisin" who carries in his fingers "the fluttering sadness of earth" with the "wandering osprey Sorrow" of Book I.

The starling, "the fluttering sadness of earth," carries us back to the melancholy song of the lost lady of Book II who, eternally rescued by Oisin, is also eternally captured by the dusky demon. She had also borne in her a fluttering sadness. Her song had gone out on the waters "like wings of birds" in a "fluttering sigh."

And the starling, in its "fluttering sadness," anticipates the fluttering dead-leaf image in which Niamh in Book III, in her last words to Oisin, hopelessly cries farewell "from the earth": " 'I would die like a small withered leaf in the autumn, for breast unto breast/ We shall mingle no more, nor our gazes empty their sweetness lone/ In the isles of the farthest seas where only the spirits come.' " Holding the entire poem in one encompassing image is, of course, impossible. But here Yeats almost accomplishes that impossible feat.

The rest of the poem, from this point to the end, is more mechanically handled. Yeats has to complete his design, so the horse carries Oisin through the great forest. Those tree images we have already examined rush by in reverse order. At last, as Oisin crosses the sea, long after the trees have vanished behind him, the bird itself vanishes: "the winds fled out of the vast,/ Snatching the bird in secret."

When Oisin approaches the real world he hears "the great grass-barnacle calling." But in his three-hundred years of wandering, the world has changed. And though he laughs at the little and mean church-dominated people "like the roaring of wind in a wood," he is doomed to be defeated by them as Finn and his warriors had been. Touching the earth, he feels suddenly the weight of his three-hundred years and realizes he will soon rejoin the Fenians in death.

But what should we make of the dominant images of bird and tree? What is their function in the poem? To what extent can we legitimately assign "meanings" to them? How do those "meanings," interacting among themselves and the images from which they are drawn, help create one poem?

All answers to such questions must, of course, be tentative. But I think we can be reasonably safe in asserting that imagery in poetry of this sort—particularly if the imagery is confined as this is to several dominant images—is structural rather than decorative.

And it is also, I think, safe to say that the explicit theme is reinforced and expanded by themes implicit in the images themselves. These themes, far more ambiguous than that explicitly stated in the poem, give the reader the feeling that he is experiencing something (as he is) both more complicated and at the same time more important than he can ever really understand.

Yeats's images accomplish this miracle in two ways: they are used both as private signs and as universal symbols. And in neither case can they ever completely be explicated. Though we might reasonably guess that the demon stands for Yeats's father, he does equally well stand for oppressive English rule. He is also, as folk figure, the returning seasons, the sun, and—in a different context —the abstract destructive force. Yet in none of these identifications do we have him. He is the composite of all of them and probably of others I have not tracked down.

Similarly the three islands are aspects of one life: youth, middle age, and old age; they represent as well the world as experienced by three types of men: the lover, the active man, and the contemplative man. Ellmann is perhaps right in seeing them as autobiographical: Sligo, London, and Howth. Yet however carefully we pin them down, we recognize always that they are more comprehensive than the limitations we assign them. I do not mean to suggest that any of those limitations are false, but I do mean to emphasize that they are limitations and, as such, less than the symbols they would seek to clarify.

Yet even if Yeats's successful image is defined as a synthesis of private sign and universal symbol, that definition does not adequately explain its function. For the great image contains not only the meaning Yeats has forced into it and the meaning he has found in it; it contains also the meaning each reader must—in his very nature as reader—add to it. And the poem we read, because of this creative act of our own, is never precisely the poem Yeats read when he put down his manuscript for the last time.

It is the role of the dominant image to force us into this creative act. Recognizing as we do that the poem has importance and a meaning we cannot quite understand (almost always because we face imagery of numerous but imprecise "meanings"), we fit to the given image not only private meanings of our own but feelings too. Want to or not, we all do this. And somewhere between the poem Yeats wrote and the poem we read stands the collaboration—Yeats-Seiden, Yeats-Ellmann, Yeats-Unterecker, whoever else may be involved—that is the nearest thing there ever will be to the "final" poem. And that collaboration is accomplished through the action of the dominant images.

When imagery is both dominant and obsessive, the poem becomes a still more complicated structure. For not only is involved the way the poet is using his image in the particular poem but—to some extent, at least—the way he has used the image in the rest of his prose and his poetry.

The birds in the trees of Oisin's first island reinforce the bird-tree image in all its other appearances, not only in those poems now grouped in the *Crossways* section of his *Collected Poems* which Yeats had written before starting *Oisin*, but in those which follow it. Such imagery unifies both individual works and Yeats's total production.

2 * Crossways

The appropriately named *Crossways* section of his *Collected Poems* represents, as Yeats pointed out in 1895, some of the "many pathways" he had tried out in his first poetic efforts. Though it is dated 1889, the bulk of the poems were written before 1887 and several of them as early as 1885.

But, with the exception of "The Falling of the Leaves," "To an Isle in the Water," and "Down by the Salley Gardens" in which only punctuation was changed, the poems as we read them are considerably different from those which appeared in Yeats's first book of poetry, *The Wanderings of Oisin and Other Poems.* Most of the poems in that first volume were in subsequent printings either deleted or wholly rewritten, the order of the surviving poems—always important to Yeats—represents a complete realignment, and two poems from a later collection ("The Ballad of Father O'Hart" and "The Ballad of the Foxhunter") were added to form at the end of *Crossways* a small group of literary ballads on Irish themes.

Though Yeats sometimes toyed with the idea of abandoning most of the poems in the group ("Every time I have reprinted them I have considered the leaving out of most, and then remembered an old school friend who has some of them by heart, for no better reason, as I think, than that they remind him of his own youth."), his final decision was to hammer them into a kind of prologue to the *Collected Poems*. Made respectable, the best of them could give the reader insight into the evolution of Yeats's major themes and techniques.

And those themes surely are anticipated. "Words alone are certain good" sings the Happy Shepherd of the first poem who, celebrating the artist, attacks the dusty deeds of materialists. And, like the later Yeats of *A Vision*, that shepherd recognizes subjective truth as the only valid kind: "there is no truth/ Saving in thine own heart."

In the final arrangement of the section, poem is carefully linked to poem. Yeats, who had seen in Blake's *Songs of Innocence* and *Songs of Experience* a model for the successful integration of a group of lyrics, must have realized as he assembled *Crossways* that in the two poems which became "The Song of the Happy Shepherd" and "The Sad Shepherd" there were possibilities for a pair of companion poems. Reworked and retitled, they fit closely together. The Happy Shepherd of the first poem who discovers in a sea shell the catalytic agent that makes poetry possible (the shell rewords "in melodious guile" man's "fretful words" until they have become pearly songs) is contrasted with the Sad Shepherd of the second poem who—incapable of communicating with star, sea, or dewdrop, each of which, intent on itself, cannot hear his "piteous story"—discovers at last a sea shell and, like the Happy Shepherd, determines to whisper to its "pearly heart" his melancholy tale. But for the Sad Shepherd—no poet—the catalyst fails. The sea shell "Changed all he sang to inarticulate moan."

The third poem, "The Cloak, the Boat. and the Shoes," origi-

nally a song from *The Island of Statues*, a remarkably unsuccessful poetic drama which had had the first version of "The Song
of the Happy Shepherd" as its epilogue, is linked thematically to
"The Sad Shepherd" "whom Sorrow named his friend" by having
as its subject sorrow itself. This graceful lyric, Yeats's first published poem, is founded on the sort of paradox which was his lifelong delight. That Sorrow should be costumed in a cloak fair,
bright and lovely; that it should sail the seas—a swift rover—night
and day; and that its footfall—in shoes woven of white wool—
should be soundless, sudden, and light constitutes the sort of ironic
truth on which poetry is founded. Yeats's musical setting for this
idea reinforces the paradox: for the swift long line of each question and the tetrameter second line of each stanza hurried on by
an anapestic second foot balance the slow echoing dimeter last
line of each quatrain.

His very earliest poetry, Yeats later recollected, centered almost
entirely on Arcadian and Indian scenes. "Anashuya and Vijaya,"
one of the Indian poems, is interesting in that it is a very young
man's attempt to work out a poem on the subject of shared love,
a subject which Yeats returned to in "The Three Bushes" and the
associated lyrics of *Last Poems*. "The little Indian dramatic scene,"
Yeats noted years after he had written it, was intended to introduce a play about a man loved by two women, "who had the one
soul between them, the one woman waking when the other slept,
and knowing but daylight as the other only night." This theme,
Yeats commented in 1925, is crucial to A *Vision*: "the antithesis
of day and night and moon and sun." Perhaps no better illustration of the difference between Yeats's early heavily-ornamented
poetry and the bare violence of his late work can be found than
these poems which, though separated by fifty years of turbulent
living, are linked by a subject matter that through his life teased
and fascinated Yeats.

"The Indian upon God" develops the notion of subjective truth
that Yeats had introduced in "The Song of the Happy Shepherd"
and slightly expanded in "The Sad Shepherd." What seems at first

to be an attack on an anthropomorphic god proves on close inspection to be an early statement of one of Yeats's firmest convictions: reality is in the eye of the beholder. Though moorfowl, lotus, roebuck, and peacock each visualize God as a colossal reflection of itself, each accurately sees God as He is. He is in fact only what He is uniquely seen to be by each individual. In spite of the fact that each individual's vision of reality is necessarily different from every other individual's, each person's vision is also necessarily the only valid one.

The third Indian poem, "The Indian to His Love," tied to "The Indian upon God" by its imagery of islanded peahens dancing on a smooth lawn near the water's edge, excellently illustrates the brilliant sort of revision Yeats practiced in bringing frequently sentimental and often carelessly worded early work to something very close to perfection.

Yeats had no illusions about the quality of those first drafts ("Nothing I did at that time had merit," he remarked in 1938), but he did see in them the framework for poetry. This, for example, is the first printed of many versions of "The Indian to His Love":

An Indian Song
Oh wanderer in the southern weather,
    Our isle awaits us, on each lea
The pea-hens dance, in crimson feather
    A parrot swaying on a tree
    Rages at his own image in the enamelled sea.

There dreary Time lets fall his sickle
    And Life the sandals of her fleetness,
And sleek young Joy is no more fickle,
    And Love is kindly and deceitless,
    And life is over save the murmur and the sweetness.

There we will moor our lonely ship
    And wander ever with woven hands,

Murmuring softly, lip to lip,
  Along the grass, along the sands—
  Murmuring how far away are all earth's feverish lands.

How we alone of mortals are
  Hid in the earth's most hidden part,
While grows our love an Indian star,
  A meteor of the burning heart,
  One with the waves that softly round us laugh and dart.

Like swarming bees, one with the dove
  That moans and sighs a hundred days;
—How when we die our shades will rove,
  Dropping at eve in coral bays
  A vapoury footfall on the ocean's sleepy blaze.

The imprecise imagery of this early draft is carefully reworked in the poem's final form. The lush, romantic language is not entirely eliminated—Yeats was enough of a craftsman to know that destruction of the tone of the poem would destroy the poem— but the disorganized images are sorted out and the entire poem is tightened. A useless stanza is cancelled. And an early work with some good lines becomes a work of art.

Yeats's interest in the poem is evident in the care he lavished on its successive revisions. The most obvious change is the disappearance of the second stanza with its abstractions: Time, Life, Joy, and Love; but other abstractions have also been banished. "We" are no longer hidden in "earth's most hidden part"; we are now hidden under very real "quiet boughs." There is also a gain in immediacy: the island is no longer "there"; it is "here." It no longer "awaits us"; we have already arrived.

In the interval between the first draft and the last the imagery is also very carefully reorganized. The tree, for instance, grows much more important. The first version of the poem, it is true, places the parrot on "a tree." But in the final version that tree is enormously expanded. "Great boughs drop tranquillity"; we are

"Hid under quiet boughs apart"; our love grows one with "The heavy boughs." In the same way the bird imagery is developed and enriched. Peahen, parrot and dove still dominate the poem; but they are made to function not only as part of the island scenery, as they do in the original, but also as elements of dawn and dusk which mark the boundaries of the poem. The unadorned dove of the first draft is now burnished in the evening light; wings that "gleam and dart" have been added to the evening. And our shades will rove "by the water's drowsy blaze" only after "eve has hushed the feathered ways." In the first draft the parrot rages; but in the last he is raging for a reason—that he may be hushed, that the entire poem may be given through the integrated images a unity, an order, which was lacking in the first draft.

"The Falling of the Leaves," imagistically linked and thematically opposed to "The Indian to His Love," functions again as a kind of a companion poem to the one printed before it. In "The Indian to His Love" the passionate central characters, hidden under the heavy boughs of mid-summer, anticipate the eternal fidelity of their love-making ghosts. But in "The Falling of the Leaves" autumn has arrived, the leaves above the lovers are yellow, their sad souls are both weary and worn, and—as passion fades —they plan a last kiss before they part.

Drawing on identical theme, imagery, and language itself, "Ephemera" (at one time subtitled "An Autumn Idyl") explores precisely the same poetic materials Yeats had examined in "The Falling of the Leaves" but in an entirely different way. "The waning of love," the theme of "The Falling of the Leaves," is the tired lover's subject at the beginning of "Ephemera" but its development in terms of a brief dialogue reminiscent, as William York Tindall has pointed out, of Verlaine's *Colloque sentimental*," gives it a kind of dramatic distance. The conversation of the lovers is, if possible, even more sentimental than the language of "The Falling of the Leaves" but "Ephemera," made impersonal through characterization, seems objective. Its autumnal imagery of faded passion and of faded leaves that fall "like faint meteors" helps fit the "wandering hearts" of the lovers into the large design of the *Crossways* section, tying this end-of-passion poem to the heights of passion enjoyed by the lovers of "The Indian to His Love" who "wander ever with woven hands" while their love, "A meteor of the burning heart," integrates them to their island world.

If the first eight poems of *Crossways,* Indian and Arcadian in subject matter, represent one road Yeats briefly wandered on, the remaining eight, grimly Irish, represent the one he finally travelled. Though Yeats later found, "especially in the ballads, some triviality and sentimentality" that was disturbing, and though he never afterwards confined himself so strictly to the versification of such legends as that he drew on for "The Madness of King Goll," Ireland became his scene in much the same way that his life and the lives of his friends became his subject matter. "The Stolen Child," set in the Sligo neighborhood, carefully substitutes for the peacock-populated Indian island of his earlier poetry the very real island in Lough Gill that had been its model and that was to serve as scenery for "To an Isle in the Water," "The Lake Isle of Innisfree," his discarded play *The Island of Statues,* and his discarded poem "The Danaan Quicken Tree." The ambivalence at the heart of things, a subject Yeats never tired of, is discovered by "The Stolen Child" who, in accepting the freedom from weeping that the fairies of the magic island promise, learns that he will also be freed from human peace and human joy. Though immortality is much to be desired, an unemotional, trivial, inhuman immortality attained at the price of feeling itself may be a poor bargain. No wonder the human child, baffled by a weeping world, leaves it for the fairies' island "solemn-eyed."

This same island, seen as a retreat from the disorder of the world to a never-never land of love and idleness, serves as scene for "To an Isle in the Water," a good example of Yeats's early manner which, unrevised, reveals the dreamy-eyed sensitive romantic that Yeats later chose to mask for purposes both of poetry and, perhaps, sheer survival. Salvaged for us in *Crossways,* he is kept that we may see how carefully Yeats gradually carved out the mask of his opposite. A fragile poem, probably borrowing from the "could"-"dare" antithesis of Blake's "The Tiger" its balancing of line 8's affection ("With her would I go") and line 16's passion ("With her would I fly"), it gives us young Yeats at his most love-lorn.

"Down by the Salley Gardens," an expansion of "three lines imperfectly remembered" that Yeats had heard sung by an old peasant woman in Sligo, turns to Irish folk song for its source in much the same way that King Goll turns to legendary material. The young and foolish boy who was too proud to take his sweetheart's advice in the willow garden or by the river is also precisely paralleled to the old fisherman's memory of himself as a youth "with never a crack in my heart" in "The Meditation of the Old Fisherman." In that poem, however, it is the maidens by the shore who are "the proud and apart."

The antithesis between youth and age and the anguish of mortality itself serve as common themes to bind together these poems and the three ballads that end the *Crossways* section. The three ballads, versified from a Sligo county history ("Father O'Hart"), "a sermon preached in a chapel at Howth" ("Moll Magee"), and "an incident in one of Kickham's novels" ("the Foxhunter") were, Yeats properly felt, too imitative of popular literary ballads and too self-consciously Irish in subject matter to be very good poems in themselves. They did, however, neatly round out a group of poems which—in spite of diverse subject matter, scenes, and metrical forms—were closely related through carefully articulated images of sea, bird, and tree; through a persistent tone of world-weariness; and through interlinked themes of time-endangered love. Though the poems show Yeats at a crossways, all the signs point in one direction.

3 * The Rose

As Yeats revised the poems of 1891 and 1892 that largely constitute the section called *The Rose* he successfully centered them on the three areas of interest defined in "To the Rose upon the Rood of Time." There he indicated that this group of poems would be personal, occult, and Irish. And they are. Specifically, they deal with his frustrated love for Maud Gonne, the Rosicrucian and cabalistic doctrine he was learning in the Order of the Golden Dawn and which he drew on for both rose and tree symbolism, and those legends of ancient pre-Christian Ireland which focused on Cuchulain, the heroic fighter and lover; Fergus, the king who—in Yeats's version—abandoned his kingdom to become a poet of Druidical wisdom; and Conchubar, the crafty Red Branch king of kings who, possessing all things, could not win love.

The red, proud, and sad Rose invoked by Yeats in the opening poem is not only "eternal beauty," though Yeats explicitly identifies it as that at the end of the first stanza, it is also, as he points out in other places, a compound "of Beauty and of Peace," of "beauty and wisdom," and of Shelley's Intellectual Beauty and man's suffering. In a note to the early editions of his *Collected Poems,* he associates it as well with physical love, Ireland, and religion. As a young man he deliberately extended the symbol still further by frequently quoting Count Goblet D'Alviella's identification of rose and sun and later was pleased to discover Dante's image of Heaven as a white rose with a sun-like yellow center. Drawing on his theosophical, cabalistic and Rosicrucian training, he explained that he had substituted rose for lotus as the proper flower to blossom on the Tree of Life: "Because the Rose, the flower sacred to the Virgin Mary, and the flower that Apuleius' adventurer ate, when he was changed out of the ass's shape and received into the fellowship of Isis, is the western Flower of Life, I have imagined it growing upon the Tree of Life." And since Yeats identified the Tree of Life with the North Star, he visualized the constellation Draco, the Dragon, which wheels about Polaris, as guardian of the Rose, and the Seven Lights (the constellation variously identified as Big Dipper, Great Bear, and—in Ireland—the Crooked Plough) as weeping over its theft.

Flower of the cabalistic Tree, the double nature of which I have already discussed, the Rose that grows "under the boughs of love and hate" represents that intersection of mortality and immortality which seemed to Yeats man's richest experience, for the mundane rose—a "poor foolish" thing that lives only one day—traps in its symbolic form "eternal beauty." Yeats's prayer, in the opening poem's second stanza, that the rose breath come near but that it not engulf him is therefore a prayer that he be allowed to function at the intersecting point, that point at which—mortal but in touch with immortal things—he is able to hold fixed in mind on Time's destructive cross the Rose, symbol of imperishable order. His project, given this double vision, is to sing both of "common things" and as well of "the strange things said/ By God to the bright hearts of those long dead." His way of doing this will be to fit sensuous detail to the "ancient ways" of old Eire and so create poems.

His rosy ambition, rather vaguely outlined in the first poem, is made much more explicit in the two concluding lyrics of the section. Trying to be Irish for Maud Gonne's sake and occult for the sake of his soul, Yeats felt that he had found an overlapping place in the ancient Irish legends of the Tuath De Danaan (the Race of the Gods of Dana—the mythological forces of goodness and light which deteriorate ultimately into fairies as their power diminishes in an increasingly secular world), and of his particular hero Cuchulain. For the pre-Christian Irish myths, he felt, complemented in many ways his occult discoveries.

Drawing on memories of long, intense conversations with members of the Golden Dawn (among them Mrs. Dorothea Hunter who, in a trance, had provided imagery for his poem by informing him that the music of Heaven is "the continuous clashing of earth's swords") Yeats managed in "To Some I have Talked with by the Fire" to combine current folk belief, legendary Irish material, the cabalistic doctrine of God's Ineffable Name, a veiled prophesy of political revolution, and an explicit prophesy of a religious revolution that would culminate in the return of the old gods and so begin a new historical cycle.

"To Ireland in the Coming Times" was even more definite. Yeats was staking out his territory carefully, and he wanted its limits to be known. He had already been taken to task by fellow members of the Rhymers' Club for "obscurity" and by Maud Gonne and John O'Leary for writing insufficiently-Irish poetry. "To Ireland in the Coming Times" was his defense. He was, he felt, as patriotic as the popular Irish poets Davis, Mangan, and Ferguson but his art, he argued, was greater because he sang not only of Irish scenery but as well of eternal truth, of the "red-rose-bordered hem" of that timeless mystical Beauty which he symbolized in the Rose and which, manifested in time, had made "Ireland's heart begin to beat." And because poetry to be effective had to be personal, he sang also, he claimed, in terms of his own experience: both "the dream I knew" and "the love I lived." Such poetry could help create, he hoped, a greater Ireland, one unified in culture, in the coming times.

"Fergus and the Druid" and "Cuchulain's Fight with the Sea" are, with *Oisin*, Yeats's first important poetic contributions to that Unity of Culture which he hoped to impose on Ireland by making her familiar with her own legends. Though the Fergus anecdote presented no complexities, that of Cuchulain did. Yeats, who found of compelling interest the archetypal tales of father-son conflict, saw in Cuchulain a Mask both for himself and for his nation. If he could make the virile lineaments of the ancient hero sharp enough, he and Ireland might be able to put on necessary Masks of courageous, reckless gaiety. Frequently reworking the poem, then dramatizing it as the crucial middle drama (*On Baile's Strand*) of his five-play Cuchulain cycle, then reworking that drama several times and alluding to it in his late poetry, Yeats made ultimately of Cuchulain's battle with the sea a structure designed to express man's anguish when, maddened by the complexities of warring emotions no violence can unravel, he takes arms against not only a sea of troubles but the sea itself, emblematic image of fecund destructive life.

Though in his play Yeats follows mythology in making Aoife the mother of the son Cuchulain kills in personal combat, in the poem Yeats presents a simpler plot. Emer, Cuchulain's wife, learns that her husband is bringing back to king Conchubar's camp a young "sweet-throated" concubine. Angered, she makes her son swear to reveal his name only at sword-point and sends him out to seek and fight in personal combat any man who has sworn the same oath. Knowing that her husband is the only man so bound, Emer has planned a revenge designed to kill Cuchulain or to drive him mad The doomed father and son, oath-bound, meet as strangers, present their challenges, and fight until Cuchulain, mortally wounding his son, asks his name: "Cuchulain I, mighty Cuchulain's son." Fearful that the enraged father will attack his court, Conchubar orders the Druids to put Cuchulain under a magical spell. Cuchulain, deluded, hears his name shouted from the waves and, rising again to battle, fights "with the invulnerable tide."

Though Yeats, referring to the poem and the play based on it, commented in 1903 that "I never re-wrote anything so many times," he continued to tinker with both poem and play for years. Eventually, Cuchulain became for him "a heroic figure because he was creative joy separated from fear." Yeats, making Cuchulain half-god and half-mortal, imagined for him a conception parallel to Helen's. The sun-god (like Zeus who to attack Leda had assumed the form of a giant swan) had put on the shape of a giant hawk and so costumed had raped mortal Dectora and begotten Cuchulain.

It is no accident, therefore, that Yeats follows his Cuchulain poem with an oblique reference to Helen in the opening stanza of "The Rose of the World." For Helen, Cuchulain's female counterpart though from a different mythology, like him bird-begotten, half mortal and half goddess, the fatal woman whose great beauty led to the destruction of Troy, is Ideal Woman just as Cuchulain is Ideal Man. Yeats, linking Maud Gonne's "red lips" with Helen and that figure from Irish mythology who most closely corresponds to Helen, Deirdre for the sake of whom "Usna's children died," speculates about the function of Beauty and concludes, as other cabalists before him, that it is a primary aspect of God.

But omnipotence, in Yeats as in Blake, is always two-faced: the god of peace struggles always with ways opposes Hell; time crashes alw of eternity; soul battles body. "Th though greatly praising Maud Gon tive by that crucial "If" that begins ity, "The Rose of Battle," is in con happy lovers from the necessary wa happy lovers, "The sad, the lonely cultists, who will, waging God's b Old Night. Mortal, they will nec they will have experienced revelati

The three poems that follow the trio of roses focus exclusively on the lucky state of the pure in heart who are wrapped in the illusions of "The Rose of Peace": "A Faery Song" offers "rest" to the legendary Irish lovers who fled from Conchubar's wrath; "The Lake Isle of Innisfree" beckons Yeats with its promise of "some peace" away from London's grey pavements; and "A Cradle Song" —partly translated from a Gaelic poem—sighs that innocent children must grow up. Yeats, in later years shocked that sentimental, autobiographical "Innisfree" should be his most popular poem, came to dislike its Biblical opening lines and the inversion in the last stanza. (The idea for it had come to him one day when he stood "very homesick" before a shop window that displayed a little fountain. "I . . . began to remember lake water. From the sudden remembrance came my poem *Innisfree*.")

Something closer to the reality of "The Rose of Battle" is hinted in "The Pity of Love," one of a group of love poems Yeats copied out in a manuscript book for presentation to Maud Gonne, for here the beloved is threatened not only by merchants but also by earth, air, and water. Those threats are expanded in the four poems —all originally written for Maud Gonne—which follow. Tears in "The Sorrow of Love," age in "When You are Old," exhaustion in "The White Birds," and death itself in "A Dream of Death" conspire to destroy the illusory happiness of those lovers protected by the "Rose of Peace."

Of these poems, only "The Sorrow of Love," the most carefully rewritten and perhaps the best, is likely to offer the reader any great difficulty. In its first draft it presented the comparatively uncomplicated story of a young man who, deceived into happiness by a full moon and "ever-singing leaves," finds his whole world picture ely shaken when "you," a girl with "red mournful lips," arrive et everything by bringing him "the whole of the world's rows, and burdens.

he plot remains much the same, the revision—made uses much more sharply on the contrast between of stanza I and man's disorder in stanza III.

Yeats does this by forcing the reader to construct, much as a painter might, two scenes identical but for a shift in emphasis. In the first scene, that of stanza I, a noisy sparrow singing under a brilliant moon, "all the milky sky" (milky perhaps because of the domination of that full moon but more likely because the millions of stars that make up the milky way fill it brimful of light) and "all that famous harmony of leaves" combine—"harmony" gives us the clue —to compose a scene of static order that successfully blots out that perishable desiring thing, "man's image and his cry." Yet all this order can be obliterated by something as frail as a girl who, doomed and proud (Helen, maybe, for Yeats links her to the death of the last Trojan king and Greek Odysseus' return home after the wars), merely arises (since the composition is presumably framed by a window we are justified in reading the lines "rose weeping from bed," though in view of the historical parallel we should bear in mind that the figure of Helen arose in the chronology of time to bring disorder to two states and destruction to a civilization)—and because of this single action: her arising weeping to step into the scene, that static picture which moon, sky, and leaves had composed is violently shattered to be replaced by an image of chaos: the sky, emptied now but for the moving, "climbing" moon, has instantly been transformed: the sparrow has vanished to be replaced by "clamorous eaves"; and the once harmonious leaves now utter only ugly noises: "lamentation." The ordered world which had once blotted out man now becomes him, and moon, sky, and leaves—swept into motion—"compose" that epitome of disorder, the articulated shape of chaos itself, "man's image and his cry."

This impressive structure is achieved through great craftsmanship. The revisions reveal it. Some of the effects, of course, may be accidental. (That repeated "arose" which pleased Louis MacNeice because of its abruptness delights me because it puns so accurately on the title of the section: my eyes, seeing double, enjoy the simultaneous vision of "A girl arose" and "A girl, a rose, that had red mournful lips . . ."; such second sight might even have entertained Yeats.) But accidentally or through design, the poem has the strength of great art.

Picking up the death imagery of "A Dream of Death," a poem Yeats had written for Maud Gonne who in the autumn of 1891 was recovering at St. Raphael from exhaustion suffered in her efforts to aid the Donegal poor, and the Irish subject matter of "The White Birds" (white because they are the immortal birds of fairyland), "The Countess Cathleen in Paradise" sets the heroine of Yeats's play dancing before the angels. The dancing figure—one of Yeats's favorite images for the synthesis of body and spirit—appears also in "Who Goes with Fergus?" another poem drawn from the early versions of his *Countess Cathleen* play. What seems at first glance a simple lyric is made rich and strange by the chiasmus of "brood" and "no more" that knits the two stanzas together, by the alliterative chiasmus of the last two lines, by the complex rhythm of the second last, and by the crowding together in the last four lines of the traditional elements of fire, earth, air, and water.

"The Man who Dreamed of Faeryland," drawing also on a symbolic dancer and the four elements for its organization, splits up man's life in four neat sections. The distracted man of the title, however, is never able to find peace in lovemaking youth, money-making middle age, angry old age, or mouldering death, for the gold and silver imagery of occult symbols, separately presented to him in each of the first three stanzas and bound up in the "glittering summer" of the fourth, lures him always away from the things of this world to the things of the spirit. A prophetic poem, its stanzas could stand as epigraphs for the chapters of Yeats's biography.

Even more explicitly autobiographical, Yeats's revision of "The Dedication to a Book of Stories selected from the Irish Novelists" turns what had been the patriotic and sentimental tune of the first draft into an indictment of "Eire,/ That country where a man can be so crossed;/ Can be so battered, badgered and destroyed/ That he's a loveless man." Yeats's imagery, drawing on the same bell branch that had put Oisin to sleep on his third island, contrasts Ireland's one-time green boughs with those barren ones of the present and introduces the final group of poems in the section, all dominated by an imagery of branch and tree.

Yeats found in the tree a particularly satisfactory symbol. "I don't know if one ever delights in trees and the sea with equal intensity, and I am of the tree party," he once jokingly wrote his father; but his devotion to the tree had begun long before that 1913 letter. Perhaps first made conscious of the tree as symbol by his occult studies and Madame Blavatsky's commentaries on comparative mythology, he quickly realized that it offered the poet complex and interesting patterns of integration: rooted as it is in the earth, leafing out in the air, sustained by water, and transforming these three essential elements into life itself through the beneficent fire of the sun, it became for Yeats the best plant on which he could perch his favorite animal, the bird.

As Yeats grew older, he liked to make the branches of his tree bare or broken, and some, at least, of their "meanings" seem fairly obvious. In one place or another they can easily be read as old man, sterility, modern times, mortality, twentieth-century Ireland, "truth," and—once in a while—reality.

Such branches are to be found in "The Lamentation of the Old Pensioner," a poem Yeats says he versified from "the very words of an old Wicklow peasant." Unlike the first draft in which the tree was green, in which the whole second stanza with its references to destructive Time was missing, and in which the pensioner at the end felt merely fretful, the revision emphasizes the broken tree which the pensioner uses to shelter himself from the rain. Contemplating Time which has transfigured him, he presents the tree as symbol for age, sterility ("There's not a woman turns her face/ Upon a broken tree . . ."), and reality. Yet since he still has contact with life-giving rain (the broken tree is poor shelter), "the beauties" that he loved remain in his memory, and he is able— like Yeats in his own old age—to spit in Time's face.

What is perhaps most interesting about this poem is that the simple allegorical solution—the age, sterility, and/or reality formula

—while functioning as it should is nevertheless considerably qualified in the context of the whole poem. The hero, for example, is
both sheltered under the broken tree and at the same time is symbolized by it. Many critics find this a serious defect. Yet one is not
really bothered by it as he reads the poem, and it does feel right.
Poetic logic, as a matter of fact, frequently demands such alogical
relationships. There is no "reasonable" correlation, consequently,
between the rain (clearly associated with Time) and the saliva
which the old man spits into Time's face, yet a poetic and functional relationship exists, a relationship further complicated by the
"face" which not a woman turns to the broken tree and the "transfiguration" the old pensioner has experienced, a transfiguration
parallel to and complementing the transfiguration of the tree
itself.

Other more deliberately logical relationships (the old-pensioner/
broken-tree image opposed to the "pikes" the "lads" are making,
for instance) supplement the dominant symbolism and help move
the poem from the passivity of stanza I ("I *shelter* from the rain,"
"every company/ That *talked* of love") to the beginning of action
in stanza II ("lads are *making* pikes," "crazy rascals *rage* their fill")
to a final violence in stanza III ("I spit into the face of Time").

My point here is that Yeats's deceptively simple images are,
upon analysis, anything but simple, are, as a matter of fact, far
more complicated and function in a far more intricate fashion than,
say, the famous "difficult" but in reality more nearly allegorical
images of T. S. Eliot. Eliot's wasteland, once its dry watercourses
and blasted trees have been accurately mapped, can safely be
trusted to present the same landscape in poem after poem. The
seasoned traveller can soon find his way through that desert to the
little door in the rose garden. Yeats's scenery is trickier. His blasted
trees have a habit of standing in the rain, or of bearing green
branches, or of emitting glistening white light, or of blossoming
near the big dipper into celestial red roses. When several such
symbols, loaded with multiple and often indefinable meanings, intersect (when the bird, for instance, lights in the branches of the

tree), the familiar world may momentarily be illuminated for us by the special penetrating light of symbolist art and all things seem for that instant in harmony. But that is only possible if the symbols are apprehended in their complexity. Each precise meaning we fix to them is a limiting device that diminishes their power. Though for a time Yeats did allow himself the luxury of explaining his poems, he tried always to make clear that their symbols made them frameworks of possibilities and ultimately determined "I must leave my myths and symbols to explain themselves as the years go by and one poem lights up another."

The poem most directly lighted up by "The Lamentation of the Old Pensioner" is "The Two Trees," a work Yeats was especially fond of, perhaps because he had written it for Maud Gonne who declared that it was her favorite among his poems. The basic imagery of the poem is drawn from the passage he had read in Mathers' *The Kabbalah Unveiled* about the birds (Mathers identified them as souls and angels) which "lodge and build their nests" in the Tree of the Knowledge of Good and of Evil. Shortly before he had read Mathers' account he had watched a young Catholic girl who, in a trance, had claimed to see "the Tree of Life with ever-sighing souls moving in its branches instead of sap, and among its leaves all the fowl of the air." Impressed by the similar imagery assigned by the girl and Mathers to the precisely opposed trees, Yeats put together his poem.

Describing first the Tree of Life—the "holy tree" growing in his beloved's heart—Yeats constructs a vast image designed to show the organic unity of the world of the spirit. Its branches start from a trunk of "joy" and reach out across a sky made starry by the "merry light" of its fruit. Its secure root plants "quiet" in the night. The rhythmic movements of its head are so archetypal as to have been the pattern both for the waves and for the lover's poetry. And filling the "great ignorant leafy ways" of its branches are bird-like, circling "Loves" which, "gyring, spiring," create—like so many of Yeats's circling birds—images of order, essential circles, in the spiritual tree.

Yet no image can exist without its opposite. Opposing the world of spirit is the world of flesh and blood, the "bitter glass" which we look into when we live exclusively for practical and worldly ends. There we see the "fatal image" of the Tree of the Knowledge of Good and Evil, its frozen roots, broken boughs, blackened leaves— all things turned to "barrenness." No longer are the great leafy ways "ignorant," for Knowledge has come to blast them with "unresting thought." Men who once saw visions of order, what Yeats later described to Joseph Hone as "the ancient hierarchy of beings from man up to the One," have broken the great circles of spiritual existence. The birds of the Tree of Knowledge no longer make flaming circles, "gyring, spiring," but rather go "to and fro . . . / Or else they stand and sniff the wind." Ravens, their wings are ragged and their claws cruel.

The important thing to see in Yeats's poem, however, is not that life is torn between two opposed images—the two "different" trees and their "different" sets of birds—but rather that those images have a direct relationship to one another. Each reflects precisely one-half of that enigmatic man-shaped cabalistic tree which stands between them. Diagramed, the pattern is something like this:

Spirit		Flesh
The Tree of Life	The	The Tree of the Knowledge of
	self	Good and Evil
Man's heart		The world
Inner truth		Outer falsehood
Peaceful ignorance		Unresting thought

Only in name are there two trees. Their images, placed back to back, form one design.

That so grand a poem was occasioned by Yeats's concern over Maud Gonne's devotion to politics rather than to him does not in any measure diminish its symmetrical excellence. Like those great oaks that from little acorns grow, "The Two Trees" dwarfs in its expansive majesty the memory of its own genesis.

4 * The Wind Among the Reeds

By 1899 when he brought together as *The Wind Among the Reeds* his first volume of new poetry since the 1892 *Countess Cathleen* volume, Yeats was a deliberate and assured craftsman. He had decided that he was primarily a lyricist and a symbolist; and, in a long set of notes to the volume, he tried to help his readers understand the difficult Celtic and occult material he was working with.

In spite of the fact that Yeats did see himself essentially as a lyricist, he had the temperament of a dramatist (something that explains a great deal about Yeats's character, particularly the "insincerity" which many of his critics think they detect both in his life and in his work). And it was this temperament he drew on as he constructed the first versions of *The Wind Among the Reeds*.

Like many dramatists, Yeats saw his own character as a compound of warring personalities. He was the dutiful son who was beginning to support the domineering father he admired yet could not live with. He was Maud Gonne's faithful, love-sick, rejected suitor; yet, while eloquently protesting to her his sincerely-felt devotion, he had become deeply involved in a complex and passionate relationship with Mrs. Shakespear whose husband refused to allow her the divorce that would let her marry Yeats. These different selves could be in part reconciled by giving each a voice, and to do this Yeats devised a group of characters whom he linked together in the short stories that comprise *The Secret Rose*. Once they had been given names and identities, they could also function as spokesmen for his poetry. By assigning quite personal poems written originally for Mrs. Shakespear or Maud Gonne to such characters as Aedh, Hanrahan, or Michael Robartes, Yeats could sort out his several selves.

Such an attitude toward character is, of course, not unusual. Yeats's friend William Sharp, for instance, carried it to spectacular extremes by inventing Fiona Macleod, a lady with whom he carried on a lifelong correspondence, even going so far as to evolve a feminine handwriting in which he composed her letters to himself. Yeats, far more conservative, was content to see his characters "more as principles of the mind than as actual personages." Yet they were always for him opposing aspects of a personality he found difficult without such dramatization to understand. For where, in such a welter of selves, did the real man lie? If the real Yeats was Maud Gonne's devoted lover, was Mrs. Shakespear's admirer a traitor to be despised? Only if he saw himself as neither figure but as a compound born of their struggle could Yeats avoid the sense of guilt which would have made him inoperative as a writer. Using his feeling of multiple personality, he created poems.

Most of the poems of the early editions of *The Wind Among the Reeds* Yeats assigned to Aedh, a character he explained in magical terms as "fire burning by itself." Michael Robartes he described as "fire reflected in water." Hanrahan was "fire blown by the wind." Since he identified fire with the imagination, all three characters were to be seen as imaginative men—Aedh offering up his richness before all that he loves, Michael Robartes proudly brooding over his possessions, Hanrahan too changeable to gather possessions at all. In Christian terms, Yeats described Michael Robartes as the adoration of the Magi, Hanrahan as the adoration of the shepherds, and Aedh as the myrrh and frankincense which burns by itself.

This complicated pattern of personalities, he reinforced by some rather arbitrary symbolism. Yeats was at this time steeped in the occult and his research in comparative mythology had gone beyond Madame Blavatsky and William Morris to include studies of the work of Rhys and Frazer. His notes to the poems, made imposing by references to Welsh November rhymes, the *Mabinogion,* and solar heroes, draw on everything from folk tales to the *Golden Bough* in support of a group of "images that . . . had become true symbols." Water, therefore, is explained as "everywhere the signature of the fruitfulness of the body and of the fruitfulness of dreams." The sea he consequently identified with life itself, but often, like the neo-Platonist he paraphrased, he sees it "as a symbol of the drifting indefinite bitterness of life." Wind is "a symbol of vague desires and hopes, not merely because the Sidhe are in the wind, or because the wind bloweth as it listeth, but because wind and spirit and vague desire have been associated everywhere." The North he identified "with night and sleep, and the East, the place of sunrise, with hope, and the South, the place of the sun when at its height, with passion and desire, and the West, the place of sunset, with fading and dreaming things."

"Once a symbolism has possessed the imagination of large numbers of men, it becomes, as I believe, an embodiment of disembodied powers, and repeats itself in dreams and visions, age after age," Yeats noted, though he was careful to add in another place, "but our understandings are temporal and understand but a little at a time." For that reason the symbol, seeming always meaningful, can frequently mean different things. As he remarked of his poem "The Cap and Bells," "The poem has always meant a great deal to me, though, as is the way with symbolic poems, it has not always meant quite the same thing."

Entangled with the symbols is a great deal of Irish material: the Sidhe, "the people of the Faery Hills" who are always associated with the wind; Maeve, their great queen who lies buried in a cairn of stones on top of Knocknarea in Sligo; Caoilte, Finn's friend; Niamh who led Oisin on his merry chase; the hornless white deer and the hound with one red ear (symbols of female and male desire, Yeats said); Aengus, "Master of Love," identified always either by the four birds which fly about his head or by the hazel rod he carries; the boar without bristles, "the ancient Celtic image of the darkness which will at last destroy the world, as it destroys the sun at nightfall in the west."

And, perhaps in an effort to make the poems more public, certainly in an effort to give Ireland the Unity of Culture he planned for her, Yeats began incorporating Christian material that he made parallel to his Celtic and occult references.

Yet in spite of their elaborate origins, these are among Yeats's least difficult poems. Read as a group in their final form, they record gracefully the shifting moods of a complex man. For Yeats in the end withdrew his assignment of the poems to Aedh, Hanrahan, and Michael Robartes, preferring to let them stand as aspects of his dramatized "poet" or "lover."

Using his first two poems to link—by proximity alone if the reader fails to see the correspondences in imagery—the Celtic "Hosting of the Sidhe" and "The Everlasting Voices" of an even older mystical tradition, Yeats moves rapidly toward a recapitulation of the familiar Rose imagery, his design for the synthesis of all things into perfect order. But the Rose is now threatened by "The wrong of unshapely things." Though the lover has in his heart its image of perfection which he has salvaged from the glimpse he has caught of it in the real world, it is no longer to be seen on earth and he has grown exhausted in his pursuit of its vanished excellence.

This theme, the subject of "The Fish" which critics have variously taken to stand for poems and Maud Gonne, is most carefully worked out in "The Song of Wandering Aengus." Aengus, who had caught at dawn "a little silver trout" on his hazel wand, found it transformed when his back was turned into "a glimmering girl/ With apple blossom in her hair" who vanished into the brightening light. Old and exhausted in his search for her, he still dreams of kissing her lips and plucking with her "The silver apples of the moon,/ The golden apples of the sun."

One way to read the poem is, of course, to remember that Yeats had first seen Maud Gonne standing beside a bouquet of apple blossoms and that he always identified apple blossoms with her complexion. A better way is to see the poem as a versification of the legends Yeats paraphrases in his notes about women of the Sidhe who, disguised as fishes, enchant living men. And perhaps best of all is to see it as a poem constructed from light itself. Driven to the hazel wood by the "fire" in his head, Aengus goes fishing in the twilight of dawn when "white moths" fly and when the "moth-like stars" flicker out, the time, as Yeats often pointed out, when miracles are most likely to take place. Carrying his fish back to the "fire"—now no longer in his head but on his hearth—he hears the "silver" trout rustle into transformation and his own name called by a "glimmering" girl who fades "through the brightening air." Grown old, he dreams still of finding her in imagery which reassembles light and apple blossoms, but now the blossoms have matured into the enormous shining fruit which light all things: "The silver apples of the moon,/ The golden apples of the sun."

Impressive enough by itself, "Wandering Aengus" is strengthened by its placement immediately after "Into the Twilight" where in the crucial half-light the "mystical brotherhood/ Of sun and moon" join forces with natural things to free man from the nets of the natural world, the nets of "wrong and right."

If the scene of the bulk of these poems is twilight by the sea, their subject is most frequently the complexity of love. Yeats's most explicit statement of his own problem was probably made in "The Lover mourns for the Loss of Love." There he describes the "still hands and dim hair" of the beautiful friend he named Diana Vernon in his unpublished autobiography (borrowing the name from Scott's *Rob Roy*), a figure George Brandon Saul positively identifies as Mrs. Shakespear. By living with her, Yeats had hoped to see his love-sickness end in love. Instead, their whole life together ended, for she discovered that he was still in love with Maud Gonne ("your image" in the poem) and went "weeping away." The poem, founded on the end of their brief love affair, helped pave the way for a reconciliation that culminated in friendship.

Though the biographical element of these poems is easy to overstress, it is probably true that Yeats's acquaintance with Mrs. Shakespear in the years immediately after 1895 is responsible for a growing sensuality that ultimately becomes the most characteristic element in his late verse. Those readers who had delighted in the more ethereal roses of his earlier poetry were startled to find the roses of *The Wind Among the Reeds* fragrant with a seductive perfume and giving way as dominant imagery to something eminently physical: hair.

The twenty-nine direct references to hair and tresses in this section start innocently enough with Caoilte tossing his "burning hair" and the Sidhe unbinding theirs in "The Hosting of the Sidhe." But Bridget's "long dim hair" sets O'Driscoll dreaming in "The Host of the Air" and later drowns neck, breast, and arms of the handsome immoral immortal who steals her away. The passionate girl who reveals herself in "The Heart of the Woman" delights in her own long "hiding hair," for it will protect both her and her lover from the "bitter storm" which rages above them while her breast "lies upon his breast." Such a "hair-tent" (Professor Tindall's phrase) also protects the lover of "He bids his Beloved be at Peace" from the Shadowy Horses of Disaster, hiding their tossing manes from the supine lover who supports in her own hair's "dim twilight" the drowsy lady whose heart beats above his heart. Presumably the same lover "reproves the Curlew" in the poem of that name for bringing to mind that passionate lady who had shaken out "long heavy hair" over his breast. And in "He remembers Forgotten Beauty," the "you" the lover's arms wrap round reminds him of, among others, ladies of old time who had woven roses in their hair. When "He gives his Beloved certain Rhymes" it is with the admonition that she first bind up her long hair, for when she does that "all men's hearts must burn and beat." The jester of "The Cap and Bells" has a heart made eloquent by the thought "Of a flutter of flower-like hair," and when his lady lays cap and bells on her bosom "Under a cloud of her hair," his heart and soul stand singing before her "And her hair was a folded flower." When "The Lover asks Forgiveness because of his Many Moods" he pleads that his mistress "Crumple the rose" in her hair "And cover the pale blossoms" of her breast with her "dim heavy hair" and, sighing, pity his restlessness. When "He tells of a Valley full of Lovers" his advice is intended to teach young women how to keep their lovers happy: ". . . bid the young men lay/ Their heads on your knees, and drown their eyes with your hair." And, perhaps most luxuriously, in "The Travail of Passion" he puns on the double sense of passion to describe his Christ-like lovers comforted: "We will bend down and loosen our hair over you/ That it may drop faint perfume, and be heavy with dew,/ Lilies of death-pale hope, roses of passionate dawn."

Offering in the large structure of *The Wind Among the Reeds* the pattern of a love affair gone wrong, a great passion that after rising to a climax necessarily fades, Yeats tries to make the poems toward the end of the section move away from things physical. "He wishes his Beloved were Dead" winds the hair that in the middle poems of the group had been sensual through stars and moon and sun. The cloths of heaven, like his dreams, are spread out at his beloved's feet in the next poem. And in "He thinks of his Past Greatness when a Part of the Constellations of Heaven" the now-desolate lover remembers two of his former incarnations: a rush trampled by horses, and that tree of the heavens on which is hung Pole Star and Plough and the symbolic Rose of Yeats's second group of poems.

Though at the end of *The Wind Among the Reeds* both poet and his lady are consequently fitted carefully into a heavenly astrological paradise, the poet himself—trapped on earth, "a hater of the wind" that sings like poetry in the reeds—is secure only in the knowledge of his anguish, sure only of one thing: "That his head/ May not lie on the breast nor his lips on the hair/ Of the woman that he loves, until he dies." The fierce apostrophe that ends the poem and that makes ironic the gay "Fiddler of Dooney" which Yeats used to bring the entire section to an end rages against flesh made vocal in the "amorous cries" of bird and beast which, voluptuous as the poems that formed the whole central action of the group, are—love ended—unendurable.

The Wind Among the Reeds represents, of course, an achievement in art rather than in autobiography. Though the first drafts of most of the poems concerned and were written for Mrs. Shakespear or Maud Gonne, in his final ordering of them Yeats is no longer speaking in his own voice. The lover and the ladies he celebrates are, finally, fictions. For Yeats's concern, here as always, is not with the representation of reality but rather with the construction of a vision of reality, a shaping of reality into a form more coherent than itself. For this reason he writes poems. And though half his problem is the organization of theme and plot, a more significant half is the manipulation of words themselves. By examining closely, for instance, even so short a poem as "A Poet to his Beloved" one can see how carefully, balancing phrase against phrase, Yeats made poetry from sheer linguistic pattern. The poet who *brings* the *books of his numberless dreams* to the *passion-worn white woman* addresses at the end of the poem the *white woman* who has *numberless dreams*, and offers to *bring* her his *passionate rhyme*. This intricate design, exchanging dream and passion, is the stuff poems are made on.

In spite of the fact that Yeats was by this time a master of poetic structure, he was still experimenting. In many of these short poems, for instance, he investigated the possibilities of one-sentence lyrics. Even such a relatively long (and such a deeply-felt) poem as "He remembers Forgotten Beauty" is successfully compressed into one semi-colon-speckled twenty-four-line sentence.

These experiments were minor ones however when contrasted

to those Yeats was about to make. For in the five years that divide *The Wind Among the Reeds* from *In the Seven Woods* he became a practicing dramatist, and drama suggested to him possibilities for a poetry founded on the lean eloquence of speech. Pursuing drama, Yeats began to evolve for himself a new poetic language.

5 * In the Seven Woods

Two events of crucial importance determine the final form of *In the Seven Woods*: Yeats's experience with theatre and Maud Gonne's marriage.

Though Yeats had written plays long before his involvement in the founding of the Irish Literary Theatre in 1899, he had had little contact with the machinery of dramatic production. But the theatre society he, Lady Gregory, Edward Martyn and George Moore organized gave him experience to spare and propelled him into years of "theatre business." Problems of casting, struggles with temperamental actresses and even more temperamental George Moore, efforts to teach actors unused to poetic speech how to read lines, and efforts to locate or write actable plays did distract Yeats from his poetry, but these distractions also helped him formulate theories about a more public kind of poetry than he had written before. In a note between the poems and his play *On Baile's*

Strand, which was published at the end of the first edition of *In the Seven Woods,* Yeats commented that he felt his experience in revising the play might foreshadow "a change that may bring a less dream-burdened will into my verses." This change, which culminated in his 1908 revision of almost everything he had written before that time, is already evident in the matter-of-fact language and the comparatively uninvolved syntax of the *Seven Woods* volume. The elaborate designs of imagery that dominate *The Rose* and *The Wind Among the Reeds* are carefully pared down in the *Seven Woods* poems; and the final product produces the effect of conversation heightened by occasional—but only occasional— startling images. "Through much knowledge of the stage," Yeats recollected in his account of these years in *Dramatis Personae,* "through the exfoliation of my own style, I learnt that occasional prosaic words gave the impression of an active man speaking. . . . Here and there in correcting my early poems I have introduced . . . numbness and dullness, turned, for instance, 'the curd-pale moon' into the 'brilliant moon', that all might seem, as it were, remembered with indifference, except some one vivid image." Most clearly evident in "Adam's Curse," this new conversational manner dominates the entire group of poems.

But though the manner is conversational the subject matter of the poems is passionately felt, for in spite of the Irish material which frames it, the core around which *In the Seven Woods* centers is Maud Gonne's marriage.

In 1899, Yeats had made a quick trip to Paris in the hopes of finally winning her hand. But she rejected him; and, as he had in the past, Yeats turned his unhappiness into poems. "The Arrow," "The Folly of Being Comforted," "Adam's Curse," and "Under the Moon" are all products of his depressed spirits of 1901 and 1902. The news of her marriage in February 1903 to Major John MacBride was, however, overpowering; at first stunned, Yeats busied himself in preparing the final text of *In the Seven Woods*— the first volume published by his sister's press—and then settled down to a flurry of theatre work from which emerged sporadically the lyrics "Old Memory," "Never Give all the Heart," "The Ragged Wood," and "O Do Not Love Too Long," all of which Yeats incorporated in later editions of *In the Seven Woods*—presumably to complete the record.

The finished version of this set of poems, therefore, is designed to give us a picture of the rejected lover who at the end gives up all hope. And yet the feeling of the entire group is not particularly gloomy. Partly, of course, this is because Yeats knew in 1908, when he established the final order of the poems, not only the circumstances of Maud Gonne's marriage but as well the circumstances which led her in 1905 to separate from her husband. Though she had turned to him for no more than friendship, Yeats was comforted that she had let him help arrange the details of that separation. He is consequently careful to keep the tone of the group of poems from sounding in any way tragic.

The title poem, referring to the Seven Woods of Lady Gregory's estate where Yeats had written many of the lyrics in the volume, sets up, as a matter of fact, a tone of judicious but faintly ironic detachment. By pointing out that he has forgotten that Tara, the seat of government of legendary Ireland, has been uprooted in favor of the "new commonness" of Edward VII, Yeats places that commonness squarely before the reader's eyes. In spite of the fact that the final configuration of its features will not be set for another decade, Yeats is beginning to adjust his manner to the man-of-the-world Mask of his middle years.

The contentment he claims to have found is also subjected to ironic undercutting, for Quiet—who wanders laughing through the woods—is eating her own "wild heart," and Sagittarius, "that Great Archer," is ready to unloose the arrow which comprises the second poem.

That arrow—the thought of mortality, Maud Gonne with grey in her hair—dominates also the brief powerful dialogue of "The Folly of Being Comforted." Though more than theatrical training accounts for the impact Yeats manages to achieve in the direct speech of Heart's answer, his work as a playwright certainly taught him how to attain the sort of characterization he displays here.

For theatre is very much in Yeats's mind in all these poems. He draws naturally on it for his imagery. The "passionate women" of his poem "Never Give all the Heart" have given their own hearts up to "the play," the sheer drama of love. Like good actresses, they must act their parts—not feel them. For the appearance of feeling, Yeats knew from his experiences with the actors of his theatre society, is achieved by technique: "If deaf and dumb and blind with love," no actress can play love "well enough." Lovers, like Yeats, lose because they have not learned to put on the actor's Mask.

A different kind of technique is the subject of "Adam's Curse," one of the first of the dramatized conversations Yeats was eventually to make his most characteristic form. Establishing time, setting, theme, and a cast of characters in his opening three lines, Yeats quickly swings into the discussion of three parallel labors: the poet's, the beautiful woman's, and the lover's. The poet's painful struggle to achieve the appearance of spontaneity—the line of plain speech that seems a moment's thought but which may have taken hours of revision—is precisely parallel to the woman's laborious achievement of beauty and the ceremonious lover's studious transformation of mere physical love into a kind of art. But none of these accomplishments are greatly valued in the modern world. Yeats's strategy in the poem is simple enough, though he moves so effortlessly from the direct statement of one of his basic aesthetic doctrines (poetry must seem casual and yet all parts must be articulated one with the other) into a general discussion of the function of technique in the production of all fine things of life, that we are hardly aware that a principle of art has been extended to a principle of behavior. Each step of the poem as it moves toward its final statement surprises us—as good conversations do—into deepened insight. But the greatest surprise, certainly, is that silence in which—talk done—Yeats lets the hollow moon rise trembling through a blue-green twilight sky. Time-worn, it evokes one last thought which, though unspoken, ingeniously integrates the three labors he has discussed. For framed in laboriously made though seemingly effortless poetry are two statements: "you were beautiful" and "I strove/ To love you in the old high way of love." Binding them into his poem by the metaphor of the "weary-hearted" moon and lovers, Yeats returns to his obsessive theme: happiness fades before the onrushing years.

Though it is perhaps entertaining to know that the poem was based on an incident reported both by Maud Gonne and by Yeats (the "beautiful mild woman" who commented that women must labor to be beautiful was her sister Kathleen), the poem survives very well without such annotation. The articulation of sweet sounds into lines that seem "a moment's thought" succeeds.

Not quite as casual as "Adam's Curse" but equally dominated by a crescent moon and the figure of Maud Gonne, "Under the Moon" is a little exercise in comparative mythology that culminates in Yeats's conclusion that the stories of all the remarkable queens of legendary lands are for him no longer "to be borne" because of a prophesy once made under "the hunter's moon." Yeats, who had assembled omens both favorable and unfavorable to his courtship from George Pollexfen's servant Mary Battle and from others, may have had those omens in mind when he wrote the last lines of his poem. The wonder-working ladies listed by him, Branwen, daughter of Lyr in the *Mabinogion*; Guinevere, Arthur's queen; Niamh, whom Oisin had pursued; Laban, Fand's sister; Fand herself, wife of the sea god, Manannan Mac Lir; and the hawk-beloved wood-woman were all betrayed or defeated in love. And the magic legendary lands that he itemizes—Brycelinde, where Viviane cast a spell on Merlin; Avalon, Arthur's resting place; all the others—were no more satisfactory as places for lovers than modern Ireland.

But if love fails, art can make of that failure a shining, incorruptible thing. When the "Third Voice" of "The Players ask for a Blessing on the Psalteries and on Themselves" pleads that her hands be blessed, it is because she realizes that art itself needs no blessing: the hands, mortal, will "ebb away" but "The notes they waken shall live on/ When all this heavy history's done."

Song, ultimately, even the song of the defeated lover, must of necessity be gay, Yeats argues, for it participates in the immortality of art which—approaching perfection—reflects patterns of supernatural order. Whether one sees that order as "The Happy Townland," the cheerful peasant-image of a Heaven running with red beer and brown beer and shaded by gold and silver trees or whether—as Yeats later—one constructs a Byzantium in which a golden bird perches on a golden bough, the pattern of perfection is much the same. Human hands must "ebb away"—and there lies tragedy—but they also manipulate the psaltery from which immortal melodies flow. Dying, tragic men make from their perishable lives gay imperishable art.

6 * From 'The Green Helmet and Other Poems'

Between the publication of the first edition of *In the Seven Woods* in 1903 and 1910 when he prepared the first edition of *The Green Helmet and Other Poems* for his sister's press, Yeats was busily occupied with two projects that he regarded as extremely important to his own development: the revision of all his early writing for Bullen's edition of the *Collected Works* and his enormously time-consuming labors at the Abbey where he actively participated as playwright, manager, play reader, fund raiser, propagandist, and sometimes as uncredited assistant director.

He was by 1910 a very public figure, and he was quite conscious of his growing reputation. His lecture tours both in England and America had been successful. Bullen's edition, though it had not sold well, had given him exactly the sort of prestige he had hoped for. In April he was invited by Edmund Gosse to be a member of the Royal Society of Literature, then being formed; and in

August of that year he was awarded a Civil List pension of £150 which he accepted only on condition that he would be free to undertake in Ireland any political activity he wished.

Though he wrote hardly any lyric poetry in the years between 1903 and 1910, in lectures and in his correspondence he was beginning to forge a new aesthetic for himself. Poetry, he felt, had become soft; it needed to be edged with satire. "What Dublin wants is some man who knows his own mind and has an intolerable tongue and a delight in enemies," he wrote Stephen Gwynn. And he began to praise such men as Byron and Ben Jonson for their poetic energy.

At the same time he reasserted his conviction that his own poetry should be both personal and Irish. When Miss Horniman, the unpopular and domineering Abbey backer who had retired from Abbey affairs to start a repertory theatre in Manchester, asked him if she could arrange English productions of his plays, his answer was an unequivocal *no:* "I understand my own race and in all my work, lyric or dramatic, I have thought of it. If the theatre fails I may or may not write plays—but I shall write for my own people —whether in love or hate of them matters little—probably I shall not know which it is."

This mixture of love and hate becomes, as a matter of fact, a key to the shifting tone of his poetry. Though he is not yet ready to regard—as he did in his old age—Swift's savage indignation as the proper attitude for the poet, he has come a long way from the pose of lovelorn young man that he affected in his early work. While not "happy," he is, at 45, successful and busy.

The poems now grouped as *From 'The Green Helmet and Other Poems'* were written between 1908 and 1912. The final structure of this section closely parallels that of *In the Seven Woods.* A pair of uncontroversial "public" poems are used to frame a set of increasingly arrogant and very personal lyrics. And— almost theatrically—the central group of lyrics draw on and intensify the conversational style that had first made its appearance in the *Seven Woods* section.

Appropriately, it is the ordinary language of conversation rather than integrated imagery that is the primary linking device by which poem is tied to poem in the central group. Consider, for example, the seven poems about Maud Gonne beginning with "A Woman Homer Sung." If one quotes from each the principal linking phrase, this design results (the italics are mine):

A Woman Homer Sung	I *thought,* 'He holds her dear,'
Words	I had this *thought* a while ago, 'My darling *cannot understand* What I have done . . .
No Second Troy	*Why should I blame her* that she filled my days With misery . . .
Reconciliation	*Some may have blamed you* that you took away The verses that could move them . . . . . . but now We'll out, for the world lives *as long ago* . . .
King and No King	. . . we . . . *Have been defeated* by that pledge you gave In momentary anger *long ago* . . .
Peace	Ah, but *peace* that comes at length, Came when Time had touched her form.
Against Unworthy Praise	O heart, be at *peace* . . .

Though a great many other devices—thematic and imagistic—integrate what at first seem separate poems into a kind of lyrical narrative, it is the echoed conversational phrases which make the transition from poem to poem especially easy.

And the conversation in all of them is about Maud Gonne. No

one, I suppose, ever read Yeats's *Collected Poems* as a kind of versified autobiographical novel of the boy-loses-girl-and-continues-to-lose-her variety, but Yeats makes it perfectly possible for anyone to do so. "The world should thank me for not marrying you," Maud Gonne had told him; and Yeats, versifying his answer in "Words," half-justifies her position: "I might have thrown poor words away/ And been content to live."

And yet, though Yeats's language is colloquial in these poems, Maud Gonne, their subject, is gradually being apotheosized. She is becoming something larger than life. "A Woman Homer Sung" fits her into a "heroic dream," while announcing explicitly Yeats's determination to paint her portrait for "coming time." And "No Second Troy" defines as Helen her mythological counterpart. "Homer's age," he points out in "Peace," would have bred a woman like her to be a "hero's wage," the proper prize of the young champion. (How Yeats must have felt his prophesy ironically fulfilled when MacBride, the "drunken, vainglorious lout" who had married her, died heroically in the Easter Week rising of 1916!) Though not precisely a model, Homer, in these poems, does offer Yeats a sort of classical parallel to himself: a middle class man singing of high deeds in the language of the streets. That Homer may not have been exactly such a man is not particularly important: it was convenient for Yeats to think he was.

The thing that makes a Homer or a Shakespeare or a Yeats a great poet is, ultimately, however, his facility with "poor words" which he brings to heel through "The Fascination of What's Difficult." For Yeats, the most difficult of poetic labors was for many years the construction of his plays, particularly the Cuchulain cycle which, anticipated by his 1892 poem, was literally a lifetime in the making. (Yeats was still revising the last of the five plays at the time of his death.) But this fascination of intractable material, as he pointed out in his lyric, keeps the poet at his task. Though Pegasus ought ideally to leap from cloud to cloud, he seems instead, as every poet knows, to "Shiver under the lash, strain, sweat and jolt." Yeats, who expresses neatly his exasperation with problems of Abbey management, does also define here as in other places the unnaturalness of art, which rends spontaneous joy and dries the sap out of the artist's veins. To seem spontaneous, the poet must calculate the precise effect of every possible combination of words. Plays do—both in the writing and in the staging—"have to be set up in fifty ways." Poems have to be made—by a supreme artifice—to seem carelessly thrown together. Describing his logic in revising one of the poems in the 1908 collection, Yeats explained to Bullen: "I have taken out, as you see, the chorus the second time it occurs, to give a more accidental look to the poem."

Such calculated accidents account for much of the power of these lyrics. The double "Ah" that begins and ends "Peace" introduces statements not quite antithetical. The references to peace itself in the first and last lines of "Against Unworthy Praise" create a parallel complicated, enriched, and expanded by the rest of that most intricate poem. Even reduced to prose, its complex internal structure is astonishingly elaborate. Schematized, its development is something like this:

The poet's work is written for "a woman's sake," and is therefore beyond the destructive power of the audience of fools and knaves who may or may not applaud it. His heart should consequently be at peace. It is enough that the very labor of composition has, the poet renewing his strength through the "you" he writes for, resulted in a kind of lion's dream so overwhelming as to make the wilderness itself cry aloud (notice how Yeats has the jungle itself roar when the lion dreams). Yet like dream itself, which though roaring is private, the work is essentially secret, something created "between" two proud people and therefore intrinsically beyond the reach of the knaves and dolts of the audience.

Yet, ironically, in spite of this knowledge, the poet does publish his work. ("What, still you would have their praise!") A "haughtier text" might, therefore, make him think twice before accepting the "unworthy" praise of this Irish audience for whom he writes: "The labyrinth of her days" (paralleling the secret dream-like structure of art defined in the first stanza) was perplexed by her own strangeness! (This phrase seems at first irrational, but it does make sense. If we read "the labyrinth of her days" as "her biography," the lines reduce—in one of many possible translations— to "her essential strangeness—her peculiar and heroic individuality —made her already complex biography even more strange and unfathomable." Yeats had in mind in these and the following lines Maud Gonne's sudden marriage to MacBride and her equally sudden decision to separate from him. One aspect of the strange labyrinth this created was that when she appeared on the Abbey stage after her separation from her husband, his partisans—and many of her strongest political supporters—hissed her down in a shouted chorus of insults.) Like the dream of the poet in the first stanza, her dream—a political rather than an aesthetic one—is a secret thing misunderstood by the insulting self-same mob of dolts and knaves. Yet she, singing on her different road—half-lion and therefore like the poet but also, unlike him, half-child and so unconscious of all the chaos through which she walks—has achieved the peace the poet longs for.

Such a reading, pointing up something of the poem's complex structure, is of course not as subtle as the poem itself. By staring at any poem long enough, however, by searching for all possible correlations, we can begin to apprehend details of the internal organization of poetic art. Only if we learn to read Yeats in this way —which is, in fact, a kind of inverse process of composition—can we ever understand what Yeats is trying to make out of poetry. In one sense, each of his poems is no more than a statement architecturally conceived. It is a linguistic design (and so static) which says something (and so seems to be in action). Like a tower which thrusts up and bears down, which falls in toward a center and which is pushed out by its weight, the poem achieves a repose assembled from precarious antithetical violences.

Sometimes, of course, information helps. "Reconciliation" is clearer if we know that the day Yeats refers to in the second line was the one on which he had received the telegram announcing Maud Gonne's marriage, a marriage that stopped, for a time, his output of lyrics, though plays—such as *The Green Helmet*—about kings, swords, and "half-forgotten things" still occupied his attention. "King and No King" is a great deal clearer if we know that the quotation in the first line is, as Richard Ellmann has noted, based on a similar line in Beaumont and Fletcher's play of that title. In context, it is part of a rose-by-any-other-name sort of speech which points up the power of mere voice, the utterance of words, in making or breaking human relationships. Other mysteries in Yeats's "King and No King" that might need clarification are the reference to "your faith" (Maud Gonne had been converted to Catholicism before her marriage) and the pledge (that she would not marry him) given long before the time of the poem. And though the marvelous epigram "To a Poet, who would have me Praise certain Bad Poets, Imitators of His and Mine" stands firmly on its own iambs, the curious will find satisfaction in A. Norman Jeffares' identification of the poet as George Russell (AE) and the Bad Poets as those Russell anthologized in *New Songs*.

This epigram and its two companions, coming as they do at the section's dead center, illustrate neatly the changing tone of Yeats's work. The most succinct of his many explorations of the flowering horse chestnut tree image (the "great-rooted blossomer" of "Among School Children"), "The Coming of Wisdom with Time" states his project precisely: a man's work (the leaves and flowers swaying in the sun through the lying days of youth) has multiple appearance, but it is founded on single truth (the root of wisdom into which he can wither as time brings old age and to which he will henceforth dedicate himself).

Yet truth can best be stated in the artificial shape of poems, and the poet's most real face is the carved Mask through which he utters his metaphors. "The Mask," Yeats's first poem to examine that image which eventually grows into a major theme, dallies an irony before the lady who wants the Mask removed: the Mask which evoked her excitement can be removed only at the excitement's peril. Though the Mask's emerald eyes and burning gold surface may hide a deceitful enemy, removing it might destroy the glamorous lover she has visualized. "What's behind" the Mask is of no consequence so long as it engenders the necessary curiosity which must not be satisfied. Partly quoted in *The Player Queen,* a play Yeats worked on for years, the poem is a kind of key to all Yeats's plays and poems about ambiguities of personality.

The five poems that follow "The Mask" are all, in one way or another, associated with Lady Gregory. The house that is shaken by the land agitation is, of course, Lady Gregory's at Coole Park where Yeats spent many summers and where he did much of his best work. His argument, that the aristocracy's special function is the breeding of good governors and eloquent men, is later considerably amplified, particularly in the prose of his *Autobiography* and *A Vision;* but his central theme (that such a leisure class is absolutely essential if we are to have disinterested government and a great literature) never changes.

"At the Abbey Theatre" invites Craoibhin Aoibhin ("Pleasant Little Branch," the pseudonym of Dr. Douglas Hyde) to volunteer an answer to the problems that perplexed Yeats and Lady Gregory in their roles as Abbey directors: the same audience that criticized them for producing such poetic dramas as Yeats's *Deirdre* had rioted when Synge's too realistic *Playboy* proved offensive in its first performance in 1907. In such a situation what is left, Yeats argues, but for the management to mock, in turn, its mocking audience. Hyde, incidentally, "answered" Yeats's poem in the January, 1913, *Irish Review.*

The "friend" of "These are the Clouds" is again Lady Gregory, who, Yeats notes in *Dramatis Personae,* was obsessed with Coole and its history and hoped that her son or her grandson might live there. This poem, written during Lady Gregory's illness in 1909, was undoubtedly intended to cheer her up by praising her accomplishment (in spite of the fact that it seems to assume her imminent death), as "A Friend's Illness," written at the same time, was intended to be Yeats's own statement evaluating her importance to him. (Perhaps deliberately, Yeats paralleled the world conflagration image first introduced here in his later poem commemorating the death of her son Robert.)

"All Things can Tempt Me" rounds the section toward "Brown Penny," the last and most public poem, by pointing out that when the poet had been young he had not "given a penny for a song" unless it had been heroically presented. This lyric, more intricate than it seems, hinges on the irony that the "things"—Maud Gonne's face and Ireland's seeming need—that had tempted him away from his poetry in his youth were precisely the subject matter from which he made poems. "Now," consequently, when the temptations are gone, he wishes, in spite of the fact that he has gained facility in composition, to be inarticulate: "Colder and dumber and deafer than a fish."

The framing poems of this section, "His Dream" and "Brown Penny," less explicitly personal than the lyrics they surround, have as their subjects the great matters which have always dominated literature: death and love. Yeats sees them in these poems as complex subjects, infinitely alluring yet never finally to be understood. The speaker on the ship of death and the crowd which races along the banks of the river beside it, cry aloud all night long with "ecstatic breath" the "sweet name" of Death. Compelled to shout praises though his wish is to be silent and, finger on lip, to hush the crowd, that speaker becomes an image for irrational man.[1] Equally irrational, the young lover of "Brown Penny" concludes that nobody is wise enough to find out all that there is in "the crooked

[1] In a note, Yeats explained that the poem was founded on a dream. "A few days ago I dreamed that I was steering a very gay and elaborate ship upon some narrow water with many people upon its banks, and that there was a figure upon a bed in the middle of the ship. The people were pointing to the figure and questioning, and in my dream I sang verses which faded as I awoke, all but this fragmentary thought, 'We call it, it has such dignity of limb, by the sweet name of Death.' I have made my poem out of my dream and the sentiment of my dream, and can almost say, as Blake did, 'The Authors are in Eternity.' "

thing," love; yet—like Death's celebrant in "His Dream"—he will nevertheless devote himself to it.

The impossible project—understanding love and death and so understanding man—moves always through Yeats's work. Here, love and death move closer together. Not yet the worm it will be in *Last Poems*, love is already worm-like, "the crooked thing." And death is both dignified and sweetly named.

7 * Responsibilities

Everything in Yeats's life and work hinges on a continuing series of evaluations and re-evaluations. Nothing is ever completely abandoned; nothing, on the other hand, escapes without revision. Yeats once diagramed for T. Sturge Moore his idea of the structure of drama. He drew a series of looping ascending lines that looked vaguely like telephone wires marching up a mountain. This, Yeats said, is the "organic" pattern of drama: a series of rising climaxes.

Though his concern was with drama, he was diagraming as well the pattern which dominates everything he did. The *Collected Poems* seem—if one stands far enough off—to follow, section by section, the ascending design he sketched in his letter to Moore. There is a kind of gathering together of forces in the initial poems of each division and then a launching out as the section loops upward toward a higher point where, recapitulating everything that had gone before, the final poems reorganize the past, establish a point of rest, and sometimes anticipate the next ascending gesture.

Yeats saw his own biography in much the same figure: a series of beginnings, each founded on a reappraisal of the past, each initiated by one vivid startling event, each involving an entanglement that threatens disaster but from which he rises—often to his own surprise—to some new higher precarious plateau where, catching his breath, he can survey the past and rest before new action. Often those plateaus are measured in terms of human lives. The death of Parnell was one, the death of Synge another, the deaths—crowded into a little space of time—of Hugh Lane, Robert Gregory, Mabel Beardsley, and the sixteen of the Easter Week rising still another. At each of these intervals, in terms of a late letter to Olivia Shakespear, "a new scene was set, new actors appeared."

The volume *Responsibilities* represents one of these plateaus of reappraisal and renewal. It is almost always singled out by Yeats scholars as a point of major division, but that perhaps is because title and structure so clearly define it as "dividing point." In fact, it is probably no more crucial than any other section of the *Collected Poems*. It evolves naturally out of the *Green Helmet* poems and just as naturally into *The Wild Swans at Coole*. Like each section, it is based on reappraisal, redefinition, and the introduction of new material.

Its structure, however, is eminently clear. Now-italicized and untitled poems that in early editions had been called "Introductory Rhymes" and "Closing Rhymes" bind it to past and future and define its contents. And the contents themselves reveal, even at a glance, the outline on which Yeats arranged them. The title of the section, obviously, is the key. Working from that we can see Yeats's plan for the group as a whole:

Responsibilities of the Poet "close on forty-nine"

Supernatural responsibilities

Dead ancestors: "Pardon, Old Fathers"
Dead friends who had been poets: "The Grey Rock"

Social responsibilities
> Lane-pictures poems
> *Playboy*-riots poems

The function of irresponsibility
> "Beggarman" poems

Personal responsibilities
> Iseult Gonne poems
> Maud Gonne poems
> "Friends"

Aesthetic responsibilities
> Supernatural models: "The Magi," "The Dolls"
> Style: "A Coat"
> Rededication: "While I, from that reed-throated whisperer"

We could, with almost equal validity, group the poems in a temporal pattern. Those I have labeled "supernatural responsibilities" could be labeled "past." The three middle groups could be called "present." The last one could be called "future."

Yeats makes clear in the very first poem of the section that he sees his life and work in dramatic terms. The poems are written for an audience of ghostly ancestors who may be assembled "somewhere in ear-shot" in order to hear "the story's end." And—perhaps to guarantee that it be a story worth the telling—he is careful to select for his audience those ancestors who practiced the "wasteful virtues": Jervis Yeats, the old Dublin merchant who had traded with Spain but who, Yeats liked to think, was no penny-pinching modern shopkeeper; the clergyman John Yeats, born in 1774, a scholarly man whose friendship with Robert Emmet made him a particularly useful forebear; soldiers who had fought at the Boyne; and especially William Pollexfen, Yeats's fierce old grandfather. Yeats's own wasteful virtue is, of course, the practice of literature; his pursuit of Maud Gonne has been a barren passion, but—childless—he has at least a progeny of words to prove a kinship with those ancestors he dreamed of as reckless men. The book he offers will show him fighting the hucksters of the world.

If the introductory poem is intended to prove that he has kept faith with his ancestors, "The Grey Rock" is intended to prove that he has kept faith with the members of the Rhymers' Club whose vision of literature's high role had helped shape his youthful aesthetic. For their sake he tells a story of a gathering of the Celtic gods at Slievenamon (the site of one of their palaces) where, drunk on "the legendary mason" Goban's wine, the gods listen to the lament of immortal Aoife (in *On Baile's Strand* the mother of Cuchulain's son) that her chosen man has preferred human companionship and the death involved in such a commitment to the "two hundred years" she had offered him as her companion. The action of the gods—dousing her with the wine of forgetfulness—points the unstated moral: art (like Goban's wine) brings a release from anguish. Aoife rises dripping—the memory of a lover's betrayal rinsed out of her—to stare at the gods "with laughing lip."

Recklessly interrupting his narrative with an interpolated digression about the actress Florence Farr's dissatisfaction with flesh and blood (the "woman none could please") and praise of his "tavern companions" who had never commercialized their art but, "unrepenting" their bad lives, died faithful still to "the Muses' sterner laws," Yeats shatters the story he seems to be telling in order to establish a series of parallels. (Florence Farr, for instance, in love with a childhood vision of immortal bodies, is precisely parallel to immortal Aoife who hungers after a mortal man; the drunken gods precisely parallel the drunken rhymers who, in death, have gained the gods' immortality.) In language seemingly offhand yet brilliantly accurate (for example, the manipulation of the word "troop" which, though repeated three times, is used as metaphorical noun, infinitive, and sign to link the italicized interpolation to the first line of the second half of the narrative), Yeats experiments with a new form: "an old story I've remade" that, broken by conversations with the dead, crosses talk—chatty and casual—onto formal narrative. Yeats, who compounds his poem from things legendary and personal, seems at the end to be dedicating himself to follow in Aoife's footsteps ("I have kept my faith, though faith was tried,/ To that rock-born, rock-wandering foot"—the grey rock of this passage and the title being Craig Liath, where Aoife is reputed to have made her home), but lurking private ambiguities swim in sight when one remembers that in *On Baile's Strand* Aoife bears a speaking likeness to Maud Gonne:

> You have never seen her. Ah! Conchubar, had you seen her
> With that high, laughing, turbulent head of hers
> Thrown backward, and the bowstring at her ear,
> Or sitting at the fire with those grave eyes
> Full of good counsel as it were with wine,
> Or when love ran through all the lineaments
> Of her wild body—although she had no child,
> None other had all beauty, queen or lover,
> Or was so fitted to give birth to kings.

"The Grey Rock" won *Poetry's* prize of $250 for the best poem published in the magazine's first year. Yeats modestly kept $50 which he used to commission a bookplate from his friend T. Sturge Moore and suggested that the rest of the money be given to a younger poet. Ezra Pound was the one he nominated.

Yeats had first met Pound, who in these years was a stimulating if irritating friend and companion, in 1909 and very soon came to see a great deal of him. He appreciated Pound's readily forthcoming advice. ("He . . . helps me get back to the definite and the concrete away from modern abstractions. To talk over a poem with him is like getting you to put a sentence into dialect," he wrote Lady Gregory early in 1913. "All becomes clear and natural.") But at the same time he saw Pound's limitations: "He spoils himself by too many experiments and has more sound principles than taste." Nevertheless, Pound's influence in these years is considerable, and there are a number of poems which benefited from his editorial suggestions. Pound, pleased with what he may have contributed, praised Yeats's "new robustness" in a review of *Responsibilities*.

The "new robustness" is particularly evident in the group of five poems that have as their subject the Lane pictures controversy. The background of that controversy is comparatively uncomplicated, though a great many complications ultimately arose. Lane, Lady Gregory's nephew, had assembled a very good collection of modern French paintings in the course of his activities as an art dealer. In 1903, he decided that Dublin needed a gallery of Modern Art, and started making plans for it. After that had materialized in 1908 as the Municipal Gallery of Modern Art, Lane enthusiastically offered the bulk of his collection as a gift to Dublin if a suitable permanent gallery were built. Lane himself strongly favored a design for a bridge gallery to be built across the Liffey that had been submitted by Sir Edward Lutyens. Lutyens, however, had unfortunately been born English, and the Dublin nationalists began an attack that centered first on the design for the bridge and that gradually extended to Lane and ultimately to the paintings themselves. By 1913 all parties concerned had lost their tempers. Lane insisted that the gallery be financed immediately, preferably by the city but if the city refused by private subscription. Private subscribers, however, were hard to come by; and the city offered a maximum of only £2,000 a year—£18,000 short of what Lane needed.

"To a Wealthy Man who promised a Second Subscription to the Dublin Municipal Gallery if it were proved the People wanted Pictures" was Yeats's first poetic contribution to the controversy. As his letters to Lane and Lady Gregory make clear, the wealthy man he had in mind was Lord Ardilaun who had argued that money should not be given unless there was a clear public demand for the gallery. Yeats, of course, takes the opposite position. The list of enlightened patrons of art assembled in his poem reflects, as A. Norman Jeffares has pointed out, Yeats's reading in Castiglione's *The Courtier*. Duke Ercole of Ferrara, who had had five plays by

Plautus produced in 1502 as part of the wedding celebrations for his son Alphonso's marriage to Lucrezia Borgia, had had—Yeats maintains—no concern about the opinions of the local onion sellers. Guidobaldo, Duke of Urbino, had built a palace—a "grammar school of courtesies"—known throughout Italy for its art treasures, particularly for its books bound in gold and silver. And Cosimo de Medici had commissioned the architect Michelozzo to draw up plans for the Library of St. Mark's in Florence, famous later for its frescoes by Fra Angelico. And neither had consulted local shepherds on design or begged the mob for matching contributions.

To Yeats's considerable surprise, his poem was "answered" not by Lord Ardilaun but by William Martin Murphy, the controller of *The Evening Herald* and *The Irish Independent*, Ireland's most popular daily papers. Murphy, who assumed Yeats's attack was directed against him, began a vitriolic campaign against Yeats, Lane, the pictures themselves, and the idea of the gallery.

"September 1913," originally subtitled "On reading much of the correspondence against the Art Gallery," was Yeats's next attack against the hucksters who "fumble in a greasy till." The poem was most directly occasioned by a lockout of strikers who were led by James Larkin, one of Lane's strongest supporters among the workers. The employers' group was headed—as one might expect —by William Murphy. By citing O'Leary in the refrain of his poem, Yeats was, of course, attempting to discredit nationalists of Murphy's stamp who "were born to pray and save" and whose nationalism had as its object the lining of their own pockets rather than the establishment of a great nation. Maud Gonne, who may have found the reference to prayer offensive, declared Yeats had lost contact with the men working for Ireland's freedom; but irony was never her strong point, and she astonishingly read the poem as a statement abandoning hope for Irish independence. "All that delirium of the brave" which offended others was not, of course, intended to suggest that the brave were delirious but rather that their sacrifice was emotional rather than rational. Had they been rational, they would—like the hucksters—have prayed and saved. But being emotional—and therefore an indigenous part of Romantic Ireland—they gave their lives for a dream of national greatness.

"To a Friend whose Work has come to Nothing," written—as Yeats notes—for Lady Gregory and not Hugh Lane, advises secret exultation in the rightness of her cause and Lane's rather than more public controversy with the "brazen throat" of Murphy's newspaper. And, as a kind of demonstration, Yeats describes his own exultation in "Paudeen." Indignant at Paudeen—his generic term for the sort of huckster he had attacked in "Pardon, Old Fathers"—Yeats, like his hero Cuchulain, has stumbled through the night to a high, windy place where, in a landscape of stones and thorn-trees, he hears suddenly in the "luminous" wind of dawn curlews crying to one another. Granted spiritual illumination ("luminous" drawing on both its meanings) in that desolate special place where bird and tree—his favorite symbols—intersect in his favorite light (twilight—this time the twilight of dawn), Yeats exults in a moment of insight as blindness drops from his eyes and "confusion of our sound" is forgotten. Order replaces chaos; blindness gives way to vision; man's confused babble gives way to the "sweet crystalline cry" of the soul. "Crystalline," with its denotation of organic form, precise order, binds sight and sound into an image of a momentarily apprehended coherent universe. Through such insight, Yeats suggests, the artist—doomed to defeat in a civilization dominated by Paudeens—necessarily triumphs. Committed to and achieving form in a messy world, the artist secretly exults in the glory of his private vision.

Like "September 1913," "To a Shade," the last of the Hugh Lane poems, calls a representative of Romantic Ireland—Parnell—from his grave beneath the "coverlet" of Glasnevin cemetery. The "brazen throat" of Murphy's newspapers is here transformed to "an old foul mouth," for Murphy had opposed Parnell as violently as he had opposed Lane, the "man/ Of your own passionate serving kind" referred to in the poem.

The controversy ended in anger and mutual defeat. Lane withdrew his offer, loaned his pictures to the London National Gallery, and in his 1913 will bequeathed them to that gallery. In 1915, however, he added a codicil once again offering the pictures to Ireland on condition that within five years of his death a suitable gallery be provided, Lady Gregory to be the sole trustee. But the codicil was not witnessed, Lane died when the *Lusitania* went down, and the English gallery refused to give up the paintings. Those paintings—still in England—are still the subject of disputed ownership, and a room empty but for a bust of Lane still waits to house them in Dublin's Municipal Gallery.

The bitterness over the Lane pictures, the attacks on Parnell, and the riots that accompanied the first performances of *The Playboy of the Western World* were, as Yeats explains in his note, the three public controversies which had alone in modern times stirred his imagination. He managed, in *Responsibilities*, to have his say on each. Though "On those that hated 'The Playboy of the Western World,' 1907" needs—as an epigram—no comment, it does afford us a good example of Yeats's working method. Yeats very seldom wrote poems without some sort of a prose statement of the main theme before him. This he manipulated gradually toward verse until drafts of poems began to appear. Frequently the prose drafts are based in turn on jottings in his diary which themselves may be records of anecdotes that entertained him or dreams he wished to preserve for evidence of unconscious psychic activity.

His *Playboy* poem originates ultimately in a painting by Charles Ricketts. He describes his reaction to the painting in a letter to Lady Gregory:

> . . . my discontents enlarge my diary. I have written a number of notes lately. I wound up my notes this morning with the sentence 'culture is the sanctity of the intellect.' I was thinking of men like Griffith and how they can renounce external things without it but not envy, revenge, jealousy and so on. I wrote a note a couple of days ago in which I compared Griffith and his like to the Eu-

nuchs in Ricketts's picture watching Don Juan riding through Hell.

When he published *Estrangement*—the extracts from that diary which he obviously wished to put before his readers so that they might see the prose development of the thought behind his poems —he eliminated personalities:

> . . . the political class in Ireland—the lower-middle class from which the patriotic associations have drawn their journalists and their leaders for the last ten years—have suffered through the cultivation of hatred as the one energy of their movement, a deprivation which is the intellectual equivalent to a certain surgical operation. Hence the shrillness of their voices. They contemplate all creative power as the eunuchs contemplate Don Juan as he passes through Hell on the white horse.

These passages—reworked—become the poem's framework.

The final draft of the poem is, however, more conspicuous for great Juan's sinewy thigh than for its attack on the middle class. Yeats, who in conversation with Synge and Pound had come to value flesh, begins to reflect in his poetry a growing concern for body as well as for soul. It is appropriate that in "A Coat," the last poem before the epilogue that ends *Responsibilities*, he is stripped: "walking naked."

One of his responsibilities, therefore, is the careful cultivation of what the Dublin lower-middle class would describe as "irresponsibilities," the values of the beggarman. To not get ahead in the world is, for the poet, more important than to get ahead. What Dylan Thomas later called the "deadly virtues" are specifically those which destroy artists.

The social code Yeats was gradually constructing recognized only one really valuable class, that of the artists. They alone— through their art—could survive flesh and so make a permanent contribution to civilization. Two classes, however, could aid them: those of the noble and the beggarman. The nobleman could—if he would—act as patron, thereby giving the artist the leisure necessary for the creation of solid work. He could also provide—Lady Gregory was, of course, Yeats's model—a gracious society which, consuming the artist's product, would justify his existence. The beggarman, on the other hand, in his freedom from middle class restrictions, his rejection of the whole social order, could provide (as the Irish peasants did for Yeats and Lady Gregory) uninhibited language and the gaiety and recklessness of behavior the artist needed for the earthy foundation of his art. The artist—coming from any class—would be fed by the nobleman and would find a reservoir of energy and imagery in the beggarman. Greater than either, he himself would be the catalyst who could shape their rough materials into an enduring art.

"The Three Beggars," the first of the beggarman poems, seems to point the moral that money is the root of all evil. All the beggars accomplish in their greed is to lose three night's sleep. The old crane—who moralizes as they snore—concludes that indifference is the best posture for one who would catch trout. Indifference seems to triumph also in "The Three Hermits," a poem Yeats enjoyed writing, "my first poem which is comedy or tragi-comedy," he wrote Lady Gregory. The two hermits who debate what their fate in the afterlife will be—the anguished prayerful one who expects to be thrown into "some most fearful shape" for his sins of omission and the flea-bitten optimist—argue while, unnoticed, the third sings, "Giddy with his hundredth year . . . like a bird." That he sings like a bird should be enough to pin him down as something near saint. That he is unnoticed in his singing assures it. Unlike the others, he has already achieved that visionary gaiety which Yeats regarded as the special property of blessedness.

"Beggar to Beggar Cried" may be linked to an entanglement that Yeats was involved in for several years before the publication of the poem. It ended in May of 1913 when the unmarried lady sent a telegram to Coole announcing pregnancy. Yeats, in consternation, turned to a medium whose prophesy ("Deception!") proved to be correct, but the affair had led to long discussions with Lady Gregory and Mrs. Shakespear, both of whom advised marriage as the solution for Yeats's emotional difficulties. The poem, perhaps an ironical comment on their well-meant suggestions, seems better seen, however, in the general framework of this group as a celebration of the beggarman's "humorous happy speech" which is threatened by his would-be marriage into the respectable middle class.

Those beggars who accept their lot are, like the singing hermit "Giddy with his hundredth year," "Running to Paradise." The refrain, which sends the artist's two supporting classes to Heaven, is made mysterious by an unitalicized "is" in a line of italics. The pause created by that illegitimately accented word forces, unnaturally, a double meaning into the line. It is hard not to read a reference to Paradise ending "*And there the king* is" as anything other than "God's in his heaven." Yet the rest of the line clearly indicates that the king is merely lower-case mundane ruler who, in Paradise, is no more than the beggar. By making that strange "is" unitalicized Yeats produces a rhythm that must have driven Robert Bridges wild and that certainly compels us to keep in mind both readings. Imagistically linked to "Beggar to Beggar Cried" by the wind that rushes through the last stanzas of both poems, this one reiterates the moral that the darling wit who gives himself up to stuffing "an old sock full" of cash is likely to prove—in the long run—a dull old man.

"The Hour before Dawn" also sends a beggar out into a "windy place." This beggar, "A bundle of rags upon a crutch," anticipates in appearance if not in behavior the scarecrow aged man, "A tattered coat upon a stick," of "Sailing to Byzantium"; but Yeats is not quite ready yet to turn his beggar into Everyman, and "The Hour before Dawn" is primarily an illustration of the kind of folk tale the artist can pick up from the peasant. Some critics, delighted by the "happy ending" of the beggarman's return to the world, see this as an indication of Yeats's rejection of dreams for the wonders of reality. That reading, cheerful as it is, may somewhat oversimplify the poem. The beery sleeper is not really young Yeats, and the "cursing rogue" who chooses not to sample Goban's brew is certainly not Yeats at middle age. Yeats's characters do debate an issue that troubled him, but Yeats does not really take sides in the debate. Each of the characters sees one side of multi-faceted truth. Yeats, like his sleeper, feels "all life longs for the Last Day" but, not so contemptuous of the other's vision as his beggarman, does choose to live in the world.

"A Song from 'The Player Queen,'" anticipating "Leda and the Swan," swings a golden cradle on a peasant's willow tree. Yeats, who later entertained himself with parallels between Helen's conception and Christ's, was fascinated by kings born in stables and bird annunciations—whether via dove, swan, or—as in this case—sea-mew. Such myths, binding the lowest to the highest classes, were—in Yeats's eyes—a justification of the system he was working out.

For without such myths, "The Realists" take over the world. The exclamatory "Hope that you may understand!" Yeats addresses to them in the beginning of his little poem clearly implies that he has no expectation that such men will know what he is talking about; but his thesis—that in the vanishing myths lies man's "hope to live," a hope which can be awakened by the books of those writers dedicated to the myths' truths—is plainly stated and becomes the foundation for the pair of short poems which immediately follow. For "The Witch" of worldly success is the realist's harlot; the beggarman-artist, constructing in "the pride of his eye" "The Peacock" of art, achieves by contrast the gaiety of aesthetic freedom.

"The Mountain Tomb" is concerned with the sort of revitalizing myth referred to in "The Realists." Yeats was, through his experiences in the Rosicrucian "Golden Dawn," more than familiar with the many legends associated with Father Christian Rosencreuz, the miracle-working patron saint of the Rosicrucian orders. (A fairly full transcription of some of the Rosicrucian initiation ceremonies Yeats went through as part of his elevation to the inner circle of the Golden Dawn has been made by Virginia Moore in *The Unicorn*, her study of Yeats's religious progression.) As he pointed out in his 1895 essay "The Body of the Father Christian Rosencrux," the crucial evidence of Father Rosencreuz' miraculous power occurred after his death: "The followers of the Father Christian Rosencrux . . . wrapped his imperishable body in noble raiment and laid it under the house of their order, in a tomb containing the symbols of all things in heaven and earth, and in the waters under the earth, and set about him inextinguishable magical lamps, which burnt on generation after generation, until other students of the order came upon the tomb by chance." Tradition has it that the good Father had remained spectacularly well preserved in that magically lighted tomb for precisely 120 years (a fine magic number, since it is the product of 1 x 2 x 3 x 4 x 5) before his undecayed body delighted the eyes of those who still kept faith.

Even as early as 1895, Yeats saw in the legend a moral for our times: "It seems to me that the imagination has had no very different history during the last two hundred years, but has been laid in a great tomb of criticism, and had set over it inextinguishable magical lamps of wisdom and romance, and has been altogether so nobly housed and apparelled that we have forgotten that its wizard lips are closed, or but opened for the complaining of some melancholy and ghostly voice."

Before the turn of the century, Yeats was optimistic in his expectations that a new day for literature would arrive: "I cannot get it out of my mind that this age of criticism is about to pass, and an age of imagination, of emotion, of moods, of revelation, about to come in its place; for certainly belief in a supersensual world is at hand again . . . for Art is a revelation, and not a criticism."

The 1912 poem, as even the most casual reading reveals, is much more cautious. In spite of wine, women, and song—an occult orgy if ever there were one—Father Rosicross sleeps on, "all wisdom" still locked behind his onyx eyes. The ceremony has been "in vain." Though still not decayed, the body has not stirred. Clues for the failure of miracle are carefully planted in the first two lines of the poem: manhood may no longer have pride; the rose, more perishable than Father Rosicross, may long since have bloomed, shattered, and turned to dust.

But though Father Rosicross still sleeps, life goes on. The dancers by the roaring cataract who cannot wake him dream of immortal wisdom; Iseult Gonne, who dances by the "water's roar" of the ocean in "To a Child Dancing in the Wind" is, as Yeats points out in the companion poem "Two Years Later," unlearned, delighting in youth's ignorance. The shut onyx eyes of dead imperishable Father Rosicross hold "all wisdom"; perishable Iseult Gonne's "daring/ Kind eyes" stare in youthful innocence on a world which seems good. Such dichotomies sting poets into wisdom, but a wisdom that is far more untranslatable to youth than Yeats's English into Iseult's French: "I am old and you are young,/ And I speak a barbarous tongue." It is barbarous for many reasons: it is foreign; it is an old man's speech; it is "barbed" with anger at life's waste (Synge, "the best labourer," dead in his prime; Maud Gonne, the "mother" who had adopted Iseult, broken by the very cause she had fought for). Brilliantly versified (examine, for example, the astonishing change of pace achieved by the suddenly introduced slow rhythm of the last line of "To a Child Dancing in the Wind"), these two poems preface a group which center on Maud Gonne.

Yeats in these years saw his perennial heroine as a tragic figure, "Fallen Majesty," a woman defeated by an unhappy marriage, deserted—like Parnell—by the mob she had once victoriously led, sick and old when seen against the fresh bloom of her adopted daughter, in love still with the martyr's "proud death" but stranded short of martyrdom.

Now associated in his mind with violence, she is characterized no longer by apple-blossom imagery but rather by blinding flashes of light that tear through black sky. "She lived in storm"; like a king who celebrates his marriage with trumpet, kettledrum, and cannon, she has bundled time away "That the night come." His memory of a night spent with her in his youth is of black sky shattered by the sudden appearance of a moon that Love "Tore from the clouds." She had been in those days, he remembers, hardly woman at all, superhuman in her beauty, a miraculous shining "thing . . . that seemed a burning cloud." And even now she is a vision of "The Cold Heaven" that leaves him "Riddled with light."

His function in these days, catching up the imagery of beggar-man and king he has been working with, is to praise her "Like some last courtier at a gypsy camping-place/ Babbling of fallen majesty," to praise the "eagle look" she still has, the "burning cloud" she was.

And these are indeed poems of praise: "I had her praise . . ."; "I praised her body and her mind"; "Yet we, for all that praise . . ."; "Now must I these three praise—"; "How could I praise that one?"

Yet in spite of so much praise there is also evaluation and careful thought. "The Cold Heaven," the most difficult of these poems, is complicated by intricate speculations about the afterlife which, in Yeats's subsequent work, grow increasingly important. To "understand" the poem, one must keep firmly in mind Yeats's treatment of his poetic material, particularly symbolic images and scenes (frequently founded on visions or reported visions). The poet uses the image or the symbolic scene, Yeats felt, by carefully studying it for possible "meanings," possible philosophical parallels, and possible correlations to other significant images or scenes. "Meaning" does not exist for Yeats in sets of abstract propositions ("scientific laws") carefully extracted from an observed physical world, but rather directly in things themselves. Birds, for instance, suggest to him a whole host of felt values: speed, lightness, freedom, flight, quickness of intellect; they link to artist—since their language is song, to the afterlife—since the medium which they inhabit is thin air; they fly against symbolic sun and moon, nest in the symbolic tree, and hatch symbolic eggs. On the other hand, Yeats was not particularly interested in scientific birdwatching: the physical principles of flight, theories on the mechanics of bird song, calculations as to why ducks float all left him cold.

"The Cold Heaven" draws, therefore, on a visionary scene and all the felt relationships—no matter how irrational—Yeats can attach to it. The poem itself, he told Maud Gonne, began with his efforts to describe the feelings brought on by the cold, detached beauty of a winter sky. Staring at "the rook-delighting heaven," he sees it transformed into a pattern of burning expanding ice. The burning ice itself ties the two seemingly antithetical subjects of the rest of the poem into a felt unity: burning passions of youth balance against the freezing naked soul of a dead old man which, "naked on the roads," is stricken by those cold burning skies for punishment. Though Yeats allows us to make up our own minds what that soul is punished for, the poem seems to offer two possibilities: his failure to bring his passions to fruition in love (the punishment, consequently, being that that naked soul will be burned by cold skies), or his recklessly taking the blame for the failure of love—a failure which he was not responsible for (the punishment for which, anticipated in advance, he already experiences: "riddled by light"—shot through with light and insight—he already sees in vision the anguish the cold skies will ultimately force on his soul). Yet within the framework of the poem both answers are the right one and neither is right. For the poet is also made skeptical by light (he is "riddled by light"—its shining conundrums plague him). Confused as a man on a death-bed, he ends his poem with a question.

Yeats offers us the experience of a shattering illumination, the memories it evokes, and—in the question that at first seems unrelated to the rest of the poem—a possible consequence of either the memories or his interpretation of them. The "meaning" we draw from the poem, can therefore be as trivial ("He remembers how much he used to be in love with Maud Gonne.") or as rich (speculations about the ethical structure of the universe) as we choose to make it. Each poem, in itself a symbol compounded from symbols, is a reservoir of possibilities.

Two other visionary poems, in early editions paired, move the section to its close. "The Magi" had been suggested to Yeats by a vision of "stiff figures in procession" marching through a blue sky. Symbols of the inexorably cyclical movement of history which Yeats would later define in A *Vision*, they here anticipate, their mask-like faces seeking "The uncontrollable mystery on the bestial floor," the themes he was to work out more fully in "Leda and the Swan" and "The Second Coming." "The Dolls"—like Yeats's envisioned Magi—are images and therefore perfect. They are also art products and so survive "accidental" human flesh, the "filthy" decaying "thing" a baby is, for example. This funny poem, made deafening by the bawling and screaming shelf of dolls who complain of the "noisy" human child, rises to a glorious pun in the wife's simultaneously vocative, affectionate, and distracted "O dear."

"A Coat" brings the section to a formal end with its announcement that Yeats will henceforth walk naked, and the epilogue ("While I, from that reed-throated whisperer") pulls the entire section into organic unity. Irritated by George Moore's publication of his insulting and inaccurate memoirs, Yeats makes in this poem a defense of those "priceless things" Moore had attacked: his psychic investigations, his pride in family, his admiration for Lady Gregory, his love of Maud Gonne; especially, his conviction of the importance of his own work. The poem is not really so complex as it has sometimes been made out to be. Though the visionary "reed-throated whisperer," Yeats's ghostly advisor, no longer clearly manifests himself in air (Yeats no longer "sees" him), that whisperer still is felt "inwardly" and Yeats is able to "surmise companions" in the spirit world (precisely those companions, those "Old Fathers" he had invoked in the opening poem and the members of the Rhymers' Club he had invoked in "The Grey Rock"). Because of their steadying presence and the aristocratic values he has discovered at Lady Gregory's home (Kyle-na-no was one of the seven woods of Coole), he is able to bear the notoriety George Moore has imposed on him. Shifting in the end of the poem from defense to an attack of his own, Yeats disposes neatly of Moore: "all my priceless things/ Are but a post the passing dogs defile." This juicy last line—an adaptation, as Yeats pointed out in his 1930 diary, of "a metaphor from Erasmus"—improves, in its "passing" pun, on a distinguished original.

8 * The Wild Swans at Coole

In the five years that intervened between the publication of *Responsibilities* and the 1919 expanded edition of *The Wild Swans at Coole* on which the present arrangement of the poems is based, a series of catastrophic international, national, and personal events took place, all of which Yeats ultimately worked into the framework of his *Collected Poems*. The first world war, the death of Hugh Lane, the Easter rising of 1916, the threatened dismemberment of Lady Gregory's estate, the death of Maud Gonne's husband and her final rejection of Yeats, Iseult Gonne's rejection of him, his hasty marriage, the death of Robert Gregory: all these events and others rushed pell-mell at Yeats who, at last almost secure financially, was during these years arranging for the purchase and rehabilitation of that Ballylee tower in which he hoped finally to settle down. In spite of the chaos through which he lived, these were immensely productive years. Delighted with the new dramatic forms he created on the model of the Japanese Nōh plays and, after his marriage, revitalized by the marvels promised in his wife's automatic writing, Yeats worked industriously on poetry, plays, his autobiography, the essays which outlined the theory of the Mask, and the growing collections of automatic writing which eventually became A *Vision*.

Many of the poems of this period were carefully excluded from *The Wild Swans at Coole*—some for personal reasons ("Reprisals," for example, never appeared in the *Collected Poems* because Yeats felt Lady Gregory might be hurt by the suggestion that her son had died in vain) but more because they simply did not fit into the plan for the volume and had to be postponed for more appropriate contexts.

The organization of *The Wild Swans at Coole* is relatively uncomplicated: a group of personal, anecdotal poems dealing with the death of Lady Gregory's young son Robert prefaces a set of observations on old age which in turn lead back to a formal elegy on the young man's death. That elegy, drawing as it does on Yeats's theory of the Mask and the new material he was assembling for A *Vision*, is followed by a group of Mask poems and a set of studies of love and death which, increasingly speculative, culminate in the last half-dozen poems of the volume, directly founded on and explicating the new system Yeats would ultimately name A *Vision*. The design of the book, therefore, is Death, Life, and The Patterns of Life and Death. Yeats's Masks are Survivor, Defeated Lover, and Scholar. The progression is from uncomplicated personal statement to an elaborate presentation of the intricate image on which A *Vision* is founded.

The title poem, "The Wild Swans at Coole," introduces all the major themes of the section. Yeats, old, stares on the fifty-nine swans which, for nineteen years, have seemed miraculously to defy time: "Unwearied," "Their hearts have not grown old." Though in fact they may like Yeats age or like Robert Gregory die, the pattern they establish survives: they give the illusion of immortality. They even manage to anticipate the structure of eternity, the gyre which Yeats saw as the pattern of all things, when—halfway through his count—they rise from the lake to wheel above him in "great broken rings." Linking the "still water" to the "still sky" which is reflected in it, they are able—unlike man—to live in two elements (and—symbolically, at least—to live on earth and in eternity: to be mortal, "lover by lover," yet somehow immortal, "Unwearied still"). "Mysterious," they lead Yeats to the question which ends the poem: where will they be, delighting men's eyes, "when I awake some day/ To find they have flown away?" This complex question (and many others Yeats will soon be asking) suggests its own mysteries: like that of the swans, the pattern of man survives; yet "I," awakening some day (into death?), will find the pattern of immortality "flown away" (and myself immortal?).

"In Memory of Major Robert Gregory" shifts the setting from Lady Gregory's estate at Coole Park upstream to Yeats's tower, but the subject remains mortal man and Yeats's focus is still on the Gregorys.

His tower and the cottage below it—the "house" of the first line of the poem—had, after considerable bargaining, been purchased by Yeats from the Congested Districts Board for the very small sum of £35. Yeats saw it as ". . . a setting for my old age, a place to influence lawless youth, with its severity and antiquity" and planned, with Robert Gregory's help, to restore though not to modernize it. The restoration costs, however, ran considerably higher than he had anticipated (initial work on the cottage alone cost him over £200), and work on the tower itself was never completely finished.

When he married on October 21, 1917, his tower was much in his thoughts; he and his bride made elaborate plans for the disposition of rooms and gardens. And though they were not actually able to move into the cottage by the tower until the summer of 1919, from the time of their marriage they regularly announced plans to move in "soon." Certainly they thought they were "almost settled" there when, just three months after their marriage, Lady Gregory's gifted, brilliant son Robert who had enlisted in the war as an aviator was killed in action over Italy. Yeats had for years admired him as a kind of symbol of aristocratic good-breeding, "Our Sidney and our perfect man," and was shocked into poetry at the thought that a man of such great promise, all his achievement still before him, should die uncommemorated.

The "Major Gregory" poem, which Yeats himself recognized as one of his finest accomplishments, gains much of its power from Yeats's evident sincerity; his "personal" feeling is genuine. But he manages, also, within the poem, to extend his subject from "the death of Robert Gregory" to "the death of the young hero." And we, reading the poem, celebrate not just Lady Gregory's son but all those young men of promise who, dying young, seem cheated shining Leonardos. "Soldier, scholar, horesman," Robert Gregory becomes himself emblem for the immense defeated possibility of war-slaughtered youth.

Structurally, the poem moves out of its chatty first two stanzas —a conversation with the new bride about the complexities of friendship for the sake of which even the most happily married couples quarrel—into a catalogue of dead friends who, since they are dead, cannot "set us quarrelling." The three Yeats lists before he comes to Major Gregory are carefully selected, for each has achieved a partial vision of that reality which, Yeats suggests, Robert Gregory saw whole. Like Lionel Johnson, who delighted in abstract thought, Robert Gregory was a scholar: ". . . his mind outran the horses' feet." Like John Synge, who "dying chose the living world for text," he delighted in the simplicity, the vivid reality, of "a most desolate stony place"; he painted in stern color and delicate line "cold Clare rock and Galway rock." And, like old George Pollexfen, he was a peerless horseman.

Yet, younger than all these men, Robert Gregory held in balance the three excellences each of them had separately risen to. In the single intense flare of his youth he had become, symbolically, "all life's epitome." Recapitulating his three models in the last stanza,

Yeats thinks of Synge (whom "manhood tried"), George Pollexfen (whom "childhood loved"), and Lionel Johnson (whom
"boyish intellect approved"). But another thought—"a thought/
Of that late death"—takes (like death itself which has made all
the passionate men Yeats names "breathless") "all my heart for
speech." This remarkable last line, ironical and grand in its announcement that Yeats's own eloquence must lift into silence before a theme larger than eloquence itself, lets the poem end where
it had begun: in the stillness that surrounds an imaginary statement before an imagined fire, for poet and new bride are, of
course, "almost"—but not—"settled" in their house, and the
"narrow winding stair" they climb led, when Yeats wrote the
poem, to an uninhabitable room.

Though it is helpful to know that Lionel Johnson is described
as "falling" because before his death he had been drinking heavily,
that the "race" Synge came to is that of the Aran Islanders who
provided him models for his great plays, and that George Pollexfen's astrological calculations "By opposition, square and trine"
were achieved by examination of the "aspects" of constellations
of the Zodiac at 180° (opposition), 90° (square), and 120°
(trine), details of this sort are not really needed for an understanding of a poem which is constructed, rather, from the "aspects" of
three dead men which, in conjunction, define the dead hero.

Another definition of him is offered in "An Irish Airman For-
sees his Death." Stressing again the "balance" of his perfect man,
Yeats—like Homer before him in the *Iliad*—lets his young man
choose a hero's death in a war otherwise meaningless. By reducing
the entire war to an occasion for Robert Gregory's "lonely impulse of delight," Yeats brings his hero to a moment of perception,
an instant of insight that balances "all" and that makes significant (because equivalent to each other) "this life, this death."

Robert Gregory died young. The next group of poems—making
connections—focuses sharply on Yeats as the surviving aging poet.
If Robert Gregory's life had been a "flare," an explosive violence
in the clouds, Yeats sees himself in "Men Improve with the

Years" as "A weather-worn, marble triton/ Among the streams."
Echoing the "picture-book" phrase from the "Major Gregory"
poem, he comments ironically on his own improvement with age.
Age's wisdom gives him possibilities of aesthetic delight in the contemplation of a girl (Iseult Gonne), but "burning youth"—the
sort Robert Gregory had—is gone. His own once-passionate flesh—
now "weather-worn"—has hardened to cold "marble." Lust must
necessarily be replaced by dreams.

The old poet's dreams themselves appropriately follow. "The
Collar-Bone of a Hare"—a wish-fulfillment dream ("Would I
could . . .")—sails him in imagination back to Oisin's enchanted
first island, its "comely trees and the lawn," its kissing, sensual,
immortal dancers. From such security, he feels, he can afford to
look back toward "the old bitter world where they marry in
churches." His telescope is the magic collar-bone. (Years before,
Yeats had told the story of "The Three O'Byrnes and the Evil
Faeries" in his *Celtic Twilight*. In that story, a peasant found "the
shin-bone of a hare lying on the grass. He took it up; there was a
hole in it." Looking through the hole, he was able to see a treasure
buried beneath his feet.) This dream-rejection of the middle-
class (". . . all who marry in churches") is precisely parallel to
beggar Billy Byrne's rejection of it in his dream "Under the
Round Tower." Refusing to "live as live the neighbours," Billy
settles down on his great-grandfather's tombstone "beside the
stream" (all these dreamers—the old triton, the Collar-Bone
dreamer, and Billy Byrne—dream only in the presence of water)
to dream of his own immortal dancers, "golden king and silver
lady," who, bellowing sweet songs and prancing sweet measures,
are in reality "sun and moon."

Whirling in a circle, "That golden king and that wild lady"
dance the night out to become for Billy omens of good luck.
"Solomon to Sheba," on the other hand, sets a different golden
king and "dusky" lady going "round and round/ In the narrow
theme of love" from "shadowless noon" until nightfall. These,
who have the wisdom the old triton was coming to, conclude that

for all their learning love is the principle which orders the world. Brilliantly balancing the "narrow" language of the final lines of each stanza, Yeats juggles "theme," "thoughts," and "thing" against the horse-pound of the world. His gay intellectuals, Sheba planted on Solomon's knees, prove that passion is wisdom's finest fruit.

The two short poems "The Living Beauty" and "A Song" return the reader from dreams to reality. The speaker of the poems is once again that "I," the poet conscious of the ravages of age, who had proposed to and been rejected by a "living beauty," Iseult Gonne. "Iseult and I are on our old intimate terms," Yeats wrote Lady Gregory at about this time, "but I don't think she will accept. She 'has not the impulse.'" And his own impulses, Yeats felt, were beginning to dry up: "the wick and oil are spent." Stranded in that wise old age he had examined in "Men Improve with the Years," Yeats finds himself driven to the contemplation of marble rather than flesh: "The living beauty is for younger men." Not even the "dumb-bell and foil" Ezra Pound had instructed him in are of avail against time. "O heart, we are old," he sighs in one poem and in the other recasts the theme as his refrain: "the heart grows old."

But if Iseult Gonne will not let him give her his love, she cannot stop him from offering advice. "To a Young Beauty," certainly addressed to her, warns her away from the Dublin Bohemian fringe which had made much of her and sets up Yeats himself as a model of the man who—picking his friends as carefully as his flowing neckties—by careful cultivation of a select circle will prepare himself for a poet's immortality in which he will have as companions Landor, whom he had long admired, and Donne, whose works he had recently read in Grierson's edition. (Donne's "pedantry and his obscenity—the rock and the loam of his Eden—but make me the more certain," Yeats wrote Grierson, "that one who is but a man like us all has seen God.")

The last of this group of poems addressed to Iseult Gonne, "To a Young Girl," returns us to Yeats's favorite subject, her mother.

and prepares the way for "The Scholars," Yeats's vitriolic attack on books of this sort, by reminding his readers and her that Maud Gonne had once loved him passionately.

Old men's annotations of the lines written by young men "in love's despair" are satirized in "The Scholars." These "logic-choppers," Yeats notes in "Tom O'Roughley," now dominate the world, but their kind of wisdom—that of the bird of prey—is not a poet's. Explaining his image, Yeats later noted, "I have a ring with a hawk and a butterfly upon it, to symbolize the straight road of logic, and so of mechanism, and the crooked road of intuition."

Celebrating as it does the artist's joy in all things—even death—"Tom O'Roughley" is a defense of the cheerful pastoral elegy Yeats prints as the immediately following poem. For in fact Robert Gregory, Yeats's "dearest friend," *is* dead; and Yeats, like Tom, dances—poetically at least—"a measure on his grave."

Taking one of his themes—the soul's progression after death back through its own infancy to a sort of oversoul—from Asia's song in Shelley's *Prometheus Unbound* and, as F. A. C. Wilson has pointed out, from an even older Platonic tradition before that, Yeats grafts the Platonic material he and his wife were examining in the early notes for *A Vision* onto a form modelled, as he told Lady Gregory, "on what Virgil wrote for some friend of his and on what Spenser wrote of Sidney."

The poem, a formal reworking of the "Major Gregory" material, is an effort to integrate through traditional imagery "the mountain and the valley" and so reveal not only Goatherd and Shepherd (age and youth, old souls and young souls, Yeats as a youth and Yeats as an old man) mourning the death of Robert Gregory, but all of that nature Robert had given tongue to (the very stone of the hills themselves which, when he had played his pipes, had "cried/ Under his fingers").

The Shepherd, who begins the poem by wishing on the cry of the first cuckoo of the year and later uses the cuckoo, "the speckled bird," as his image for Robert Gregory, sings "of the natural life" as both young Yeats and the Goatherd (who "made like music in my youth") had once done. A sensualist, he praises Robert Gregory for physical accomplishment (best in every sport and craft—the horseman and artisan Yeats had admired in his "Major Gregory" poem) and speculates that, since Robert had gathered up no gear, set no carpenters to work, and "left the house as in his father's time," perhaps he had realized his own impending death. His song, "maybe 'I am sorry' in plain prose/ Had sounded better," concerns itself with the shortness of life, the cuckoo which appears for an instant, sings briefly, and vanishes. It offers no consolation, only regret.

The gay old Goatherd, however, who remembers Robert Gregory's isolation, feels sorrow not so much for the young man dead as for the mother who survives him. (Yeats has him praise her for having fed him physically and spiritually in the "winter" of his youth.) Like Yeats, who in the "Major Gregory" poem had memorialized Robert in terms of long dead friends, the Goatherd thinks of "that young man/ And certain lost companions of my own." Unlike the Shepherd, however, his song will not be of the natural but of the spiritual life. He has "talked with apparitions," found patterns of supernatural order, "paths my goats' feet cannot find"; he has seen in vision Swedenborg's angels which, as Yeats pointed out both in *The Tragic Generation* and in *The Bounty of Sweden,* "move perpetually . . . towards 'the day-spring of their youth.'" His song—explicating some of the more intricate material in *A Vision*—is concerned with what Yeats ultimately called the "dreaming back" process by which a soul was reincorporated into the eternal flux from which it had first sprung. Death in such a system is an unwinding of the spool; at the top of the gyre of life, dead, one spirals down—reversing time—in the narrowing circles of an inner cone. Yeats wanted no one to miss this idea, and he carefully prepared a note that would explain that " 'pern' was another name for the spool, as I was accustomed to call it, on which thread was wound." Dead Robert Gregory, consequently, will work merrily backwards, "Jaunting, journeying/ To his own dayspring," from death toward birth: the "outrageous war" will fade, he will court again the girl he married, he will indulge in childish play, until—newly born, "clambering at the cradle-side" —he will be ready to recover the "sweeter ignorance" of immortality. For Lady Gregory's orthodox sake, Yeats abandoned what would have been the next step in the "dreaming back," the discovery of the current incarnation of Robert Gregory's soul.

A whole group of poems, all loosely based on the evolving Mask imagery and that of *A Vision,* follow "Shepherd and Goatherd." "Lines Written in Dejection" represents Yeats's conviction that at fifty he had moved into a solar phase, "Banished heroic mother moon and vanished," and that all the moon's imagery (dark leopards, wild witches, holy centaurs) will be replaced by a new "masculine" realism, embittered but perhaps (he was wrong) "timid."

"The Dawn" fits the Mask of this solar phase to Yeats's features. He would be "ignorant and wanton" as the moon-banishing dawn which looks down on ancient lunar mythologies like those of Celtic Ireland (whose old Ulster queen Macha had measured a town with the pin of her brooch) and Babylon of mathematical starlight.

"On Woman," ingeniously exploring in its imagery the "shuddering" machinery of sex, accomplishes in the same vein new feats of frankness. Woman, who offers man a friendship that "covers all he has brought/ As with her flesh and bone" leads Yeats once more to thoughts of Solomon and Sheba. But Sheba is now the active partner, and Solomon is hard pressed to praise her "When she the iron wrought, or/ When from the smithy fire/ It shuddered in the water." For those who fail to see how these images illustrate "Harshness of their desire," he goes on to define more explicitly "Pleasure that comes with sleep,/ Shudder that makes them one." And his prayer that in his next life he be allowed to "live like Solomon/ That Sheba led a dance" is interrupted by one more variant of the image he has so carefully constructed, this one drawn from the basic reincarnation symbolism of *A Vision:* "The Pestle of the moon/ That pounds up all anew/ Brings me to birth again."

"The Fisherman," another dawn poem, defines more carefully the features of the Mask Yeats is constructing for himself. Years before Yeats had tried in fact to be such a man as his fisherman "In grey Connemara clothes" and, ordering proper garments from his tailor, had delighted in his homespun Irishness. "I believed myself dressed according to public opinion," he recollected in *The Stirring of the Bones,* the memoirs on which the poem is directly based, "until a letter of apology from my tailor informed me that 'It takes such a long time getting Connemara cloth as it has to come all the way from Scotland.' " But now, Yeats argues, his youthful dream of an Ireland integrated by "great Art" is no longer possible. Ireland, essentially disordered, has "beaten down" both "the wise/ And great Art." The man in Connemara cloth of the first stanza, the sentimental image for united Ireland, is re-placed in the second stanza by his double, newly imagined, "Maybe a twelvemonth since," and imagined "In scorn of this audience" of hypocritical frauds. This new figure—like the old but different—will be Yeats's solar Mask, a Cuchulain reborn, for whom no sentimental moonlit verses need be made but rather "one/ Poem maybe as cold/ And passionate as the dawn." An important poem, linking in its imagery "The Dawn" to "The Tower" and the poems to the plays, it is, perhaps, richer than it seems.

Cuchulain, who is associated in Yeats's plays always with "the grey hawk's feather," is certainly Yeats's Mask and may well him-self be masked as "The Hawk" in the next poem. Each stanza spoken by a different figure, the poem makes from the three analyses of the hawk a rudimentary symbol. The first stanza rep-resents the voice of all "practical" people who would find utili-tarian functions for everything from hawks to poets. The second stanza is the answer of the hawk himself who, discovering free-dom, rejects their demands on him. Yeats's own comment in the last stanza, recognizing the "Yellow-eyed hawk of the mind" as image and symbol, deals with the problem of the artist who must live in the world. What value is his symbol, he seems to ask, when he can be "Dumbfounded before a knave" yet display for his friend "A pretense of wit"?

If the imagined symbol seems at this point to have dubious utility, the woman-made-symbol, Maud Gonne, still stands Yeats in good stead. The six poems beginning with "Her Praise" allow her to sink violently into middle age. Still seeing brilliant flashes of the beauty that had thrilled him so many years before and fascinated by her violence (she was at this time, he wrote Lady Gregory, "in a joyous and self forgetting condition of political hate the like of which I have not yet encountered"), Yeats made his poems about her the vehicles for his persistent theme of time's treachery.

The first of them, "Her Praise," not only develops that persistent theme but illustrates remarkably Yeats's growing interest in functional repetition. Held together by echoing interwoven words (foremost, uppermost, foremost; praised, praise, praised, praise, praise; book, books; talk, talk, talk; name, name, name; new, new, new; old, old, old; young, young, young) and a complex pattern of internal rhymes and half-rhymes too intricate to reproduce without reproducing the entire text, this astonishing eighteen line poem seems at first glance simple.

"Her Praise" fixes the memory of her name not in the literary "educated" classes but rather in "the poor both old and young." These, "The People," are—as that poem points out—her own persistent theme. One of Yeats's problems always was his effort to reconcile his growing aristocratic sentiments with Maud Gonne's passionate democratic spirit. In this poem, drawing once more on imagery from Castiglione's *The Courtier*, Yeats imagines himself in an ideal aristocracy free from Dublin's bitterness. But Maud Gonne, his "phoenix," delights in her own defeat. Recollecting those painful moments when, separated from her husband and suddenly for the first time unpopular with the crowd, she had been hissed on the Abbey stage, she reproves—in spite of everything—Yeats's criticism of the people. Though he defends himself, "whose virtues are the definitions/ Of the analytic mind," a defense that is as well the defense of all satirical art, nevertheless his heart—in spite of all his good reason—"leaped at her words," and he remains at poem's end "abashed."

Maud Gonne is elevated to symbol through definition and redefinition. "His Phoenix" supplies one more. Here Yeats praises her by constructing a long catalogue of "most beautiful" women (the Chinese or Spanish queen beautiful as "that sprightly girl" Leda who, trodden by Zeus in the form of a swan, eventually gave birth to another of Yeats's heroines, Helen, and incidentally to one of his greatest poems; Gaby Deslys; Ruth St. Denis; Pavlova; Julia Marlow, whose child-like Juliet had thrilled Yeats when he had been in America on his 1903 lecture tour; and all the others: Margaret, Marjorie, Dorothy, Nan, Daphne, and Mary, some at least half-identifiable). Beautiful women, "that barbarous crowd," will, Yeats contends, come and go; and they will even be "my beauty's equal." But they will not—Yeats, as always, celebrates saving human individuality—be "the exact likeness." Maud Gonne's simplicity, her hawk-like proud look (an image he will later make her signature) "as though she had gazed into the burning sun" and her perfect body have now all drifted into the past. Though she lives, her once-unparalleled lineaments are dead; and Yeats mourns for her as for a dead body, a "thing" most lonely and lost. A poem built, at least in part, on Yeats's response to Maud Gonne's 1909 assertion that they must in the future "be apart," something of its genesis can be seen in the sections from his unpublished journal quoted by Virginia Moore in her study *The Unicorn*:

> She is my innocence and I her wisdom. Of old she was a phoenix and I feared her, but now she is my child more than my sweetheart. . . . Always since I was a boy I have questioned dreams for her sake—and she herself always a dream and deceiving hope . . . the phoenix nesting [?] when she is reborn in all her power to torture and delight, to waste and ennoble. She would be cruel if she were

not a child who can always say, "You will not suffer because I will pray."

The other three poems devoted to her, "A Thought from Propertius" (the Roman poet Sextus Propertius), "Broken Dreams" (with its "paddling" echo of the title poem of the section, its anticipation of Helen, the daughter of the swan, who paddles through "Among School Children"), and "A Deep-sworn Vow" reaffirm her continuing power while "Presences," which develops the hint of "A Deep-sworn Vow" that Yeats has had affairs with other women (the "friends" he mentions) only because Maud Gonne had once recklessly refused to marry him, again makes the accusation that she had really "returned" his love in spite of all her assertions of purity, that, returning it, she had also in "monstrous" fashion refused to requite it. The ladies of the last three lines, the "harlot" who had pretended to be with child in the hope of trapping Yeats into marriage, Iseult Gonne, and Maud herself are, of course, made carefully recognizable.

The epigrammatic lyrics that follow separate life from death, vital Maud Gonne from dead Alfred Pollexfen and dying Mabel Beardsley. Uncomplicated, they were occasional poems written for Yeats's own amusement. ("On being asked for a War Poem," for instance, was Yeats's tongue-in-cheek "answer" to Edith Wharton's request through Henry James that Yeats comment on the war. Yeats's return letter with its careful salutation "Dear Mr. Henry James" is quite as entertaining as the poem. See Wade's edition of Yeats's letters, p. 599.)

But it is life and death and those life-death symbols birds which *The Wild Swans at Coole* centers on. And "In Memory of Alfred Pollexfen" brings us quickly back to dominant image and theme. After recapitulating all the dead Pollexfens (old William Pollexfen, Yeats's grandfather, who was buried by his wife in St. John's Churchyard; George Pollexfen, Yeats's uncle, whose grand Masonic funeral, formal and ceremonious—eighty Masons actively participated—seemed to Yeats right treatment for a much-loved man; "lost" John Pollexfen; and Alfred himself), Yeats adapts for the poem a little of the material he had assembled for his new volume of autobiography *Reveries over Childhood and Youth.* There, in an analysis of Pollexfen character, he recollected that "Only six months ago my sister awoke dreaming that she held a wingless sea-bird in her arms," a dream Yeats interpreted as symbolic of the mortal illness of one of his Pollexfen relatives who soon after died in a madhouse, "for a sea-bird is the omen that announces the death or danger of a Pollexfen." Expanding his prose statement in "In Memory of Alfred Pollexfen," Yeats makes the bird not merely symbolic of death but assigns it as well his recurring theme; for the bird does more than appear: it cries out against the very fact of mortality, "Lamenting that a man should die." "And with that cry," Yeats adds, ending the poem, "I have raised my cry."

Still another of those cries is to be found in the set of seven poems "Upon a Dying Lady." Yeats, who as he grew older narrowed his theme more and more strictly to the meaning of life, watched with a fascinated mounting horror the death-toll of relatives and friends. Life, as for many sensitive people, became for him when he approached old age and his own death a kind of catalogue of dying; and he tried, examining all those deaths, to extract from dying faces and from dying statements insights into universal patterns. If any men could see into the heart of things, dying men should be able to. Graceful deaths especially might let the keen-eyed surviving man stare through the grave into the shining reality all men have dreamed of.

Mabel Beardsley's was for Yeats one of those horrible, graceful, meaningful deaths. Yeats had first known her through her brother Aubrey in his Rhymers' Club days. Then a promising young actress, she brought gaiety and light-heartedness to the often sober meetings, and later she was an occasional visitor to Yeats's at-home Mondays at Woburn Buildings in London. Younger than Yeats, she was discovered in the summer of 1912 to be suffering from an incurable and painful cancer. Her friends and those of her brother,

Yeats among them, did their best to make her last years full ones. Moved by her courage, her faith, and her reckless, gay defiance of death, Yeats made her an image for heroic man who, doomed, triumphs in his disaster.

Two letters to Lady Gregory reveal most clearly the particular events which Yeats translated into poems. The first is dated January 8, 1913:

> She had had a week of great pain but on Sunday was I think free from it. She was propped up on pillows with her cheeks I think a little rouged and looking very beautiful. Beside her a Xmas tree with little toys containing sweets, which she gave us. Mr. Davis— Ricketts' patron—had brought it—I daresay it was Ricketts' idea. I will keep the little toy she gave me and I daresay she knew this. On a table near were four dolls dressed like people out of her brother's drawings. Women with loose trousers and boys that looked like women. Ricketts had made them, modelling the faces and sewing the clothes. They must have taken him days. She had all her great lady airs and asked after my work and my health as if they were the most important things in the world to her. 'A palmist told me,' she said, 'that when I was forty-two my life would take a turn for the better and now I shall spend my forty-second year in heaven' and then emphatically 'O yes I shall go to heaven. Papists do.' When I told her where Mrs. Emery was she said 'How fine of her, but a girls' school! why she used to make even me blush!' Then she began telling improper stories and inciting us (there were two men besides myself) to do the like. At moments she shook with laughter. Just before I was going her mother came and saw me to the door. As we were standing at it she said 'I do not think she wishes to live—how could she after such agony? She is all I have left now.' I lay awake most of the night with a poem in my head. I cannot over-state her strange charm—the pathetic gaiety.

The second was written about a month later, February 11, 1913:

> . . . Mabel Beardsley said to me on Sunday 'I wonder who will introduce me in heaven. It should be my brother but then they might not appreciate the introduction. They might not have good

taste.' She said of her brother 'He hated the people who denied the existence of evil, and so being young he filled his pictures with evil. He had a passion for reality.' She has the same passion and puts aside any attempt to suggest recovery and yet I have never seen her in low spirits. She talked of a play she wanted to see. 'If I could only send my head and my legs,' she said, 'for they are quite well.' Till one questions her she tries to make one forget that she is ill. I always see her alone now. She keeps Sunday afternoon for me. I will send you the little series of poems when they are finished. One or two are I think very good.

Letting his poems move swiftly through the events he had experienced, Yeats constructs a case for life as "play," play that through good living becomes elevated almost to the level of art. The sixth lyric, "Her Courage," linking his heroine to the immortal dead who "laughed into the face of Death," joins her to a company of great free spirits, half drawn from history and half from myth: Grania, the heroine of the Fenian cycle of Irish myth; an imagined cardinal who might have dying praised the Venetian painter Giorgione's luxurious coloration; Achilles, who faced death carelessly, almost gladly, after his friend Patroclus' death; Timor (Tamerlane); Babar, the founder of the Indian Mogul Empire; and Barhaim (perhaps Bahrám, the "great Hunter" of FitzGerald's *Rubáiyát*). She, Yeats argues, like these heroes, "lived in joy" and, so living, constructed the only human equivalent to immortality's "predestined dancing-place." Yet, Yeats suggests in the last poem of the set, if death is the means by which we join the immortal dance, it is nevertheless also our "great enemy." Fated to die, fragile man arranges his "pretty things" that he may have a moment's joy, laughter on his lips, as he turns to stare in death's grim face:

> Give her a little grace,
> What if a laughing eye
> Have looked into your face?
> It is about to die.

But "pretty things" alone could not account for Yeats's feeling of order in the universe, and the rest of the poems in *The Wild Swans at Coole* seek—drawing on Yeats's theory of the Mask which he had outlined in *Per Amica Silentia Lunae* and the even more detailed plan of the nature of things that he was evolving for *A Vision*—to suggest something of the order Yeats thought he had discovered.

"Ego Dominus Tuus," written in 1915, focuses primarily on the Mask, though it anticipates aspects of *A Vision*. With its opening reference to Michael Robartes, who in Yeats's first draft of *A Vision* is supposed to have discovered that much-battered manuscript, it sets up as its two characters "primary" and "antithetical" men. *Hic*, the "primary" specimen, solar, objective, associated with the body, seeks to "find myself and not an image"; antithetical *Ille*, on the other hand, lunar, subjective, associated with soul, is the man determined to locate his own opposite, his Mask, "an image," and so discover his own true nature. Like Yeats, who saw himself in an antithetical phase, *Ille* walks in the moonlight beneath the tower and awaits the arrival of a double almost precisely like that one Yeats summoned in "The Fisherman," "the mysterious one who yet/ Shall walk the wet sands by the edge of the stream/ And look most like me, being indeed my double,/ And prove of all imaginable things the most unlike, being my anti-self."

As part of their debate, *Hic* and *Ille* define the nature of the modern world in terms that would later become familiar to readers of *A Vision*. *Ille* explains that the world itself has entered a primary phase. *Hic* and men of his kind are ascendant: Artists now are out of style; "We are but critics, or but half create." (As I have pointed out in discussing "The Mountain Tomb," Yeats earlier had more optimistic thoughts about the chances for a creative era arriving in the near future.)

Trying to prove that great men of the past have, like him, sought their own images, *Hic* cites the "hollow face" of Dante; but *Ille*, suggesting that that face was not the face that Lapo

Gianni and Guido Cavalcanti knew, answers that that "hollow face" is more than likely the sensuous real man's Mask, "fashioned from his opposite." Dante, himself, mocked by Guido for his sensuality, he maintains, had "set his chisel to the hardest stone" and so carved out a "spectral image" most unlike himself. Keats, too, *Ille* argues, had fashioned for himself a Mask of happiness that hid a mind starved for the things of the world, "His senses and his heart unsatisfied."

Ultimately, *Ille* contends, "those that love the world serve it in action." Such men are inadequate artists because their object is the accomplishment of some mundane purpose, not the static achievement of a work of art. Propagandists, they use their servile art to falsify reality rather than to present it: "The rhetorician would deceive his neighbors,/ The sentimentalist himself." But the artist, the subjective man concerned with realities more genuine than flesh and blood, constructs the cold impersonal work which is nothing more nor less than "a vision of reality."

Still looking for reality in nature rather than in vision, *Hic* recommends the imitation of old masters as the proper technical training for the modern artist, but *Ille* points out once more that he seeks "an image, not a book." His anti-self, the Mask, will free him from himself and so disclose all that he seeks: "Those men that in their writing are most wise," he sums up, "Own nothing but their blind, stupefied hearts."

Yeats's tower itself, mentioned at the beginning of both "Ego Dominus Tuus" and "The Phases of the Moon," is the subject of the short poem linking those two major works. For "A Prayer on going into my House" is part of a large group of poems which Yeats uses to incorporate that recent ancient acquisition into the Mask he is creating for himself. Seeing it and its furniture as a "norm" (Yeats uses the word in its original Platonic sense: pattern, type, model), he constructs from it a symbol intended to show correspondences between the ideal and the physical worlds. By handling while he is at the tower only those things which the "great and passionate" have used for centuries, he hopes to experience something like the "norm" of aristocracy. Yet as soon as he uses the term, a second "norm" rises in vision before him: "should I dream/ Sinbad the sailor's brought a painted chest,/ Or image, from beyond the Loadstone Mountain, that dream is a norm." Ancient objects and imagined objects can in the tower be correlated. That which is above can, in his symbol-home, be integrated to that which is below. The visionary chest from beyond the Loadstone Mountain can, in the tower, be fitted in among real tables and chairs and stools "simple enough/ For shepherd lads in Galilee." No wonder that Yeats curses at the end of the poem the "practical" man of the future, "some limb of the Devil," who might be tempted to alter the careful landscape he and his wife had prepared. Symbols, as Yeats was fond of pointing out, must be handled with great respect.

"The Phases of the Moon" is, like "Ego Dominus Tuus" to which it is most carefully related through form (dialogue), character (Michael Robartes), theme, and interpenetrating images (especially the bird which appears at the end of each poem and the lighted window which begins each), set outside Yeats's tower. Its subject is a poetic explication of the great central image of *A Vision*.

Its characters, Owen Aherne and Michael Robartes, costumed now in that symbolic "Connemara cloth" we have already examined, pause before Yeats's tower. Drawn from three of his very early Rosicrucian stories, they were revived by Yeats as the fantastic friends who delivered the manuscript to him in his first account of his "discovery" of *A Vision*. (In his revision of that work, though he finally admitted authorship, he was trapped into keeping his characters because of the poems he had written in which they figured.) A note to "Phases of the Moon" makes clear the use to which Yeats put Aherne and Robartes: "They take their place in a phantasmagoria in which I endeavour to explain my philosophy of life and death. To some extent I wrote these poems as a text for exposition." And though there is no space here for a full exposition (it would involve a summary of most of *A Vision!*), a few difficulties can, perhaps, be set straight.

In the opening lines Yeats carefully identifies the visit of Robartes and Aherne as taking place beneath "a dwindling and late-risen moon" (a moon, presumably, therefore, in phase 26, 27, or 28—the phases Yeats is most concerned with in this poem and the phases he investigates in detail in the saint, hunchback, and fool poems that follow). Looking up toward the window, they see Yeats's light, and Robartes comments that he is seeking in "book or manuscript"—the manuscript, obviously, of *A Vision*— "What he shall never find," the basic design of all things. Robartes, for those readers who may have failed to see the tower as symbol, explains that Yeats has chosen it as his "place to live" because of the symbolic associations he had perhaps found in Milton, Shelley (*Prince Athanase*), and Palmer's illustrations for Milton's "Il Penseroso."

Aherne, echoing "Ego Dominus Tuus" and its imagery of Dante's "bitter bread," recommends that they collaborate to drive Yeats mad: "speak/ Just truth enough to show that his whole life/ Will scarcely find for him a broken crust/ Of all those truths that are your daily bread," but Robartes refuses to subject Yeats to that much anguish. Instead, at Aherne's suggestion, he sings the "changes of the moon," the basic image on which Yeats's *A Vision* is founded and the very manuscript which Yeats is presumably studying in the tower.

I have already outlined that structure, and Yeats has Robartes make it quite clear in the poem. At phase 1 the moon is dark and human life cannot exist. From phase 2 through 8, man's incarnations are dominated by animal happiness. Beginning at phase 9 (Yeats keeps his mathematics clear in the poem by locating it as that time when man's increasingly handsome body is scarred by "the cat-o'-nine-tails of the mind"), when the moon passes the half and heads to full brightness, tragic handsome heroes dominate. Phase 12, drawing on incidents at the beginning and end of the *Iliad*, is illustrated by Athene's outline to Achilles (*Iliad*, I, 197ff.) of the course of action he must follow and the consequences of that course of action (Hector in the dust: *Iliad*, XXII, 330). The man of phase 12, Nietzsche for instance, must be "twice born, twice buried" because two human incarnations intervene before the fifteenth phase, full moon, when human life is again impossible. As the body approaches that crescent, soul begins to achieve complete domination (precisely as body will at phase 28), and when the fifteenth phase is reached body itself vanishes, the interpenetrating gyres reverse ("the soul/ Becomes a body") for—as Aherne points out—each aspect seeks necessarily its own opposite: the soul dreams always of becoming body and that transformation takes place in the fifteenth phase.

This fifteenth phase is of considerable interest to Yeats, for the approach to it illustrates, he feels, a doctrine he has long held: beauty is always born of the pain of increasing psychic awareness. Aherne interrupts Robartes' account to discuss those psychologically wounded beauties whose loveliness is born in the extreme opposition of the double cones. As such figures approach the fifteenth crescent, he maintains, "Their beauty dropped out of the loneliness/ Of body and soul." That is, as body and soul reached opposite ends of the double interpenetrating cones on which Yeats founded his system, out of their extreme conflict (their loneliness) beauty is literally born ("dropped out" of their loneliness, as a calf is dropped by a cow). Beautiful men and women, figures of the thirteenth and fourteenth phases, have a "terror in their eyes" because they anticipate the total extinction of body in the fifteenth phase "When all is fed with light and heaven is bare" (when the moon is full and moonlight has blotted out the stars). Such figures, ghost-like, superhuman, must wander, "the mind's eye/ Fixed upon images," for they are now exactly at the extreme limit of the antithetical half of Yeats's design, their entire focus upon Mask itself.

The rest of the cycle reverses all that has gone before. Body assumes increasing importance, and the soul—seeking to become its own opposite—"would be the world's servant." Yeats carefully records man's progress through incarnations 17-22—reformer, merchant, statesman, learned man, dutiful husband, honest wife— then skips the last quarter (23-28) to comment on phase 1, the first stage of the next trip around the cycle. Here again no life is possible because there is pure body (as at phase 15 there had been pure soul). Life, compounded from opposites (good/evil, beauty/ ugliness, mind/flesh) is possible only when those opposites are both present. Life itself, by its very nature, Yeats contends, cannot exist without such necessary conflict.

Such a pattern, Yeats realizes, is a nightmare vision. Somewhere there must be "escape." Men cannot face a design of infinite reincarnation. He lets Robartes, therefore, offer just a hint of salvation from the fleshy round. After the last three crescents —Hunchback (26), Saint (27), and Fool (28)—comes an instant "betwixt/ Deformity of body and of mind" when the miraculous escape into a kind of freedom can take place, when the "burning bow" can shoot its arrow out of the double cone ("the up and down") which creates the pattern of the moon's phases ("the wagon-wheel" of opposites, "Of beauty's cruelty and wisdom's chatter") and so allow man to be finally freed from life's "raving tide" of blood and become a fixture in what Yeats will in a later poem define as the "artifice of eternity."

Bringing the poem back to the material of "Ego Dominus Tuus," Aherne—Yeats's fictional enemy—thinks how he might amuse himself, how he might be, in fact, that Mask Yeats's alter ego *Ille* had so diligently sought while walking the wet sands beneath the tower, how he might in his Connemara clothes pass for "some drunken countryman" who would mutter just enough of the system to drive Yeats mad. (In "Ego Dominus Tuus" *Ille* had dreamed of his anti-self "whispering" beneath the tower precisely such clues—whispering them for fear that the birds would carry away the secrets to "blasphemous men.") As Aherne laughs at the Mask he might so easily be, a bat rises from the hazels under the tower, circles round him in a neat symbolic gyre, and, uttering a "squeaky cry," prepares the way for revelation. For in the last line of the poem "The light in the tower window was put out." *Ille's* antics on the sand have, after all, succeeded in luring beneath the tower his anti-self Aherne who, all unknowingly, revealed the secrets he delighted to think he had so successfully kept.

"The Cat and the Moon," a cheerful animal version of the "lunar parable," is designed to remind us that the moon's phases govern not only a man's incarnations but as well the phases of his own life. As the moon shines on cat Minnaloushe, he "lifts to the changing moon/ His changing eyes."

But of all the phases of the cycle, those of most interest to Yeats are crucial phases 1 and 15 where man is out of the body and the last three, Saint, Hunchback, and Fool, where spiritual revelation might take place.

Almost as cheerful as "The Cat and the Moon," "The Saint and the Hunchback" sets its two characters reminiscing about vanished incarnations. The Hunchback, who in Yeats's system is bitter because committed always to judge his own past, asks the Saint's blessing for his past corruption. Saint, on the other hand, is busy trying to get rid of his past. As Yeats puts it in A *Vision*, the Saint has "an emotion of renunciation, . . . an ecstatical crying out that he must do penance. . . . His joy is to be nothing, to do nothing, to think nothing." Since Yeats offers Socrates as A *Vision's* example of the Saint, there is every reason for him to want to thrash out of his flesh "That great rogue Alcibiades" who, as those who recollect Plato's *Symposium* will remember, wanted to be something more to Socrates than mere Platonic friend.

For phase 28, Yeats writes "Two Songs of a Fool" and "Another Song of a Fool." The character of the Fool, of great importance in Yeats's late work, is defined precisely in A *Vision:*

He is but a straw blown by the wind, with no mind but the wind and no act but a nameless drifting and turning, and is sometimes called "The Child of God." At his worst his hands and feet and eyes, his will and his feelings, obey obscure subconscious fantasies, while at his best he would know all wisdom if he could know anything. The physical world suggests to his mind pictures and events that have no relation to his needs or even to his desires; his thoughts are an aimless reverie; his acts are aimless like his thoughts; and it is in this aimlessness that he finds his joy.

Minor works, the poems suggest the fool's two aspects and his one preoccupation with aimless joy. "Sweet and harsh, harsh and sweet," he sings in "Another Song of a Fool"; and in "Two Songs of a Fool" he is excited to think that his tame hare might have found, equally sweet and harsh, "The horn's sweet note and the tooth of the hound." Fascinated by wisdom, he rightly calculates the butterfly to have been in earlier incarnation a schoolmaster. There are also, as Jeffares has noted, autobiographical possibilities in the speckled cat who, like Mrs. Yeats, sleeps on the poet's knee and the tame hare, poor forgotten wandering Iseult Gonne. Such parallels, however, seem to me to add unnecessary complications to sufficiently complicated material.

"The Double Vision of Michael Robartes" appropriately ends this *Vision*-based material. Yeats sets his hero on the rock of Cashel, Tipperary, where Cormac mac Carthy had in the twelfth century built the now-ruined "house" in which Michael Robartes has his Double Vision. The time of the first section of the poem, in lunar terms, is phase 1, "When the old moon is vanished from the sky/ And the new still hides her horn." Then, when soul has vanished and body so dominates the double cone that human life is impossible, the will-less flesh is "pounded till it is a man" ready to enter phase 2, the first phase in which breathing man can exist. Here at phase 1 all is physical, incapable of moral act, and the creature is "Constrained, arraigned, baffled, bent and unbent." And the abstract dead forces which shape it—equally physical—are so emptied of soul that "They do not even feel . . . Triumph that we obey," the triumph of the lunar system itself. Mechanically, phase 1 grinds up and reassembles the fools of phase 28 to spew out into the world the happy human animals of phase 2.

The second vision is set at exactly the opposite phase of the lunar design. Phase 1 is dark of the moon; phase 15—when the second vision takes place—is at full moon. Phase 1 represents the manipulation of pure body; phase 15 represents the dance of pure soul. Amoral, will-less things pummel the body at phase 1; symbols of intellect (the Sphinx) and love (the Buddha) set in motion the dance of the soul at phase 15.

As Yeats had pointed out in "Phases of the Moon," when the body approaches phase 15 it grows increasingly beautiful; when it reaches phase 15, it is brought to perfection impossible in life— irradiated with pure soul. In this harmonic triumph of spirit over flesh, the symbol of the dancer emerges, Yeats's favorite image for organic unity.

The first part of the poem presents a vision of elemental chaos; the second part presents a vision of elemental order. Yet life—as Yeats never wearies of pointing out—is neither one nor the other. Living man, the subject of the third part of the poem, "Being caught between the pull/ Of the dark moon and the full," is a compound of body and soul, of flesh and spirit; experiencing simultaneously a sense of chaos and of order, only in rare moments of insight can he see the whole design or contemplate its extremities. Michael Robartes, granted his double vision, does the best he can. He reacts emotionally to the revelation he has experienced of cosmic design ("I made my moan"), and he pays homage both to things physical (he "kissed a stone") and things spiritual (he "arranged" his vision "in a song").

Yeats's image of the dancer—collecting all the wild whirlers from earlier in the section and anticipating the great dancing figures of his late poems—becomes a symbol for the artist's vision of order in a partly (but only partly) disordered world. A figure out of Anima Mundi, she is indeed "That girl my unremembering nights hold fast," that visionary girl who flings into his meat a "crazy juice," who makes him feel as if he had been seduced by

Helen of Troy, her human counterpart. The dancing image of a coherent universe, she is the supersensual equivalent of mundane ordered things, the "image" which the artist—seeking form—copies, the vision which both inspires and justifies him. Balancing like "a spinning top" between impersonal love and impersonal intellect, she moves yet stands still. Impersonal herself, she achieves the static action of art.

9 * Michael Robartes and the Dancer

The poems collected in *Michael Robartes and the Dancer* fall into two very clear groups: a set of poems based on the Easter rising and the subsequent troubles, and a set which explored aspects of *A Vision* other than those Yeats had already examined in the poems explicating Mask and Phases. The actual structure of the section, however, juggles the poems on these two subjects into a carefully arranged pattern which was intended to reflect what Yeats saw as a developing personal maturity in a time of national and international crisis. Private happiness grew, but with that happiness came insight into impending social chaos. From this point to the end of his career, Yeats focuses more and more sharply on themes of personal joy set against a background of irrational destructive violence until, driving himself into postures of prophetic ecstasy, he finally looks on life's tragic scene with gay eyes. Here, the outline of this pattern is vividly clear for the first time.

On the personal level, the volume begins with an opening poem which seems finally to dispose of Iseult Gonne, moves through a series of affectionate poems intended to praise Mrs. Yeats and disparage her rivals, and culminates in a prayer for his daughter's happiness and a reaffirmation of his love for his wife. At the same time, ominous events are assembled: Solomon and his Witch are recollected who once, Yeats cheerfully suggests, almost blotted out the world; ghosts walk; the grim violence of Easter, 1916, and the attendant civil disorder is recapitulated; supernatural forces—demon and beast—display their power; and at last the rough beast of "The Second Coming" slouches toward Bethlehem to be born in the violent overthrow of our own civilization, an overthrow which, in terms of the last words of the section, will bring us to a time "When all is ruin once again."

Fit carefully into the collected poems, *Michael Robartes and the Dancer* ends with a poem which commemorates that tower which will be title and theme of the following section and begins with the physical manifestation of the dancer Michael Robartes had last seen in the second part of his double vision—the double vision which ended *The Wild Swans at Coole*.

That dancer, as I have indicated, is now no longer visionary but eminently physical—and argumentative as well. Almost as beautiful as her supersensual counterpart, she is determined—in spite of Michael Robartes' warnings—to educate herself in the most modern way. Though incapable of understanding his ingenious explication of the allegory of the altar-piece (she reduces everything to simple-minded platitudes), she would nevertheless put herself "to college." Robartes' argument—which Yeats has by now often enunciated—is that beautiful women who achieve Unity of Being, the "uncomposite blessedness" of those who approach the fifteenth phase of the system, must learn to think with the whole body rather than with the mind. All of his illustrations support this thesis: Athene's beating breast and vigorous thigh reveal a "knowledge" superior to that contained in any "mere book"; paintings by Michaelangelo (whose art in a much later poem excites "globe-trotting Madam") and Veronese make flesh eloquent.

This fine poem—as most of Yeats's work of this period—does not really need the framework of A *Vision*. Nor do we need to know that Yeats had in mind Bordone's painting of "St. George and the Dragon" in the National Gallery, Dublin, or that—as Mrs. Yeats told T. R. Henn—he had seen earlier in the Cathedral at Ferrara (in 1907) a similar "altar-piece," Cosimo Tuva's "St. George and the Dragon." It is comforting to have one's suspicions confirmed by Mrs. Yeats that the "lady" is Iseult Gonne (Henn, p. 236), but even that piece of news does not particularly improve the poem. Its strength lies, it seems to me, in a beautifully balanced ironic tension: Too stupid to realize that she does not need the sort of education she would have, the lady coyly rejects the only education that could possibly be of value to her.

If this woman misses her greatest opportunity, Sheba—in the companionable poem which follows—grabs hers with a vengeance. In spite of the fact that she and Solomon had failed, under a wild moon, to end the world in their near-perfect passion, they had come, as Solomon points out, spectacularly close. When she had "cried out in a strange tongue," the sound had been in reality made by a supernatural bird, "A cockrel," which "Crew from a blossoming apple bough/ Three hundred years before the Fall,/ And never crew again till now." Thinking that the situation for the end of the world had at last arrived—the moment when a pair of lovers bring to the bride-bed "imagined" Platonic images that precisely coincide with each other's "real" physical images—"He that crowed out eternity/Thought to have crowed it in again." And though that attempt had failed, Sheba is no one to give up: " '. . . the moon is wilder every minute./ O! Solomon! let us try again.' " The fifteenth night on them, they might achieve world-shattering union.

Recklessly inventive (especially in the remarkable definition of Solomon's wisdom in lines 6 and 7) the poem is nevertheless meticulously constructed around a framework of interrelated imagery. Moon, cockrel, and Eve's "brigand apple" establish a complex symbol which Yeats quickly loads with a rich freight of mythological meaning drawn from the Apocrypha, the Old Testament, Theosophical literature, and Yeats's own contribution to myth—A *Vision*. And yet the poem is personal, too. Yeats knows all about the anguish of Choice and Chance in love, the "murder" that the unmarried lover experiences, the "despair" the bride-bed brings to lovers who come to it wrapped in memories of earlier loves.[1]

But for those attuned to ghosts, ghosts themselves can disrupt marriages. Though not quite the crowing of a supernatural cock, the scream of a "terrified, invisible bird or beast" heralds the arrival of the husband's sweetheart from an earlier incarnation, a sweetheart who thoroughly frightens the newly-wed bride, in "An Image from a Past Life." For this poem, accompanied in an early edition by a long note which outlined the technique by which live men, haunted by the ladies they had loved in earlier lives, might ultimately come to "a natural deep satisfying love" and at long last to "the Beatific Vision," Yeats draws on personal experience which, made objective by the dramatic form, seems perhaps more universal than it was.

By the time we reach "Under Saturn," Yeats abandons dramatic form to speak again in his own voice. His subject, however, is still jealousy. We can be reasonably sure that "An Image from a Past Life" was intended to reassure Mrs. Yeats that her husband did not prefer to her "the hovering thing" she had seen in the night. In "Under Saturn" he is explicit: not only does she not have to fear ghostly rivals; she also does not have to fear the more physical ladies of his immediate past. It is not memories of Maud Gonne, Mrs. Shakespear, or Iseult Gonne which make him "saturnine"; rather it is the memory of those Sligo figures of his ancestry. These spur his wits on "a fantastic ride" (the double composition of his autobiography and of A *Vision*, the systems which will explain for his readers both himself and his people).

[1] See *Estrangement*, vii, for the notebook prose statement that evolved into the poem.

His wife, his work, a whole conspiracy of events have returned him to that Ireland which he swore as a child "Never to leave." Yet that Ireland itself is different. It has been swept by revolution, "changed utterly." And the group of poems commenting on the change—personal, intense poems—"murmur name upon name" as if incantation itself could make meaningful events vivid, terrifying, and portentous of the universal disaster which his wife's automatic writing had predicted.

"Easter 1916," the earliest and in many ways the best of these poems, sets up a careful antithesis between the "polite meaningless words" which constitute the "casual comedy" of pre-revolutionary Ireland, the Ireland where "motley" had been worn, and the tragic "terrible beauty" that is born of the Easter Rising. Cataloguing in the second stanza the men and women he had undervalued—Con Markievicz who, grown shrill in political argument, had seemed to have betrayed the "young and beautiful" Constance Gore-Booth he had admired years before at her Sligo family home of Lissadell; schoolteacher Padric Pearse; the young writer Thomas MacDonagh; and Maud Gonne's husband John MacBride, "A drunken, vainglorious lout"—Yeats extends one step further his "drama" image by having them "resign" their parts in the casual comedy, reject the roles called for by the script, become independent, beautiful figures, terrible and violent in their freedom.

In the first two stanzas, "change" has been the metaphor behind Yeats's metaphors; in the second two stanzas, he engineers a neat ironic reversal. For it is not their change—indeed it is precisely their lack of change—which has made them stone-hearted, tragic. Their obsession with "one purpose alone" makes of them the only unchanging object in a world of flux. "A stone," they trouble in their inflexibility "the living stream" which sweeps disturbed by them. Gorgeous in its structure, the long sentence defining the life of that "living stream" in terms of time and action ticks off "minute by minute," "minute by minute," "minute by minute" those things which range, change, change, slide, plash, dive, call, and—finally—live. And yet, "in the midst of all," is dead stone.

The heart, in the last stanza no longer "enchanted," has been sacrificed. Death is both metaphor and fact. The men are not sleeping. This is "not night but death." And—stuff of tragedy— it is a death which, though perhaps needless (all tragic death, in one sense, is needless), is certainly brought on by a heroic dream, a dream founded—again perhaps (again like all the greatest tragic motives)—on "excess of love."

Changed by not changing, dying uselessly, bewildered by love, Ireland's unexpected heroes create the ironic "terrible beauty" of tragedy in an otherwise "meaningless" time. These are of course the "Sixteen Dead Men" executed for their part in the rising. Yeats, letting them find in the poem specifically commemorating them new comrades among the heroic dead of the United Irishmen movement of the eighteenth century, assigns them grave conversations with Lord Edward Fitzgerald and Wolfe Tone who, both born in 1763, both captured by the British, both accused of treason, both dead in prison in 1798, would have much to discuss with the sixteen newly dead. And their conversations would, no doubt, resemble those of Pearse and Connolly who, calculating how to make "the green come out again" conclude that the only way to water "The Rose Tree" in a time of drought is with their "own red blood."

Yeats never abandoned his notion of the heroic sacrifice of that Easter Rising. Yet the movement itself, he began to feel, had fallen into disorder; the mob, greedy opportunists, corrupted the men and women who fought for them. Such corruption is the theme of "On a Political Prisoner" and "The Leaders of the Crowd." Written about Con Markievicz (he was, he wrote his wife from Lucan in 1918, "writing one on Con to aovid writing one on Maud. All of them are in prison . . ."), the first of the poems contrasts the bitter "abstract thing" her mind had become with the impatient wildness it had displayed in youth. Turning the gray gull that enters her prison window into an image for her own past, Yeats creates a symbol for the greatness from which she has fallen. That symbolic bird—something universal, "the hollows of the sea" themselves crying out beneath its "storm-beaten breast"—had maintained an isolated, lonely balance on thin air. But she, caught by the crowd's passion, has become "Blind and leader of the blind." No longer associated with "the hollows of the sea," she now drinks "the foul ditch" where the blind crowd lies. (Yeats must have delighted in the pun on *lie*.)

Drawing on exactly the same imagery, "The Leaders of the Crowd" contrasts "The abounding gutter" where those leaders "have no solitude" with lofty Helicon where the muses once in isolation sang. Concerned with "news," the crowd's lying leaders are incapable of recognizing that "truth" revealed by the student's lonely lamp.

And it is that truth, snared from "the tomb," the spirit world, which is the concern of the rest of the poems in this section. "Towards Break of Day" hints at one of its sources. Lovers' parallel dreams may offer keys to supernatural correspondences. That the double dream Yeats records actually took place in January, 1919, when Yeats and his wife were staying in the Powerscourt Arms Hotel, Enniskerry, County Wicklow is the sort of biographical detail that strikes me as eminently unimportant; more important is the fact that he regarded the shared dream as an example of the sort of "complementary" vision which could lead poets to basic insight into the nature of things. Yet what is the relationship between Mrs. Yeats's white stag and Yeats's waterfall? Certain connections seem obvious. Yeats, who by this time had read Freud, had learned to see water as a female symbol. And certainly Arthur's stag leaping from mountain to mountain is eminently masculine in its associations. Such correspondence might, for Yeats, have been enough; but it seems likely that he was intrigued also by the naturalistic detail of his own dream (he awoke, after all, with "The cold blown spray in my nostril") and the mythological detail of his wife's. He might also have noted that his dream is possessive (he goes wild that he cannot touch the beloved waterfall of his childhood), a dream of "over-much" love, and that his wife's "bitterer" dream is detached. And he would certainly have been conscious that the dreams were linked visually he saw the white foam, she the white stag; the foaming white water in his dream fell in a waterfall, in hers the white stag leaped; both dreams were mountain dominated.

"Towards Break of Day" gives us, therefore, the dreamed raw material of Yeats's obsessive studies. But in the studies themselves dream-material takes on an almost nightmarish reality. "Demon and Beast," as he points out in that poem, plagued him "day and night." These symbolic creatures—perhaps the True Mask and the False Mask which his system offered him—represent, on one level, "desire" and "hatred," opposed possibilities of personality. And though freedom from them brings momentary relief, laughter under reality's sun, the "aimless joy" that delights in "a stupid happy creature" "gyring down" in a symbolic but for Yeats momentarily insignificant pattern, ultimately he must seek demon and beast again to gain "Right mastery of natural things." The mysterious last stanza suggests that a similar vision had been granted St. Anthony who, like the other hermits in that monastic colony he had founded in the desert near Thebes, had sworn to live in isolation away from all men and from the men in the colony itself. Discovering as he "withered to a bag of bones" the sort of "sweetness" Yeats had found in his own occult studies, Anthony too had achieved mystical exultation.

Anthony, Yeats is asserting, had experienced the kind of momentary prophetic insight that Yeats himself had been given through his discovery of the system outlined in A *Vision*. The most vivid record of such insight Yeats left us is, of course, that which he recorded in "The Second Coming." Though bound to "Demon and Beast" by beast itself and gyre, and to the rest of his prophetic poems and A *Vision* by theme, "The Second Coming" manages to use the system without becoming servant to it. Perhaps because it relies on what Maud Bodkin and Jung would define as an archetypal pattern, its horror vision of the destruction of the familiar world seems infinitely meaningful. For what man does not carry in him the buried conviction that the continuance of the world depends on his own existence? Jealous of the real world which kills and survives him, he delights in speculations of a grand finale which—blotting out all things—brings all to the same extinction he necessarily faces. Every age has taken consolation, and a kind of hideous pleasure, in the conviction that it is the worst and last. All prophecy points always to tomorrow when graves will open and the infinite dead will walk through the burning world's purgatorial fires.

Yeats, carefully vague, manages to hint the end of all while explicitly prophesying the reversal of the world's gyre, the birth of a new, violent, bestial anti-civilization in the destruction of the two-thousand-year Christian cycle. His rough beast, compounded from Christ's Matthew 24 prediction of His future return and St. John's vision of the coming of Antichrist, the beast of the Apocalypse, gives a double meaning to the "revelation" that is at hand.

Yet Yeats is faithful to his system. The pattern of the double interpenetrating gyre is carefully worked out, even to the inclusion of paired circling birds: the first stanza's falcon which lifts beyond the call of its master, the indignant desert birds of the second stanza which wheel about the lumbering sphinx. These double gyres, binding *then* to *now*, point toward the destructive birth about to take place.

For in the real world, revolution, "mere anarchy," is loosed upon the world. As the gyre widens "Things fall apart; the centre cannot hold." In a note to the Cuala Press edition of *Michael Robartes and the Dancers*, Yeats describes in great detail this historical process as it is symbolized in his double cones:

> . . . the end of an age, which always receives the revelation of the character of the next age, is represented by the coming of one gyre to its place of greatest expansion and of the other to that of its greatest contraction. At the present moment the life gyre is sweeping outward, unlike that before the birth of Christ which was narrowing, and has almost reached its greatest expansion. The revelation which approaches will however take its character from the

contrary movement of the interior gyre. All our scientific, democratic, fact-accumulating, heterogeneous civilization belongs to the
outward gyre and prepares not the continuance of itself but the
revelation as in a lightning flash, though in a flash that will not
strike only in one place, and will for a time be constantly repeated,
of the civilization that must slowly take its place . . . when the
revelation comes it will not come to the poor but to the great and
learned and establish again for two thousand years prince and
vizier.

So it is that the "blood-dimmed tide" of violence (a tide both
dimmed by blood and in the blood itself) is loosed on our world
to drown "the ceremony of innocence," ceremony because in ceremony alone lies the vestiges of the sort of order Yeats briefly
found at Coole Park, innocence because innocence alone opposes
all the sexual and social violence symbolized by the blood-dimmed
tide.

But that tide, for Yeats's purposes, has begun to move: fanatical
men have seized power the world over; "the worst," full of "passionate intensity," seem ready to rule an earth on which good men,
grown skeptical, "lack all conviction."

The "vast image" Yeats draws from *Spiritus Mundi,* his ware-
house of supersensual Platonic forms, is of course a nightmare
symbol of the coming time (due "perhaps not for another two
hundred years," according to his conversation with Lady Gregory,
though in later comments made far more imminent). This future, he predicted in *A Vision,* would be "hierarchical, multiple,
masculine, harsh, surgical." Constructing as its symbol an image
with a man's head and a lion's body, and assigning it a pitiless,
blank gaze, Yeats let his beast slouch toward the seat of that
"dogmatic, levelling, unifying, feminine, humane, peace its means
and end" Christian era which it was doomed to supercede.

Yeats with reason placed immediately after "The Second Coming" "A Prayer for my Daughter" which opens with the image
of a child sleeping innocently through a howling storm. For how
are the innocent, among them his daughter, Anne Butler Yeats,

born February 24, 1919, just a month after he had written "The Second Coming," to escape the wrath of coming times? Only with difficulty, Yeats suggests, for a "great gloom" is on his mind. The violence of nature seems symbolic of a larger violence, the "murderous innocence of the sea," a symbol for that which in "The Second Coming" had been the "blood-dimmed tide." The stream beneath his tower is "flooded," and a rising sea-wind screams. In such a setting, how can this birth, the child in this cradle, escape the nightmare violence to be born in Bethlehem when the rough beast of "The Second Coming" lies rocking where Christ had once been cradled? No way, he argues, but in the frail, beautiful manipulation of form—doomed though it may ultimately be to be drowned—which survives "in custom and in ceremony." Praying that she be like her mother rather than like Maud Gonne, that she "be granted beauty and yet not/ Beauty to make a stranger's eye distraught," that she be kind, capable of closest intimacy rather than like Helen bored and troubled by "a fool," that she escape the sort of "intellectual hatred" which had turned Maud Gonne into a jailed propagandist, her once-lovely voice into "an old bellows full of angry wind," Yeats focuses his poem on two images: the rich Horn of Plenty which he associates with courtesy, aristocracy and ceremony; and the hidden laurel tree which, "Rooted in one dear perpetual place," can provide through custom a "radical" (rooted) innocence for the soul. If through custom that innocence can be recovered, then his daughter stands a chance, though "every windy quarter howl/ Or every bellows burst," to be happy in spite of the world which surrounds her.

Held together by a set of wind and tree images remarkable even for Yeats (before he finishes he has even turned the Horn of Plenty into a wind instrument bartered by Maud Gonne for the "old bellows full of angry wind" with which she lectures the world), the poem balances the real storm "bred on the Atlantic" which strikes Yeats's tower and the elms beneath it against the symbolic storm of future time which will threaten but not immediately destroy custom's "spreading laurel tree."

It is also these symbols which Yeats draws on to animate still one more vision drawn from *A Vision*. For "A Meditation in Time of War," set as it is beneath "the old wind-broken tree," manages, in spite of its shortness, to recapitulate in wind and broken tree the disaster he had prophesied both in "The Second Coming" and in "A Prayer for my Daughter," and at the same time to suggest the prophet's consolation: he has seen into the essential pattern of all things. Reality is in the Platonic forms ("One is animate"); mankind is the shadowy imitation, the "inanimate phantasy," of the grand design.

Against such vision, and against the coming murderous time when all will be "ruin once again," Yeats can do no more than to record on "that old grey stone" where insight had been granted him, his name, his profession, and his symbol. These, "To be Carved on a Stone at Thoor Ballylee," will give him—if not immortality—at least one anchor in the flux of past/future, one stone poem from the past in which he lived that will enable him to communicate to that future which he dreaded and for which he wrote a brief fragment of his perished self.

10 * The Tower

Perhaps the most important single fact to bear in mind as one
looks at that bitter section of his work Yeats called *The Tower*
is that it is only half of a complex pattern that is completed in
the following section, *The Winding Stair*. The two groups of
poems balance each other not only in their obviously related titles
but in carefully opposed points of view. For instance, the eleven
poems of *A Man Young and Old* in *The Tower* are carefully
parallel to the eleven poems of *A Woman Young and Old* in
The Winding Stair, even to the Sophoclean passages, drawn appropriately from *Oedipus at Colonus* and *Antigone*, that end each
set. "Sailing to Byzantium," the first poem of *The Tower*, not
only establishes the tone for that collection, but—almost point for
point—is "answered" by the opening poems of *The Winding Stair*,
particularly "A Dialogue of Self and Soul" in which Yeats explicitly chooses for his soul reincarnation rather than a resting place

in the artifice of eternity. Images of sterility (the tower crumbles from one end of that collection to the other) dominate *The Tower*; regeneration and sexuality (the famous passions of Crazy Jane and Tom the Lunatic) act as shaping forces in *The Winding Stair*. The focus is primarily on things masculine and political in *The Tower*, on things feminine and aesthetic in *The Winding Stair*. (It is no accident, I suspect, that that circling stair which is enclosed by but yet gives form to the crumbling masculine tower was selected by Yeats as the title of the more "optimistic" collection.)

That Yeats saw the two sections as related can easily be documented. "Re-reading *The Tower*," he wrote Mrs. Shakespear shortly after it was published, "I was astonished at its bitterness, and long to live out of Ireland that I may find some new vintage. Yet the bitterness gave the book its power and it is the best book I have written. Perhaps if I was in better health I should be content to be bitter." But Yeats was not content to be bitter, and he was already planning the "new vintage" that would culminate in *The Winding Stair*. Even before he published *The Tower* he had ready for publication *A Woman Young and Old* and he looked forward, as he told Lady Gregory, to the poems that would answer the political pessimism of *The Tower*. At doctor's orders, he moved to Rapallo, and he anticipated an altogether happier frame of mind: "Here I shall put off the bitterness of Irish quarrels, and write my most amiable verses. They are already, though I dare not write, crowding my head. *The Tower* astonishes me by its bitterness." And in the same vein he wrote Mrs. Shakespear, "Once out of Irish bitterness I can find some measure of sweetness and light, as befits old age—already new poems are floating in my head, bird songs of an old man, joy in the passing moment, emotion without the bitterness of memory."

Ironically, the bitter *Tower* poems were composed during the years in which Yeats met his greatest success. His lecture tours brought him not only fame but money to roof Ballylee, his autobiographical volumes and *A Vision* provided him frameworks for poetry. In 1921, his son was born. In 1922, he was invited to become a member of the Senate of the new Irish Free State. And in November of 1923 he was awarded the Nobel Prize for Literature.

But happily married, honored at home with a D. Litt. from Trinity College and abroad with the praise of critics, Yeats in a burst of furious productivity pushed himself to the limits of exhaustion. In 1927 his health broke down. Sick with what his doctor termed "the overwork of years," spitting blood, suffering from a combination of high blood pressure and an almost complete nervous collapse, he was ordered to write nothing more tiring than letters, to read nothing more controversial than detective stories. It was in this condition that, re-reading *The Tower*, he determined that it had to be countered with *The Winding Stair*.

Almost everything in *The Tower* is assembled in support of the great opening poem, "Sailing to Byzantium." Restatements of its theme, evidence supporting his contention that the modern world "is no country for old men," the angry poems that follow catalogue incidents from the Irish "troubles" to show the violence from which Yeats sails, the terrible world that was being brought into existence by the powerful historical forces he had defined in "The Second Coming." Moved into coherence by its one central theme and the controlled, carefully-integrated imagery of tower, tree, bird and dancer which dominate the volume, *The Tower* manages to be explicit yet infinitely suggestive. ("The Tower is Thoor Ballylee, or Ballylee Castle," Yeats once noted, "where I have written most of my poems of recent years. My poems attribute to it most of the meanings attributed in the past to the Tower —whether watch tower or pharos, and to its winding stair those attributed to gyre or whorl. What those meanings are let the poems say.")

And the poems, even the most crucial one, "Sailing to Byzantium," are clear enough. The reader's only real problem in that poem is to see why Byzantium itself was so attractive to Yeats. Some of the reasons are, of course, obvious. It was, for instance, mathematically convenient that the high point of Byzantine art should come almost dead center in the 2000 year cycle which, for him, defined beginning and end of modern times. But Byzantium had for him greater attractions than systematic convenience. Perhaps a passage from A *Vision* most explicitly defines the appeal that its brilliant integrated art made to him:

> I think if I could be given a month of Antiquity and leave to spend it where I chose, I would spend it in Byzantium a little before Justinian opened St. Sophia and closed the Academy of Plato. I think I could find in some little wine-shop some philosophical worker in mosaic who could answer all my questions, the supernatural descending nearer to him than to Plotinus even, for the pride of his delicate skill would make what was an instrument of power to princes and clerics, a murderous madness in the mob, show as a lovely flexible presence like that of a perfect human body.
>
> I think that in early Byzantium, maybe never before or since in recorded history, religious, aesthetic and practical life were one, that architect and artificers—though not, it may be, poets, for language had been the instrument of controversy and must have grown abstract—spoke to the multitude and the few alike. The painter, the mosaic worker, the worker in gold and silver, the illuminator of sacred books, were almost impersonal, almost perhaps without the consciousness of individual design, absorbed in their subject matter and that the vision of a whole people. They could copy out of old Gospel books those pictures that seemed as sacred as the text, and yet weave all into a vast design, the work of many that seemed the work of one, that made building, picture, pattern, metal-work of rail and lamp, seem but a single image . . .

It is to this world Yeats would sail, a world in which artist, "almost impersonal," manages to reflect "the vision of a whole people" in a culture so integrated as to produce an art that will have the impact of a single image. The world he leaves, transfixed by the sensual music of its singing birds, is compounded of and celebrates decaying multitudinous bodies. Unlike the golden bird he would be, the "dying generations" (birth and death compressed remarkably into a phrase) of the world's real birds sing hymns to body, hymns which distract "all" from the contemplation of that sort of art which alone can justify an old man's existence, the "Monuments of unageing intellect" which cannot be produced in modern chaotic times.

And yet what is an old man to do? He cannot be a singer of the sensuous world without appearing ridiculous. No bird in the tree, he is as a matter of fact precisely opposed to the first stanza's singing birds. A scarecrow, "A tattered coat upon a stick," he must sing not of the flesh but rather of the soul, and his singing school must be among those monuments that only perfect civilizations of the past—Byzantium, say—have produced. There, flame-wrapped sages can (bird metaphor only modestly disguised) like immortal phoenixes rise from their holy fire, "pern in a gyre," and —"singing-masters"—consume his heart away as, returning to the fire, they gather him into "the artifice of eternity."

At last "out of nature," he can renounce all physical incarnation. He can be the imperishable thing itself, the golden bird—the very work of art—beyond decay, and so unlike the dying generations of real birds who perform similar song in stanza one (who sing "Whatever is begotten, born, and dies" but who must themselves perish). On his golden bough, he will have become himself one of those monuments he had so admired.

Drawing on memories of Italian and Sicilian mosaics that he had seen on his 1925 Mediterranean visit and a painstaking study of Byzantine art that included research in such texts as George Finlay's *History of the Byzantine Empire,* Yeats buttressed his poem with what by now were for him conventional arrangements of the elemental symbols of earth, air, fire, and water; the complex image compounded from natural bird/ scarecrow/ perning phoenix-like sages/ golden bird; and a new "monumental" set of references—all loosely associated with the evolving architectural treatment of the tower. (Monuments, as a matter of fact, echo through *The Tower:* "These stones remain their monument . . . ," "No honour leave its mighty monument," ". . . the great/ That

. . . toiled so hard . . . To leave some monument behind," for instance.)

Greatest perhaps in its synthesis of these elements into a paradoxical structure that lets him sing of flesh yet be freed from its limitations, "Sailing to Byzantium" prepares the way for a whole group of comments on the passionate old man as symbol for the tyranny of time; for "sick with desire," his at-last-comprehending heart is ironically fastened to the "dying animal" that he has become.

Exactly this theme is picked up in "The Tower," the title poem of the section. "Decrepit age" has been fastened onto the poet's "troubled heart" like "A sort of battered kettle at the heel." And —again like the scarecrow old man of "Sailing to Byzantium"— the poet can in this absurd situation no longer sing sensual songs: "It seems that I must bid the Muse go pack." Yeats, who found it amusing to write poems about the impossibility of writing poems, concludes that the old man's project should be the study of Plato and Plotinus (thus, incidentally, giving his reader a clue to the sort of homework he will have to do if he is really adequately to be prepared for the poems that follow).

The second part of "The Tower" gathers—as Yeats explains in his note to the poem—a crowd of persons all in one way or another associated with the tower's neighborhood so that, before the symbolic "Tree, like a sooty finger" (an echo of imagery from work as early as *The Wanderings of Oisin* and a foreshadowing of imagery from as late as *Purgatory*) Yeats can "ask a question of them all." The question and the image are related, for the blackened tree by the ruin is—in many different ways—symbolic of those "old men and women" who, all driven mad, are involved as essential characters in the question itself: Did they "in public or in secret rage/ As I do now against old age?" But the simple question, as so many of Yeats's, leads to another more difficult and more personal one and, dismissing all but one of the ghosts he has conjured up, he asks a final question of the "old lecher" he had himself invented, Red Hanrahan, an expert in sexuality, a single-minded student of all the varieties of ways in which one can "Plunge . . . Into the labyrinth of another's being": "Does the imagination dwell the most/ Upon a woman won or woman lost?" The answer, he implies, is that it dwells on the woman lost. And he demands that Hanrahan admit that he "turned aside/ From a great labyrinth" for vain inadequate reasons, that the memory of such a loss blots out the sun's reality to substitute for it lunar insanities.

(Yeats here carefully echoes the story he has already related earlier in the poem about the drunken farmers who, maddened by blind Raftery's song about the peasant beauty Mary Hines, "mistook the brightness of the moon/ For the prosaic light of day" and marched into the great bog of Cloone. Suggesting that the poet's art always makes men mad, Yeats links blind Raftery to Homer, Mary Hines to Helen, and himself—and presumably his own lost love, Helen-like Maud Gonne—to the illusion-creating artist who, making "the moon and sunlight seem/ One inextricable beam," will be able in that triumph to rise above his own anguish and so madden men. For that reason every crucial action in the poem is set at a time of mingled light, a time when sun and moon can both share in lighting the sky, a time of dawn or sunset: In the first part the young poet—dragged up out of memory—climbs Ben Bulben's back at dawn; in the second, Hanrahan—when first created by that same young poet—had raged "drunk or sober through the dawn"; in the last the poet bequeaths "Pride, like that of the morn" to those young men who, as he had climbed in the past, climb the streams "at dawn," and under that "bursting dawn" fish the mountain streams. Similarly, in the second part, the tree is seen by the old poet "Under the day's declining beam"; old Mrs. French receives the insolent farmer's ear at dusk as she is sitting down to her candlelit supper; the forgotten bankrupt master of the tower ends his "dog's day" somewhere at evening unremembered by all. And in the third part the dying old swan fixes his eye upon sunlight's "fading gleam" and the poet, anticipating his own death, visualizes it as an illusion of evening: ". . . but the clouds of the sky/ When the horizon fades,/ Or a bird's sleepy cry/ Among the deepening shades.")

The last part of the poem, defining Yeats's pride and faith, creates only two minor difficulties for the reader. The first, that after having in part I selected for friends of old age Plato and Plotinus he should now "mock Plotinus' thought/ And cry in Plato's teeth," Yeats himself disposes of in his note to the poem. Explaining that "it is something in our own eyes that makes us see them as all transcendence," he quotes Plotinus' declaration that the soul "is the author of all living things, . . . the maker of the sun" to prove that Plotinus ultimately agrees with him that "man made up the whole,/ Made lock, stock and barrel/ Out of his bitter soul,/ Aye, sun and moon and star, all." It is important to see, however, that this declaration does not defeat the "reality" of either Platonic form or "Translunar Paradise." Though created by man, Translunar Paradise does, Yeats argues, exist. Man invents it; but, once invented, that paradise is free to operate independently. Like those products of the arts, with which he also made his peace, Platonic forms and Translunar Paradise are made by man but survive their inventors to shape men in the future.

The second problem is in the strange syntax of the passage that refers to the daws at the loophole. Probably linked to the passage on those art products which though reflecting man are yet greater than their creators, "superhuman," it seems to assert the instinctive nature of the artist who builds his poems or paintings as undeliberately yet as accurately as the birds build their nests. (Yeats, who was given to experiments, had used his own canaries to test theories about the initiating function of natural symbolic forms. Suspending appropriate shapes by the cage he hoped to inspire nests and eggs.) Structurally, of course, the daws-at-the-loophole passage bridges the two dying swan references that begin and end part III by offering a bird-birth in the middle of the section and so, once again, affirming birds as "dying generations" which can yet be symbolic of the artist who, to the end, utters his "last song" on the "long/ Last reach of glittering stream"—the "bird's sleepy cry/ Among the deepening shades."

Though at the end of the poem he may be at sea with the swan sailing his old body to Byzantium, in the central section he is happy to be proprietor of the tower itself. "I like to think of that building as a permanent symbol of my work plainly visible to the passer-by," he told T. Sturge Moore. "As you know, all my art theories depend upon just this—rooting of mythology in the earth."

"Meditations in Time of Civil War," is, in spite of the fact that its subject is uprootings, part of that rooting process. "The Tower" presents the significance of the symbol; "Meditations" sets it in a landscape of "Ancestral Houses" and in a time of chaotic terror. The poem is designed to move carefully from symbols of order (the ancestral houses, the tower itself, and the "changeless sword . . . Curved like new moon, moon-luminous" which, resting on Yeats's table, represents "a changeless work of art"), through details of the war (associated with imagery of cracked masonry), to the final vision of "the coming emptiness" in which the tower stands isolated in the midst of an "indifferent multitude" who see the moon put out by the "innumerable clanging wings" of "brazen hawks."

Written in 1922 when the tower itself was threatened, the poems, Yeats told Mrs. Shakespear, "are not philosophical but simple and passionate, a lamentation over lost peace and lost hope." "Simple" may, however, be an understatement. Consider both the ingenious theme and the working out of it in the first poem in which both "sweetness" and "gentleness" are born of a "violent bitter" man's determination to hire architect and artist, "Bitter and violent men," to build the fountains and terraces which survive him to be a community's delight. Parallel to the sixth poem of the series in which Yeats calls on honey-bees ("sweetness") to build in the loosening masonry of the violence and bitterness-swept tower, the imagery organizes both poems (no-

tice particularly how in the last lines of each of the last two stanzas of "Ancestral Houses" it brings the poem to an end) and also
manages to suggest that greatness is a compound on the one hand
of violence and bitterness and on the other of gentleness and
sweetness.

If "Ancestral Houses" provides theme and landscape, "My
House" brings the reader to the symbolic scene itself: bridge,
tower, its winding stair, "the symbolic rose," old thorns, and bird
offer us a cluster of Yeats's favorite symbols. And "stony ground,"
wind, rain, and the candle combine earth, air, water, and fire into
the supporting and powerful basic symbolic structure of all occult
doctrine. Here, like "*Il Penseroso's* Platonist" whom he had earlier celebrated in "The Phases of the Moon" Yeats can assemble
sweetness from bitterness, gathering his symbols, the "emblems of
adversity," into patterns coherent enough "To exalt a lonely
mind."

One new symbol has, however, been added to the collection,
and in honor of it Yeats writes the third poem, "My Table." The
symbol is, of course, the sword which Junzo Sato had given Yeats
on his 1920 American tour. Yeats, thrilled, wrote an enthusiastic
letter to Edmund Dulac:

A rather wonderful thing happened the day before yesterday. A
very distinguished looking Japanese came to see us. He had read
my poetry when in Japan and had now just heard me lecture. He
had something in his hand wrapped up in embroidered silk. He
said it was a present for me. He untied the silk cord that bound it
and brought out a sword which had been for 500 years in his family.
It had been made 550 years ago and he showed me the maker's
name upon the hilt. I was greatly embarrassed at the thought of such
a gift and went to fetch George, thinking that we might find some
way of refusing it. When she came I said 'But surely this ought
always to remain in your family?' He answered 'My family have
many swords.' But later he brought back my embarrassment by
speaking of having given me 'his sword.' I had to accept it but I
have written him a letter saying that I 'put him under a vow' to

write and tell me when his first child is born—he is not yet married—that I may leave the sword back to his family in my will.
[Yeats's will did include a provision for returning the sword.]

Using the sword to symbolize the art product produced by a
stable society which had genuine Unity of Being ("Soul's beauty
being most adored"), Yeats treats it as a catalyst that may "moral-
ize/ My days out of their aimlessness." Primarily, however, the
poem re-examines the relationship between the perishable artist
and his imperishable art: "only an aching heart/ Conceives a
changeless work of art." Man who does change creates that which
is changeless. His desire (as the old man's who sails to Byzantium) is to be the work of art itself, yet limited by flesh he can
only construct that which is ultimately greater and more durable
than himself. The mysterious reference to Juno's peacock, tied to
the first poem in the set, is somewhat clarified in the light of a
comment in the first version of A Vision. Describing that time
when the millennium approaches, Yeats comments, "The loss of
control over thought comes towards the end; first a sinking in
upon the moral being, then the last surrender, the irrational cry,
revelation, the scream of Juno's peacock." "The most rich inheritor" may, of course, be Yeats.

The fourth poem, "My Descendants," anticipates the running
out of Yeats's line in descendants who may "lose the flower" (the
symbolic rose of the first poem which stands not only for the
brevity of life but as well for its flowering in the artist) and so
leave the "stark tower" to become "a roofless ruin" of "cracked
masonry" inhabited only by an owl which, like Juno's peacock,
cries "Her desolation to the desolate sky." Yet even owls "in circles move"; the gyre represents historical necessity, and Yeats concludes that "love and friendship are enough." Building in the
chiasmus of love/friendship: friendship/love a neat structure in
praise of Lady Gregory and his wife (for whom he literally
"decked" the tower by building floors in it and figuratively
"decked" it by surrounding it with roses), Yeats makes his symbolic

home a local stone "monument" and an international poetic
one.

The following two poems, "The Road at my Door" and "The
Stare's Nest by my Window," move us into a set of incidents
drawn from the Civil War which Yeats expands into evidence
of the larger disintegration of Western society explicitly forecast in
the last poem of the group. The Republican Army Irregular and
the National Army Lieutenant are both intruders from a world of
action. Reminding Yeats of the active man he might have been,
they momentarily tempt him to prove himself in "affairs." (For
refusing to give in to such temptation he had, he felt, lost Maud
Gonne.) Yet that violent real world (associated with "foul weather,
hail and rain" and the storm-broken tree) is not his; and, forcing
himself to focus on symbolic birds, he turns toward the tower and
the "cold snows" of the poet's dream. But in a time of war the
tower itself offers no sanctuary from reality. Rumors of killings and
burnings, tales of violence (the "dead young soldier" Yeats describes as being trundled down the road "in his blood" had actually been dragged to Yeats's horror down a nearby road, his body
so battered that his mother could recover only his torn disembodied head) force their way in though door be closed and the
key turned. The tower's wall—like the world about it—loosens
before a chaos vaster even than the "troubles," and though Yeats
pleads for order in a time of chaos ("O honey-bees,/ Come build
in the empty house of the stare") his conviction is that there is
"More substance in our enmities/ Than in our love."

In the last poem of the series, recapitulating earlier images
(stream, tree, and crumbling tower; a mist like blown snow; his
sword and the seemingly "unchangeable" moon that resembles it),
Yeats prepares the way for a set of three visions—drawn this time
not from reality but from the imagination which, paralleling it, creates poems. The first, a vision of hatred, offers an image of gigantic
violence, a mob, "Trooper belabouring trooper," which "Plunges
towards nothing, arms and fingers spreading wide/ For the embrace of nothing." These visionary troopers, like those real ones

who passed Yeats's door in the fifth poem, exert a great attraction. "I . . . all but cried/ For vengeance on the murderers of Jacques Molay." (Yeats's notes to the poem supply an account of his reasons for selecting the characters he refers to in it.) He is almost—though not quite—lured into the kind of disastrous action which he recognizes as symbolic of impending world disorder (in his lunar cycle, a phase immediately before dark of the moon). The second vision, developing the first poem's discovery that sweetness is found in violence and the sixth poem's appeal to the honeybees to build in the loosening masonry, focuses on an image based on the time of full moon (phase 15, in A *Vision*) when "hearts are full/ Of their own sweetness, bodies of their loveliness." Yet the unicorns and their lovely ladies are no more real than the hysterical "rage-hungry troop." Reality may lie, however, in his third vision—one more prophecy of a new and more horrible 2000-year cycle, parallel to but in all ways opposing the Christian one. Recapitulating his poem at the end of his penultimate stanza, Yeats concludes that neither the "self-delighting reverie" of his first stanza (Yeats on the tower), nor the "hate of what's to come" of his second (the troops), nor the "pity for what's gone" of the third (the unicorn-mounted ladies) can prevent the terrible cycle of "coming emptiness" (symbolized by the brazen hawks) from materializing. Content to be prophet, Yeats uses his last stanza to celebrate occult investigations of "Demonic images," and, in a parody of Wordsworth, to insist that such investigations have brought him intimations of immortality quite as accurate in old age as in youth.

"Nineteen Hundred and Nineteen" is an effort to justify the isolation he has accepted at the end of "Meditations in Time of Civil War." Having assumed the "ghostly solitude" of his prophetic role, he is able to face with a kind of equanimity the destruction both of familiar social institutions and of the great art products of the past. He is even able to face the destruction of his own work: "no work can stand, . . ./ No honour leave its mighty monument." His project, therefore, is to see destruction

accurately, to record precisely the civil war and the larger international destruction that it foreshadows as "the Platonic Year/
Whirls out new right and wrong,/ Whirls in the old instead."
"All the time I do not spend on proofs," Yeats wrote T. Sturge
Moore in 1922 as he was finishing the poem, "I spend on a series
of poems about this Tower and on the civil war at which I look
(so remote one is here from all political excitement) as if it were
some phenomenon of nature."

Taking his examples of destructive violence from two civilizations, Yeats emphasizes at the beginning of the poem that "lovely
things," even though apparently protected from the last phase of
the moon (the difficult syntax is probably best read: "That seemed
miracle and that seemed protected . . ."), are in reality guaran-
teed no survival. Though "sheer miracle" to the Athenian multitude, the marvels of Athens have vanished. Not one authentic
work of Phidias remains (in spite of the fact that his chrysele-
phantine statues were acclaimed the greatest sculpture of the ancient world). So too in our civilization, the multitude at the end
of the nineteenth century had felt that a time of democratic triumph had arrived, that the "pretty toys" of law and public opinion
had effectively outlawed war. Yet "Now" that time is gone. Men
who had thought "All teeth were drawn" discover to their amaze-
ment that they are "but weasels fighting in a hole" who, as Yeats
points out in the fourth part, "Shriek with pleasure" if they show/
The weasel's twist, the weasel's tooth." For 1919 had brought the
end of the First World War and, for the Irish, a time of what
seemed deliberate reprisals on England's part for the nationalistic
efforts that had gained strength while English attention was
focused on Germany. The Black and Tans and the Auxiliaries were
recklessly used to frighten Ireland into submission to "law and
order." Atrocities like that Yeats describes in the fourth stanza
became on both sides the order of the day.

Yet there is a kind of cold comfort. Those weasels fighting in
a hole are, in the abstract, man; and "Man is in love and loves
what vanishes." Seeing always the double nature of all things,

Yeats cannot paint a picture so black as entirely to eliminate the artist or the artist's audience. Though the end come, though the second coming bring its rough beast out of two thousand years of stony sleep, this time in the image of the dragon, even that dragon is capable of being incorporated in art (Loie Fuller's Chinese dancers had transformed strips of gauze into "a dragon of air . . . fallen among dancers"). Chaos is come, Yeats argues: men move "to the barbarous clangour of a gong." Yet at the same time those men move as artists. Though the music they dance to is "barbarous," though it seem to ears raised on nineteenth-century harmonies sheer "clangour," "All men are dancers."

In bare, brilliant images, Yeats contrasts the dragon-headed mob with the swan-like solitary soul. (A real lesson in poetic structure can be gleaned, incidentally, from a close examination of the way Yeats manipulates his "dragon-ridden" day image. For day is turned into a night that sweats with terror, a terror like that which preceded the good time when we had "pieced our thoughts into philosophy," and the old order's drowsy chargers are set against the *night*mare that *rides* upon sleep and the days that are *dragon-ridden*. The image is of course expanded further in the unnatural horses that ride the last stanza and which, as Yeats once noted, "now that the times worsen, give way to worse.")

The swan—probably compounded from Yeats's own "Wild Swans at Coole," T. Sturge Moore's "Dying Swan," and Mallarme's frozen one—manages, like the artist or like Yeats in *A Vision*, to see "An image of its state" before it leaps "into the desolate heaven" to "ride/ Those winds that clamour of approaching night." But that leap—setting the swan itself on nightmare wind—"brings a rage/ To end all things," and Yeats sweeps through the fifth stanza in an orgy of destructive violence as he pictures the artist, now one who traffics in mockery, mocking the great, the wise, the good, and even mockers themselves who will not lift a hand ("maybe") "To bar that foul storm out." In the last stanza storm itself triumphs in a thunder of ghostly hooves that give way to Herodias' unreal passionate daughters, "the eter-

nal enemy" according to Arthur Symons whose "The Dance of
the Daughters of Herodias" was almost certainly Yeats's source
for them. Finally Robert Artisson, the fourteenth-century "fiend"
arrives to end the poem. Pure nightmare (he was—like nightmare
itself in its original meaning—an incubus who had been evoked
by "love-lorn Lady Kyteler" to satisfy her unnatural lusts), he
moves always with his thoughtless stupid eyes under that circle of
the moon "That pitches common things about." Bringing his
poem also full circle, Yeats sees man caught in patterns larger
than himself—designs of the Platonic Year. And though he allows
man little free will, he does allow him feeling and a sense of form.
"Man is in love and loves what vanishes,/ What more is there to
say?"

If the large circle of the Platonic Year sweeps civilizations in
and out, the little circles of the seasons dispose of individual men.
In "The Wheel," "Youth and Age," and "The New Faces" Yeats
considers what it is to be old and, for a moment, seems almost to
accept death; some of his early horror is gone. As they grow older,
men experience, he concludes, a "longing for the tomb." And as
he thinks in "The New Faces" what it would be to be without
Lady Gregory, he seems almost to accept the fact that "night can
outbalance day."

But if there is any pattern in Yeats, it is that of life's ultimate
triumph over death. And "A Prayer for my Son" follows hard on
those poems which explore the death-wish. Some of the minor
problems of the poem can be disposed of if one recalls Yeats's
note in A *Packet for Ezra Pound* to the effect that he had been
warned in the automatic writing that the "Frustrators" who had
made difficult the dictation of that script were planning an attack
on his health and on his children's. The ghost he calls on at the
beginning of the second stanza is therefore a kind of hearth god
who will guard young William Michael (born August 22, 1921)
from the evil forces that oppose a poet's son.

The importance of the poem, however, is that—returning to
"The Second Coming" for theme—it introduces a whole group of

poems concerned with the difficult correlation between Christ and modern times on the one hand and, on the other, between Christ and the historical cycle that his coming invalidated. The "You" of the last two stanzas is therefore Christ-as-artist who taught the morning stars to sing, who could fashion "everything/ From nothing," and yet who as inarticulate child was dependent on the protection of his parents until he had mastered speech (until he had become the artist-in-fact as well as the potential artist). When the god does put on flesh, Yeats argues, he must accept as well the accidents of flesh which only human beings—for instance, loving parents—can in part control.

"Two Songs from a Play" moves us from Christmas to Easter, from the birth of Christ to His death and resurrection. And, as for all events associated with those crucial years, Yeats managed to find parallels.

"Managed to find" is perhaps an understatement, for Yeats as early as 1896 had assembled in "The Adoration of the Magi" much of the materials that he ultimately expanded to the play (*The Resurrection*) from which the songs are drawn. This early "Magi" story, which Yeats for years mined for poems, included prophecies of the end of the Christian era in a return to an antithetical harsher civilization. Even more significantly it contained the character of "a dying woman" who might in an annunciation "so transform the world that another Leda would open her knees to the swan, another Achilles beleaguer Troy," and three old men ("The Magi" themselves) one of whom "crowed like a cock" beside the dying woman's bed before saying in a strange prophetic voice, "I am Hermes . . . and you have heard my sigh. The woman who lies there has given birth, and that which she bore has the likeness of a unicorn and is most unlike man of all living things, being cold, hard and virginal. It seemed to be born dancing . . ." Dying, the woman holds out her arms to the being who had left her. "Harsh sweetness," she calls, "Dear bitterness," "O solitude," and "O Terror." The old men had in the first place been sent to her when a voice, speaking through the mouth of one of them who had fallen asleep while reading Virgil's *Fifth* Eclogue, had ordered them to travel from Ireland to Paris.

Though all the correlations between Virgil's *Fourth* Eclogue (Yeats was never one for close detail), *The Golden Bough* (which Yeats had studied carefully), and the neo-Platonist Proclus from whom he extracts the "fabulous, formless darkness" cannot be itemized here (a fine account of their function which I have in part drawn on is made by Richard Ellmann in *The Identity of Yeats*), it is of some value to know that both Dionysus and Christ had died and been reborn under the same astrological signs (both deaths therefore "at the spring") when the moon is next to Virgo (the Virgin, who holds in her hand the star Spica). The first stanza gives us, consequently, the death of Dionysus (who in legend is born twice—the second birth made necessary by his having been dismembered by the Titans, only his heart being rescued by Athena) and links it to Magnus Annus, the Platonic Year. The prophecy that begins the second stanza echoes Virgil, Yeats's adaptation of Virgil in his short story, and the whole design of *A Vision*; and it draws as well on Christian legend that connects Virgil's prophecy of the return of Astraea (sometimes identified with Virgo) and with her of the golden age to the coming of Mary and the Christian golden age she will inaugurate. The design behind the first song is therefore:

Fierce virgin	Virgo	Astraea	Staring virgin (Athena)
and	and	and	and
Her Star	Spica	Golden age	Dionysus' heart

anticipate

Mary	Mary	Mary	Mary
and	and	and	and
Christ	Star of Bethlehem	Christian age	Christ's heart

The second song, linking large cycles to little ones, draws parallels between the cycles each man experiences in his life and those large historical ones that had been inaugurated by such deaths as those of Dionysus and Christ. But in the large cycle and the little one it is the resinous heart of man (whether he be Dionysus, Christ—whose heart in the play *The Resurrection* continues to beat though Christ himself has become ghostly—or an anonymous lover, painter, herald, or soldier) which feeds that which "flames upon the night."

"Fragments" offers an image for the end of the Hebraic-Christian cycle as things mechanical take over. Though the poem might have come "Out of a medium's mouth," it took Yeats to see all the glorious correlations between Eve and the "spinning-jenny" which God takes out of Adam-Locke's side in the dying Garden of the modern world. Reminding us that Locke and Adam did delve while Eve and modern clattering jenny span, the poem whirls out gyres uniquely Yeatsean.

Like "Fragments," "Wisdom" is a playful treatment of a theme Yeats takes seriously. Yeats, who had been reading Henry Adams, speculates that perhaps "the true faith" is more the product of Byzantine or medieval artist than of "some peasant gospeller," that the gorgeous unreal majestic Mother is in some ways a more satisfactory image than Mary as real mother putting up with the wild infancy of the child who would grow up to be working-carpenter. Intrigued always with the relation between reality and symbol, Yeats sees Christianity compounded from both.

The "horror" that Christ's "wild infancy" drove from "His Mother's breast" is however precisely that horror, that "terror," Yeats is concerned with in "Leda and the Swan," a complex poem which, ideally, all the poems before it in this section should explicate. Yeats, who likes to see annunciations in human terms, tries to visualize the reality of Mary's experience at the end of "Wisdom"—something far different from the convenient medieval abstraction: King Abundance (God) begot Wisdom (Christ) on Innocence (Mary). Mary's real experience he concludes was, like Leda's, an experience of horror—of terror at the violent arrival of the god, an experience that might, he suggests at the end of each poem, have been compensated for by insight (knowledge) gained in the violent encounter with the supernatural.

Explaining his poem and his system in A *Vision*, Yeats comments:

> I imagine the annunciation that founded Greece as made to Leda, remembering that they showed in a Spartan temple, strung up to the roof as a holy relic, an unhatched egg of hers; and that from one of her eggs came Love and from the other War. But all things are from antithesis, and when in my ignorance I try to imagine what older civilisation that annunciation rejected I can but see bird and woman blotting out some corner of the Baylonian mathematical starlight.

The annunciation he refers to is, of course, the rape of Leda by Zeus who, disguised as a gigantic swan, had in that remarkable conception begotten not only Helen but as well the whole consequence of Helen: the fall of Troy, the death of the Greek heroes.

Yeats regarded the poem as one of his major accomplishments, "a classic enunciation," he told L. A. G. Strong, adding that he had "40 pages of commentary" on it in A *Vision*. Certainly it does summarize the "Dove or Swan" antithesis that A *Vision* drives to, the view of history as essentially cyclical. Yet it is even greater, perhaps, as a nearly perfect sonnet. If we visualize the division between octave and sestet as a kind of fulcrum, we can see how carefully Yeats maneuvered into lines 8 and 9 a point of balance. For one instant, the instant of Helen's conception, the opposing flows of passion intersect. Zeus at the beginning of the poem had been passionate, Leda helpless and terrified. At the end of the poem Leda is "caught up" in his passion, Zeus is "indifferent." But at the structural center of the poem a kind of communion takes place. Leda must feel, Yeats insists, "the strange heart beating where it lies" at exactly the instant that "A shudder in the loins" engenders the future.

Everything in the poem contributes to this design. Even rhythm itself underlines the shifting passions of the two characters. The five anapests literally move Leda through the poem staggering her, loosening her thighs, letting her be caught up and finally letting her drop ("the staggering girl," "her loosening thighs," "Being so caught up," "the indifferent beak"). The deliberately Freudian imagery (the white rush, the broken wall, the burning roof and tower, to name only the most obvious), the puns on such words as *laid* and *lies*, the ambiguities inherent in "those terrified vague fingers" (visually vague because buried in feathers or blurred from beating, emotionally vague because, in spite of the fingers' terror, thighs already loosen to the equally ambiguous feathered glory), the unanswerable question that ends the poem all serve to bind up into "a classical enunciation" a poem no part of which does not function in all other parts.

"Leda and the Swan" was perhaps based on the Michelangelo painting (Yeats had a colored reproduction), but it is even more likely, it seems to me, that he visualized an ideal scene. Or—as he did with the poem which follows "Leda"—he may have combined the memories of two paintings to produce a poem independent of either one. Certainly—as Cecil Salkeld has copiously and Mrs. Yeats casually testified—"On a Picture of a Black Centaur by Edmund Dulac" is founded on two paintings, though Yeats neglects to credit Salkeld's.

The poem itself, complicated and considerably richer than any prose "meaning," can be at least in part translated into a simple statement for those who like that sort of thing thanks to a note Yeats included in the "Four Years: 1887-1891" section of *The Trembling of the Veil*. There, in a comment on his early desire for personal and national Unity of Being, he observed, "I thought that all art should be a Centaur finding in the popular lore its back and its strong legs. . . . One thing I did not foresee, not having the courage of my own thought: the growing murderousness of the world." If we, therefore, tentatively identify the Centaur with the sort of national culture Yeats had once hoped to found, there is no great difficulty in seeing how its hooves had stamped his works down into the sultry mud. He was in 1920, when the poem was written, a man more honored in England and America than in Ireland. Nationalist horse-play—for that matter, the world's horse-play—had become, in a time of domestic and international wars, "murderous."

The "horrible green parrots," on the other hand, are far more difficult to pin down. Linked perhaps to the green-pated bird of "Demon and Beast" and certainly to the parrot that rages "at his own image in the enamelled sea" ("The Indian to His Love"), modelled perhaps on Yeats's own parrot, they may here represent the sort of demoniac forces that Yeats felt threatened his own family, the "Frustrators," the "devilish things" he describes in "A Prayer for my Son," the forces of disruption which constantly impeded his work on A Vision. Driven half insane by them, Yeats admits to having focused primarily on abstractions, "old mummy wheat" from "the mad abstract dark" (his image drawn from accounts—inaccurate ones as it turned out—of the miraculous sprouting of grains of prehistoric rivet wheat that were supposed to have been found in Egyptian mummy wrappings). Now, however, thanks to his work on A Vision he has discovered a way to fit reality into coherent patterns, "full flavored wine." (The seven Ephesian topers are the Seven Sleepers of Ephesus, ancient Christian martyrs whose 200-year-old sleeping bodies reputedly kept Theodosius II from losing his faith. Having wakened to keep him Christian, they returned to their cave to sleep on to Judgment Day.) The ambiguous last quatrain is sometimes taken to be addressed to the Centaur and there are critics who worry about it sleeping yet keeping unwearied eyes on the birds. (The lines, of course, may be addressed to the sleepers themselves.) The most likely reading, however, seems to me to be Yeats telling the Centaur—political Ireland—to stretch out and sleep, for he has in spite of all his words, his accusations of murderous horseplay, loved Ireland better than his soul. It *can* sleep, moreover, because he himself—now fortified with his new *Vision*—will keep a personal watch on the horrible birds. The sense of the passage would then read: Stretch out your limbs and sleep (. . . I have loved you better than my soul). And there is none so fit (as I) to keep a watch and keep unwearied eyes on the horrible birds. To make it painfully literal, it seems to me to be saying, "Ireland has hurt me, but I have loved it in spite of that hurt and my counter-attacks; and now that the nation seems to be established, I too will perform a service—a poetic one, but a service still—in keeping watch in my own way against the forces of evil."

"Among School Children," which follows, is as a matter of fact founded on exactly the sort of public watching Yeats seems to be setting himself to in the Black Centaur poem. Written after a 1926 semi-official senatorial visit to Waterford, a progressive convent school, the poem is an effort to synthesize the "sixty-year-old smiling public man," the aged one-time lover, and the would-be philosopher into something as organic as a chestnut-tree, as coherent as a dancer's movements. Structurally, the poem is organized around a series of parallel trinities: Yeats's own "selves" noted above; the baby, child, and "old scarecrow" metamorphosis common to all men; the three kinds of images worshipped by lovers, nuns, and mothers; the "Presences" known to passion (lovers), piety (nuns), and affection (mothers); the three systematizers of the sixth stanza who offer different ways of locating reality—Plato finding it in unnatural "ghostly" forms, solider Aristotle locating it in nature, and Pythagoras discovering it in art; and a whole host of minor trinities. These trios, suggesting relationship and interrelationship, lead Yeats to the final discovery that blossoming and dancing can be seen only in terms of the total organism, whether that organism be poem, person, tree, or dancer. The poem, consequently, is not image, not theme, not rhythm, not rhyme scheme, not sound, not even words on a page; it is poem. Just that. And the "person"—say, Yeats—is not Maud Gonne's life-time lover, or Mrs. John Butler Yeats's one-time child, or philosopher, or school-inspector, or poet. He is rather the compound of those separate selves and a multitude of others. Never is he an isolated one of them. The chestnut-tree is neither leaf, blossom, or bole; it is its own complex self, the "great-rooted blossomer" which finds its essence in no aspect but in all parts of itself, which indivisibly exists. The dancer swept by music is indissolubly integrated to his dance.

Stripping Mask (the smiling senator) from the time-tortured self behind it (scarecrow Yeats visualizing Maud Gonne as a child), the poem constructs from the destructive ravages of time a final justification of life. And yet that justification of life is, as Yeats is quick to point out, ironically heart-breaking; for it is ultimately an abstraction, an image. Like those images worshipped by nuns, mothers, or lovers, it represents a vision of reality rather than reality itself. Maud Gonne's Ledean body has been corrupted to something "Hollow of cheek as though it drank the wind/ And took a mess of shadows for its meat." Philosophers, for all their vision, become "Old clothes upon old sticks to scare a bird."

It is ultimately, however, in the double vision that the truth resides. The part (what Yeats calls "Labour," day-to-day flesh-and-blood life) must not be taken for the whole yet is itself an indispensable ingredient of the whole. The chestnut-tree is not leaf, blossom, or bole; yet without leaf, blossom, or bole it is not chestnut-tree.

This allusive poem which links to all of Yeats's other Helen, Leda, swan, and paddler poems; which echoes "honey of generation" from Porphyry's essay on "The Cave of the Nymphs"; which, as William York Tindall notes, reflects Pythagoras' golden thighs from Plutarch's life of Numa Pompilius; and which is meticulously constructed to prove that Yeats is now a scholar familiar with art, history and philosophy is, like Yeats's chestnut-tree, greater than its parts.

"Colonus' Praise," the chorus from Yeats's translation of *Oedipus at Colonus*, is probably inserted after "Among School Children" because its image of the dancing ladies and their companion Dionysus ("Semele's lad") parallels the "School Children" dancer.

Other parallels exist also. The miraculous olive-tree suggests, for instance, not only the chestnut, but as well, being "self-sown, self-begotten" and symbolic, the "Presences" of "School Children," those Platonic forms, "self-born," which because of their perfection are "mockers of man's enterprise." A miraculous earthly equivalent of Platonic form itself, the olive-tree "gives/ Athenian intellect its mastery."

"The Hero, the Girl, and the Fool," on the other hand, examines appearances in the modern world. Both Girl and Hero are fearful that their Masks are loved and not themselves. The Fool by the Roadside, however, working out an image of that "dreaming back" process Yeats had made central to "Shepherd and Goatherd" concludes that—because of the very nature of reality itself —"a faithful love" can be found only when one is outside the human condition altogether, "mere shade," a "Coagulate of stuff/ Transparent like the wind."

"Owen Aherne and his Dancers," drawing on considerably more personal material, explores further complexities of love. Yeats had written the poems immediately after his marriage (Mrs. Yeats dates them as written between October 24 and October 27, 1917), when he was greatly concerned that perhaps he should have tried harder to persuade Iseult Gonne to marry him. He had the feeling, he wrote Lady Gregory, that he had betrayed three people: himself, Iseult, and George. He was, he said, "in great gloom." It was at this point, perhaps because she became involved in a real trance situation, perhaps merely to distract him, that Mrs. Yeats first practiced the automatic writing which ultimately became *A Vision:*

> She got a piece of paper, and talking to me all the while so that her thoughts would not affect what she wrote, wrote these words (which she did not understand) 'with the bird' (Iseult) 'all is well at heart. Your action was right for both but in London you mistook its meaning.' I had begun to believe just before my marriage that I had acted, not as I thought more for Iseult's sake than for my own, but because my mind was unhinged by strain. The strange

thing was that within half an hour after writing of this message my rheumatic pains and my neuralgia and my fatigue had gone and I was very happy. From being more miserable than I ever remember being since Maud Gonne's marriage I became extremely happy. That sense of happiness has lasted ever since. The misery produced two poems which . . . are among the best I have done.

The poems, recording the frustrations he had experienced with Iseult, fearing to hurt her yet fearing even more the ways in which her refusal would hurt him, depend for their success on a contrast of wild youth and tame age, of wild bird and cage bird; yet at the same time Yeats is conscious of a real responsibility to the woman he did marry: " 'O but her heart would break to learn my thoughts are far away.' " And he defends her against the attack of His Heart, maintaining that he had not found "in any cage" the woman at his side. His final decision, to accept reality, to encourage Iseult to "choose a young man now and all for his wild sake," lets all end well. Both women are wild birds at the end, and the fifty-year cage bird has himself shown a streak of considerable wildness.

Similarly autobiographical, as indeed everything at the end of *The Tower* is, *A Man Young and Old* works a kind of free fantasia on Yeats's own love life. (Yeats had originally intended to publish with it *A Woman Young and Old*, but he withheld the companion piece for the Fountain Press edition of *The Winding Stair* (1929) when he discovered a deadline approaching and not enough poems written to fill that volume.)

Held together by a set of interrelated images of moon, stone, thorn tree, and—astonishingly—a shriek, *A Man Young and Old* contrasts the experience of love as known to youth and age. The young man's poems—the first four—present the stone-hearted lady (Maud Gonne as moon goddess) who coldly drives her lover lunatic by emptying thought from his head in the same way that the full moon (by outshining them) empties the heaven of stars. Transformed by her he himself lies, in the same poem, "like a bit of stone" under a broken tree (two of Yeats's favorite sterility images neatly combined) while she sails by in kind lunar majesty. Though a shriek to something mortal (a passing bird) could free him, he chooses the dignity of silence. In the fifth lyric, the first of the old man's songs, the lunatic "moon-accursed" youth that he had been is recollected, the youth who had found with another woman the communion his first love had denied him. Yet even with that other woman he had feared to drink from the cup of love. And now that they are old that cup is "dry as bone." (For those who like precise identifications, it is perhaps worth noting that Yeats quoted the first draft of the poem in a letter to Mrs. Shakespear after commenting, "I came upon two early photographs of you yesterday, while going through my file—one that is from *Literary Year Book*. Who ever had a like profile?—a profile from a Sicilian coin. One looks back to one's youth as to [a] cup that a mad man dying of thirst left half tasted. I wonder if you feel like that.") These two loves are the old man's secrets. But secrets, as he points out in the ninth lyric, are now his stock in trade; and he announces with a good deal of relish in poem VI that the goddess-like figure (now Helen, Yeats's favorite "equivalent" for Maud Gonne) who had driven him lunatic as a youth had in fact once lain in his arms under the symbolic thorn tree which had in poem II been his own symbol for dreadful silent sterility. She had, as a matter of fact, he reveals, joined that unshrieking silence, had "cried into this ear,/ 'Strike me if I shriek.' "

The seventh lyric makes him crack-voiced as well as crack-pated, a mad old man laughing under a pot-bellied full moon. (Autobiography at this point slips away in favor of the lunatic Mask Yeats is creating for himself.) Barren Madge joins him under the moon, but now she too is lunatic, carrying a stone in her arms which she attempts to nurse. Shrieking Peter, another relic of youth, cries " 'I am King of the Peacocks,' " and the old man laughs till tears run down his cheeks, "Remembering that her shriek was love/ And that he shrieks from pride."

The eighth poem returns again to that crucial night under the broken thorn tree when after talking half the night the lovers had fallen in each others' arms to bring metaphorically the dead tree to life: "O what a bursting out there was,/ And what a blossoming . . ." Yet reality is not in that lost spring and summer but in the winter of the aged in which he finds himself trapped, chatting with his old mistresses, sharing with them the three-sided solitude of poem IX. Madge finally confesses that she had reciprocated his love ("what I dared not think/ When my blood was strong"); but the recollection of that casual embrace which in poem III had seemed to drown him sounds now "like an old song."

Shared love, in fact, is the theme in the end, a theme embodied in "stories of the bed of straw" beneath the thorn-tree that had belonged to the "pair who loved many years" but who made love only once, stories "Of the bed of down" that belonged to that pair who loved but one year but who made love that whole year long.

But now all the beds he shared have been swept into the dustbin of the past, and "Peg and Meg and Paris' love . . . / Are gone away." Alone in the tenth poem, he turns once more to the meaningful images, struggling to incorporate them at least (since flesh has vanished) into himself. He would, like his first love's symbol, the moon, sail "the cloudy wrack," in that splendid isolation of sky shriek Peter's "peacock cry," or shriek the ecstatic cry neither he nor his mistress could utter under the thorn tree; nursing that which in poem I had been the moon itself, "a stone," he would like lunatic Madge sing lullaby—finally articulate—to his illusions.

The eleventh poem, a chorus from Yeats's translation of *Oedipus at Colonus*, acts as a kind of benediction, freeing the old man from memory of the "delights of youth" which can only bring pain to the old. Shrieking ended, laughing dancers throng "the long echoing street" (in terms of the rest of the lyrics a life image) to bring bride to bridegroom's chamber and, significantly, the "silent kiss that ends short life or long."

Though most editions of Yeats's collected poems place "All

Souls' Night" immediately after "The Three Monuments" (Yeats's satirical poem which uses the statues of Nelson, Parnell, and O'Connell to ridicule the Senate's reluctance to pass a Divorce Bill), in the original edition of *The Tower* and in the final ordering of the English Definitive Edition Yeats inserted "The Gift of Harun Al-Rashid" as the second-last poem. The reason is, it seems to me, obvious. For just as *A Man Young and Old* is intended to be *The Tower's* contribution to the long saga of Yeats's relations with Maud Gonne and the less-explicitly identified ones with Mrs. Shakespear, so "The Gift of Harun Al-Rashid" is intended to remind the reader that Yeats has at last settled down with an ideal wife. Almost painfully allegorical, the poem accounts for the circumstances of Yeats's marriage and the inception of the automatic writing. One has only to read "W. B. Yeats" for "Kusta Ben Luka" and all is clear. But more than mere allegory, the poem also records a triumph of love over the early obsession. Mrs. Yeats "Can shake more blossom from autumnal chill/ Than all my bursting springtime knew." And in that passage Yeats carefully diminished the "blossoming" he had commented on in the eighth lyric of *A Man Young and Old*, the lyric in which he praised Maud Gonne, who "had all the spring." Now praising his wife for inventing the "emblems on the sand" which had figured so largely in "Ego Dominus Tuus" and which prefigured the pattern of *A Vision*, Yeats is careful to reassure her that he loves her for more than the automatic writing, that it is she who gives the writing its character. Like the dancer who is indistinguishable from the dance, the voice which speaks through his wife is also her voice:

> . . . The voice has drawn
> A quality of wisdom from her love's
> Particular quality. The signs and shapes;
> All those abstractions that you fancied were
> From the great Treatise of Parmenides;
> All, all those gyres and cubes and midnight things

Are but a new expression of her body
Drunk with the bitter sweetness of her youth.
And now my utmost mystery is out.

"All Souls' Night," the epilogue to A *Vision*, sets therefore on the most appropriate night this unparalleled pair of lovers on either side of their table ready to toast each other and all the ghosts they have evoked in their long labors on the mystical philosophy. And in ten stanzas of ten lines each, Yeats performs the ritual act that will call all the old occultists of his youth from their graves: William Thomas Horton, for whose A *Book of Images* he had in 1898 written an introduction and who had died only the year before; Florence Emery (Florence Farr) who after not quite successfully teaching Yeats to speak verse had gone to Ramanathan College in Ceylon where until her death from cancer in 1917 she had taught in that native school and occasionally had written Yeats of the progress of her Indian studies; and finally MacGregor Mathers, "half a lunatic, half knave," who had translated Rosenroth's *Kabalah Denudata* and who had, often costumed in full Highland regalia, fought sometime before his death in 1918 with everyone he had ever known. But, as Yeats says, "names are nothing." He would have the whole dead occult crowd, each of whom having proved competent to operate those gyres which wind through the mind "As mummies in the mummy-cloth are wound," come to his party and join him in the unravelling of his mummy truths "Whereat the living mock." Celebrating the complex pattern of A *Vision* which incorporates Hell ("where the damned have howled away their hearts"), Heaven ("where the blessed dance") and earth in the recurrent destructive cycles of one coherent design, Yeats manipulates from the casual conversational tone he had perfected in the Major Gregory poem an ominous excitement. Employing witty puns (his "mummy truths" are both old truths and truths that involve mummies; MacGregor Mathers, half insane, had changed his mind in more ways than one; and Yeats, literally blind in one eye, admits to being "half

contented to be blind" in the observation of Mathers' faults),
linking through its mummy windings to all other gyres and
through its reference to the cannon sounding "From every quarter
of the world" to all other prophetic poems, this poem prepares the
reader for the new subject matter that will be of immediate concern to Yeats at the beginning of *The Winding Stair*, the nature
of death itself, the great riddle all his work, he felt, had at last
enabled him to assault.

11 * The Winding Stair

Late in 1927, the text of *The Tower* in galleys, Yeats set about putting in shape a group of poems for "an American with a private press" (William Edwin Rudge whose Fountain Press issued two years later the first version of *The Winding Stair*). "The American" had given Yeats an advance of £150 for "six months' use of sixteen or so pages of verse," and had promised another £150 on delivery of the manuscript. "I am giving him 'The Woman Young and Old,'" Yeats wrote Mrs. Shakespear, "a poem called 'Blood and the Moon' (a tower poem) which was written weeks ago; and I am writing a new tower poem 'Sword and Tower,' [This became "A Dialogue of Self and Soul"] which is a choice of rebirth rather than deliverance from birth. I make my Japanese sword and its silk covering my symbol of life . . ."

Yeats's crucial choice in the poems he grouped as *The Winding Stair* is that of this rebirth, an emphatic shifting of interest away from the predestined dancing place, the place of escape which had figured so largely in *The Tower*, to the much more viceral "fury and . . . mire of human veins." Conscious of "Vacillation," his own alternate focus first on escape from life and then on life itself, Yeats in this section of his work swings back to an acceptance of life. At the end of the poem "Vacillation" Heart triumphs over Soul and Yeats dismisses saintly Von Hügel: "So get you gone, Von Hügel, though with blessings on your head." "The swordsman throughout repudiates the saint, but not without vacillation," Yeats wrote Mrs. Shakespear. The swordsman—the man wielding the symbol of life itself—triumphs.

There are biographical reasons for this changing emphasis: Yeats, very ill, suffering from a nervous breakdown and influenza that was complicated by lung congestion, suddenly realized that he might die. But, he felt, the pattern of life and work was not complete. *The Tower* had been a distortion, half the picture, its emphasis on a man making his soul; flesh, too, demanded its due. Life, the silken sheath, a woman young and old, the immortality of generation, body surviving through body, all these needed to be sung. And Yeats fought his body to gain strength to sing them: "My dear Olivia: When I wrote to you—being staggered by my first nervous illness—I hardly expected to recover but now I do expect to," Yeats wrote Mrs. Shakespear on November 29, 1927:

> . . . I did not know how tired I was till this last blessed illness began, and now I dream of doing nothing but mystical philosophy and poetry. . . . George goes back to fetch the children out here for Xmas so that my lung may have time to mend. Three days ago I spat a little red and that roused me to defy George and begin to work and now though I am better again I write verse a little every morning—I want to finish that book for the American before some doctor gets at me—and I am going to allow myself when I am in the mood to write a little in the afternoon. How strange is the subconscious gaiety that leaps up before danger or difficulty. I have not had a moment's depression—that gaiety is outside one's control, a something given by nature . . .

It is this spirit which dominates *The Winding Stair*. Yeats's note to the section explains the general plan and the importance of the gyre and tower symbolism:

> I have used towers, and one tower in particular, as symbols and have compared their winding stairs to the philosophical gyres, but it is hardly necessary to interpret what comes from the main track of thought and expression. Shelley uses towers constantly as symbols, and there are gyres in Swedenborg, and in Thomas Aquinas and certain classical authors.

But the main project for *The Winding Stair* is the celebration of "the return to life":

> A *Dialogue of Self and Soul* was written in the spring of 1928 during a long illness, indeed finished the day before a Cannes doctor told me to stop writing. Then in the spring of 1929 life returned to me as an impression of the uncontrollable energy and daring of the great creators; it seemed to me that but for journalism and criticism, all that evasion and explanation, the world would be torn in pieces. I wrote *Mad as the Mist and Snow*, a mechanical little song, and after that almost all that group of poems, called in memory of those exultant weeks, *Words for Music Perhaps*. Then ill again, I warmed myself back into life with *Byzantium* and *Veronica's Napkin*, looking for a theme that might befit my years. Since then I have added a few poems to *Words for Music Perhaps*, but always keeping the mood and plan of the first poems.

Following one of his favorite patterns, the poems move from personal ancedotal observations about his friends (this section, primarily melancholy, reflective, ends with the poem "For Anne Gregory"), through a group of speculative "philosophical" works (the titles give away the changing point of view: "At Algeciras— A Meditation upon Death," "The Choice," "Vacillation," "The Results of Thought," "Gratitude to the Unknown Instructors") to the two final affirmative groups, *Words for Music Perhaps* and *A Woman Young and Old*, their sensual acceptance of life made universal through characterization, their enthusiastic celebration of love and lust shaping *The Winding Stair* into an "answer" to *The Tower*.

The Winding Stair begins, however, in something very like the bitter tone that had dominated the earlier section. "In Memory of Eva Gore-Booth and Con Markiewicz" is a memorial poem not to the two sisters (both of them, after all, were still alive) but rather to the girls they had been when, young, middle-class Yeats had visited Sir Henry Gore-Booth's Sligo home Lissadell, one of the first "big houses" he had known and through his life an image for him of aristocratic elegance. If the poem is a memorial to what the girls once were, it is as much a memorial to what Yeats had been: young, eager, enthusiastic, his head full of plans, all his life and work before him.

It is not just the two girls grown old and grim in what seemed to Yeats meaningless, stupid political activity, efforts to construct a Utopian world from the dregs of society, the mob, that Yeats is attacking, but the whole destructive force of time itself, the "raving autumn" that shears off youth from them as well as from him, that turns into an angry old man the young dreamer who on November 23, 1894, had written his sister Lily, "I have been staying at Lissadell for a couple of days and have enjoyed myself greatly. They are delightful people. . . . Miss Eva Gore-Booth shows some promise as a writer of verse. Her work is very formless as yet but it is full of telling little phrases. Lissadell is an exceedingly impressive house inside with a great sitting room high as a church and all things in good taste . . ."

But the "delightful people," corrupted, have become "withered old and skeleton-gaunt," the selves that they were only "Dear shadows," ghosts clinging to wrecked bodies. It is ghosts, therefore, and the ghost of his own youth that he calls on when threatening to destroy the nineteenth century's "great gazebo," whether crystal palace or aristocratic society. We had made the turreted glassed-in summer house, Yeats argues, the nineteenth century's dream of an ordered civilization, but "they," the mob, had "con-

victed us of guilt." At the end of the poem, joining the aristocrats
turned revolutionists, Yeats calls to the ghosts of their youth in a
shout of destructive ecstasy at the thought of that conflagration
that could end not only the past but all murderous time as well:
"Bid me strike a match and blow."

The short poem "Death" seems at first to contradict much of
Yeats's speculations about the afterlife and the nature of the soul.
It is only on a careful reading, I think, that one realizes that Yeats
is not saying that man has created the notion of a heaven and a
hell but rather that man has created the notion of extinction. No
dying animal worries about an afterlife (because he instinctively
knows that the soul survives); only man worries. But the great
man realizes his soul will triumph over the flesh: he knows death
—Yeats constructs a marvelous irony—"to the bone" and in knowing that knows that "Man has created death." Written in part
to praise, as Yeats notes, Kevin O'Higgins' brave stand before his
assassins, the poem makes a fitting introduction to "A Dialogue
of Self and Soul."

That great poem opposes the self and its "life-symbol" Sato's
sword to the winding stair that leads to darkness, an afterlife with
no return, "breathless" mindlessness, a kind of nirvana which
Yeats's system had promised as the end of the soul's journey
through the fleshy incarnations.

Soul, which eventually loses the debate, begins by urging the
contemplation of the winding stair that symbolizes the path of escape (straight up past pole star, a direction in which man is per-
mitted to move in that phase of the moon when all thought is
finished, the blacked out moment at dark of the moon). But *Self*
prefers a different object of contemplation, Sato's sword, to which
Yeats had already introduced his readers in the third section of
"Meditations in Time of Civil War." This "consecrated blade,"
now used as a masculine symbol for life, war, love, and sex, is
appropriately covered, as Yeats remarked in his 1930 diary, with
"a Japanese lady's court dress," female, enveloping, which, though
almost as tattered as those scarecrow bodies Yeats assigns all old

men and women, can "still protect, faded adorn." (Sword, here, is seen as the untarnished vital principle which the Japanese lady's dress—symbol of the body—can, though battered by time, still guard.)

Soul's response makes the identification of these symbols explicit: they are "Emblematical of love and war." And *Self's* answer expands both their symbolism and that of the tower. "All these [sword, sheath, the dress, the purple flowers embroidered on it] I set/ For emblems of the day against the tower/ Emblematical of the night."

Self, in the affirmative second section of the poem, reasserts its "right" to live life again, to suffer as man, to accept the world-imposed Mask which blinds each man to his true nature. Drawing on the "blind man's ditch" imagery of "On a Political Prisoner," Yeats explicitly rejects the solution "Sailing to Byzantium" seems to offer. Having discovered through A *Vision* the eternal patterns of reincarnation and return, and, once having seen them, "cast out remorse," he comes to tragic joy (a theme developed most fully in "Lapis Lazuli" in *Last Poems*), the bitter sweetness that is involved in the acceptance of life. Yet this sweetness is, for the artist, the only blessedness he can experience and leads inevitably to insight. Artists who accept this insight, who experience this sort of joy, *must* sing: "we must sing,/ We are blest by everything,/ Everything we look upon is blest."

That Yeats's insight made him blessed, he knew; that such blessedness extended to Thoor Ballylee and to his symbolic tower had to be proved. "Blood and the Moon" sets out both to invoke that blessedness ("Blessed be this place,/ More blessed still this tower") and to justify the invocation.

Though in the first section of the poem the "bloody" power that rose, like the tower, out of the peasantry (symbolically the "Storm-beaten cottages" at its foot) is not identified, we learn in the rest of the poem that it is to be associated both with the "seven centuries" of political revolution that have swept across Ireland since the tower was built and particularly with the aristocratic eight eenth century which produced in (and in spite of) Ireland the great figures of Goldsmith, Swift, Berkeley, and Burke. These four, in articulating intellect and passion, in defining the state and the nature of God, travelled, Yeats argues, his "winding, gyring, spiring treadmill of a stair," symbol here of those intellectual pursuits which, he felt, freed him as it did them from the limitations of "the race."

Yet if they were freed from "the race," they also expressed it and shaped it ("Uttering, mastering it"); they succeeded better than men of any other time in achieving that Unity of Culture of which Yeats had dreamed (symbolically, they come closest to constructing the whole tower, an organic state which, unlike modern nations, would not be "Half dead at the top"). Berkeley and Swift especially seemed of crucial importance, and Yeats set himself to a deliberate study of their works while he was working on the poem. From this point on, not only do they figure in plays and poems, but they also dominate a whole group of letters, diaries, and essays. In his 1930 diary, for instance, Yeats reports a conversation with his son, then nine years old. Michael had asked his teacher what Ireland had excelled in, and the teacher had had no answer. Yeats himself could think of nothing, but as he sat writing in his diary he realized what he might someday say to his son: "I may suggest to him, if I live long enough, that the thought of Swift, enlarged and enriched by Burke, saddled and bitted reality and that materialism was hamstrung by Berkeley, and ancient wisdom brought back; that modern Europe has known no men more powerful . . ."

The last two sections of the poem link it to the pattern outlined in A *Vision* and reveal that what had at first seemed rather a simple symbol (the tower in section I) embodies the sort of "complexity" Yeats at this time of his life found in everything. For if all mundane things are compounded from opposites, their patterns determined by the changing moon and the equally changing flux of life beneath it, no act can be a simple one and, as Yeats loved to point out, no perception can be a really accurate one. Even Yeats's own vision of reality is a vision limited by the second-by-second changing oppositions in his own nature. It is therefore constantly accurate and inaccurate, accurate for the moment but necessarily inaccurate for all others.

In section III this "complexity" is vividly demonstrated, for the "pure" moon is made the ultimate agent of corruption, the cause for the "blood-saturated ground" at the foot of the tower. Though for the seven centuries that the tower has stood the moon has washed its foundations in innocent blood, the "arrowy" murderous "shaft" of moonlight has itself remained pure. Though blood falls through that white light in a red rain, moonlight itself, the determining force, is uncorrupted; though the symbolic stair by which man climbs the tower toward a coherent vision of the whole reeks with "odor of blood" and though men of modern time "who have shed none" must clamor on that stair "in drunken frenzy for the moon," moonlight itself, the maddening pure force responsible for man's disorder, so successfully disorders him that he shrieks for his own destruction.

Section IV completes the paradox. In spite of all Yeats's insight, he assures us, it has been necessarily inaccurate: "No matter what I said,/ For wisdom is the property of the dead,/ A something incompatible with life." Wisdom belongs to the dead and to the dead vital force of the moon, beyond stain, inhuman, a shaft of white unearthly light; while power, on the other hand, belongs to man and finds its symbol in blood, its force in the earth. But between earth and sky, rooted in blood, the tower sweeps toward the white light of the moon. And, like human souls, butterflies cling at the tower's top to the transparent "glittering" windows, seem, in fact, to cling to the "moonlit skies," to the pure destructive "glory" of the unstained determining "visage of the moon."

"Oil and Blood," an astonishingly rhymed little poem (lazuli/ clay, exude/ blood, violet/ wet), acts as a kind of footnote to "Blood and the Moon." Vampires, "full of blood," lie in bloody shrouds under that emblem of power, earth itself, "heavy loads of trampled clay." Holy men, on the other hand, who have presumably climbed the tower toward moon's wisdom, lie preserved in golden tombs and tombs of lapis lazuli. Yeats draws on this image again in the last section of "Vacillation." His source, as he indicates in a letter to Mrs. Shakespear, is "the tale that when St. Theresa's tomb was opened in the middle of the nineteenth century the still undecayed body dripped with fragrant oil."

"Veronica's Napkin," based on another saint's legend, that of St. Veronica whose napkin was used to wipe the bleeding face of Christ as he carried the cross and which ever after retained the impression of his features, opposes imagery from Old Testament and New. The important pole star of the Old Testament Apocrypha (tent-pole of Eden) is opposed to "a different pole" (the Cross). The starry designs of the constellations, the "faces" which look down on us from the heavens, are opposed to the earth-bound face—its pattern drawn in blood—that appeared on Veronica's napkin. Specifically antithetical to Christ, whose masculine blood was shed for man, is Berenice, the murderous queen of Egypt (d. 221? B.C.) who had slaughtered her mother and suitor and who was ultimately slaughtered by her own son, but who—loyal to husband at least—was immortalized in the constellation Berenice's Hair (*Coma Berenices*) for having offered her hair for his safe return from war. Compounded from circles and poles, the poem balances a macrocosmic circle (Heavenly Circuit) against a microcosmic one ("the circuit of a needle's eye"), a macrocosmic erection ("Tent-pole of Eden") against a "different" microcosmic one (the Cross).

For those who have difficulty seeing such images as masculine and feminine, Yeats makes a quick recapitulation in "Symbols," the little poem which reassembles tower, sword, and sword-case. The tower and its stair, male and female symbols interwoven, link earth to sky and suggest the possibility of intellectual insight (though such insight will necessarily be supernatural, the tower's hermit being "blind" to things of this world). "All-destroying" sword represents a masculine destructive life force. Feminine sword-case, the silk which encloses the sword, represents beauty and regeneration.

The significance of such symbols in our time is the subject of the three epigrammatic poems that follow. Because of the world of literalists he lives in, the modern symbolist finds his work "Must ramble, and thin out" like the "Spilt Milk" of Yeats's title. Ironically drawing on both the magazine "The Nineteenth Century and After" in his title and Arnold's "Dover Beach" in his last two lines, Yeats extends the image of a time gone dry. "Statistics" continues the attack against the literalists. (Modern man, not Yeats, is of course the "he" of the first line. Yeats, like the Platonists, found his symbolic diagrams necessary connecting links between the physical and the ideal world.) And "Three Movements" brings those literalists, here represented as naturalists, gasping on the strand that had been revealed by the receding wave of "The Nineteenth Century and After."

The modern man's "rational sort of mind" is also under attack in "The Seven Sages." Only the seven old men, "massed against the world," hold out for the eighteenth-century values of Burke, Goldsmith, Berkeley, and Swift. "Whether they knew or not," Yeats has his sixth old man argue, these four great Irishmen hated the sort of democratic Whiggery that finds the middle classes excellent. Careful to keep his speakers in character, Yeats saves for his seventh and most perceptive old man one of his favorite dogmas: "wisdom comes of beggary." The ultimate source of insight is in the peasant class and of them in those propertyless men, beggars, who walk the roads and can—because uncorrupted by possessions—speak truth.

Like most of the poems in this group, "The Crazed Moon" opposes to present "rancorous" middle class Whiggery the greatness that had been. A poem more complicated than it seems, it is based on themes fully treated in *A Vision*. The moon is staggering and crazed, for instance, because it is approaching the end of a cycle. It has given birth to all of its various types of children (a different type for each phase) and we, the product of its old age, its last and most democratic breed, are necessarily crazed from staring at its "wandering eye." Members of the levelling middle class, we are, as in "The Seven Sages," essentially vicious. We grope for the moon's great children (men such as Burke, Goldsmith, Berkeley, and Swift) but they, happily, are dead. For, as the third stanza points out, could we reach them we would use our emaciated fingers ("slender needles of bone") to "rend what comes in reach." Making his poem circular in design, Yeats uses the "now" of stanzas I and III to surround a memory of the moon's maidenhood (phases 1-8), the time of the beginning of the cycle when amiable animal spirits had filled all men and "manhood led the dance."

But the twentieth century was, for Yeats, no dancing time. Only in isolated places, little pockets of aristocratic grace that had held out against modern chaos, could "A dance-like glory" still preserve pattern in a world of disorder. For Yeats, the most important of these was, of course, Coole Park. But in these years Coole Park was doomed. In 1927, though she was allowed to stay on as a tenant for the remainder of her life, Lady Gregory had been forced to sell house and land to the Forestry Department. Partly to honor her, partly to console her, but more simply perhaps merely to thank her in a work of art for all that she had done for him—a complement which he knew would please her— Yeats wrote the poem "Coole Park, 1929" and later followed it with "Coole Park and Ballylee, 1931."

The first of these poems, a "meditation" similar in form to the Major Gregory poem, assembles like that great model a group of typical visitors, five men of radically different personalities carefully selected for their common interest in the arts. The first three are poets: Douglas Hyde, who went on (Yeats's metaphor is ingenious) to beat the sword of poetry into the ploughshare of scholarly prose; Yeats himself, who "ruffled in a manly pose/ For all his timid heart" and who remained a poet; and the "slow," meditative dramatist John Synge. The other two, both Lady Gregory's nephews, were "Impetuous men." Yeats in 1911 had written an essay on the first of them, John Shawe-Taylor, in which he described a great leap from ship to boat that had been the talk of the neighborhood, and in which he went on to analyze Shawe-Taylor as a man of accurate intuitive insight who resolved every question through his visionary mystical identification with God. Hugh Lane had, of course, already been commemorated in Yeats's poems on the "pictures" controversy. Though they function well in the poem, Yeats probably selected these two for the very personal reason that they had been much in Lady Gregory's mind while he was writing the poem. In the July 23, 1929, entry in her diary, for instance, she remarks that she remembered their accomplishments as she stood above Shawe-Taylor's grave and then goes on to add: "In dedicating a play, *The Image*, to their dear memory, I wrote, 'And so we must say "God love you" to the Image Makers, for do we not live by the shining of those scattered fragments of their dream?' "

Reassembling his characters in his last stanza (travellers Lane and Shawe-Taylor, scholar Hyde, poets Yeats and Synge), Yeats anticipates the destruction of the house and visualizes their ghosts joining his own in a future meditation, "a moment's memory," to honor Lady Gregory's "laurelled head." (Three of them were already dead, of course, when he wrote the poem. Because all of them would be ghosts when the last stanza's meeting would take place, Yeats has them turn their backs upon reality and sensuality, "the brightness of the sun/ And all the sensuality of the shade.") Held together by the first and third stanza swallow's flight, the characters of the five men who, after swallow-like wandering, come finally in the last stanza to take their stand, and by the first stanza's trees which in the last stanza have sent up saplings in the broken stone of what had been Coole, the poem creates that meditation which it projects for the future and knits, as in the first stanza Yeats maintained all arts should, "Thoughts . . . into a single thought,/A dance-like glory." Here that glory is begotten quite literally from the walls of Lady Gregory's home and Yeats's conversations with its owner.

"Coole Park and Ballylee, 1931" was started in that year as an introductory piece to the Cuala Press edition of Lady Gregory's *Coole*, though Yeats ultimately substituted for it "Coole Park, 1929" when, deadline at hand, his second Lady Gregory poem was still unfinished. Using as basic materials his own relationship to her and Ballylee's geographical relationship to Coole (once part of the estate and still linked by the underground river), he incorporates in it romantic themes which he explicitly identifies, "Traditional sanctity and loveliness" and less obvious but by now familiar speculations on the nature of the soul. Holding the work together is a symbolism based on water, winter trees, and a white swan.

The water symbolism is perhaps easiest to grasp. The stream that runs beside the tower does travel for a ways underground through " 'dark' Raftery's 'cellar' " (Raftery is, of course, the blind poet Yeats had credited in "The Tower" with maddening through his voluptuous rhymes the man who ultimately "drowned in the great bog of Cloone.") and then rises again in Coole to be the source of one of the estate's lakes. Yeats, seeing it as an "emblem" for the soul's progress out of light (life) into darkness (death) and again into light (reincarnation), complicates an almost allegorical statement by returning to the "darkening flood" in his last line. Here, however, there is no "flooded lake" but rather the wine-dark sea celebrated by Homer (as in "The Tower" parallel to blind Raftery and half-blind Yeats) who, giving voice to great myths, had set on his dark waters an immortal drifting swan.

Unlike Homer's drifting swan (perhaps Zeus about to appear to Leda; though swans on dark waters symbolized always for Yeats the artist who, dying, sings in fading light), the one on Coole's lake "under a wintry sun" rises thundering into the white sky to become "Another emblem" for the progress of the soul which "sails into the sight/ And in the morning's gone." But this emblem for the soul, "arrogantly pure," does not lead Yeats to the tragic mood the water symbolism had generated but rather to one of joy. The emblematic swan is "so lovely that it sets to right/ What knowledge or its lack had set awry."

Having presented two opposed images for the soul (and having hinted a third in the domestic moor-hens floating on the stream beside his domestic tower), Yeats goes on to contrast the barren winter wood (its bare trees identified with sterile modern times) to Coole's opulent summery past, a world of "ancestral trees" and "gardens rich in memory." The "dry sticks" of the winter wood link also to Lady Gregory, Coole's "last inheritor," and with Yeats the last of "the last romantics," who—confined to her second-floor room—was dying as Yeats worked on the poem: "Sound of a stick upon the floor, a sound/ From somebody that toils from chair to chair." Though her stick associates her with the dry sticks of the sterile wood, to old age and death, Yeats remembers her at the end of the poem in terms of an artistic achievement that cannot die: she and he, grounding their writing "in what poets name/ The book of the people" had written work to "bless/ The mind of man." Like Homer, they had mounted Pegasus, the "high horse" of poetry, to sing emblematic songs of darkening flood and drifting swan. Though their high horse now runs "riderless," Lady Gregory too weak to rally and Yeats caught in a chaotic meaningless world, they had ridden him well, Yeats argues, had given the "great glory" of tradition and gracious manners, "loveliness," a lyric last song.

"For Anne Gregory" (Lady Gregory's granddaughter) brings not only the Coole material to an end but also the larger group of meditative, personal poems that dominate the first part of *The Winding Stair*. A reworking of "The Hero, the Girl, and the Fool," its focus on the nature of the self and that self's relationship with God anticipates a theme Yeats examines in great detail in the poems that immediately follow "Swift's Epitaph."

"Swift's Epitaph" itself, except for the introductory first line a translation—and a great one—of the great Latin original ("Ubi saeva indignatio/ Ulterius cor lacerare nequit./ Avi viator/ Et imitare, si poteris,/ Strenuum pro virili libertatis vindicem."), was for Yeats a defense of the artist-philosopher, the heroic figure who —like Burke, Berkeley, and Goldsmith—isolated himself from the mass of men to give voice to the human spirit. Swift served liberty, in Yeats's eyes, by freeing the artist from the mob. "I remember his epitaph," he wrote in his 1930 diary, "and understand that the liberty he served was that of intellect, not liberty for the masses but for those who could make it [liberty?] visible."

The three closely-related poems "At Algeciras—A Meditation upon Death," "The Choice," and "Mohini Chatterjee" not only share a concern with the "value" of life but, in concert, act as introductory material for the otherwise difficult poem "Byzantium." The group also very effectively demonstrates Yeats's careful organization of his material, since "At Algeciras—A Meditation upon Death" and "Mohini Chattejee" were originally companion poems titled "Meditation upon Death"; and "The Choice," which now separates them, was the sixth stanza of what was then called "Coole Park and Ballylee, 1932." When he came to rework the poems for *The Winding Stair*, Yeats withdrew the stanza from the Coole Park poem, titled it, and inserted it after "At Algeciras," probably, as I shall try to demonstrate below, as an "answer" to that poem.

"At Algeciras—A Meditation upon Death" with its focus on "Newton's metaphor," forces the reader, as G. B. Saul did, to locate in S. Brodetsky's biography *Sir Isaac Newton* (London, 1927, p. 153) the metaphor so impressive to Yeats. Newton is the speaker: "I do not know what I may appear to the world; but to myself I seem to have been only like a boy playing on the seashore, and diverting myself in now and then finding a smoother pebble or a prettier shell than ordinary, whilst the great ocean of truth lay all undiscovered before me."

Aware of Newton's metaphor, one can readily translate the syntactically difficult second stanza: When I was a boy I often carried to an older friend real shells rather than the insubstantial metaphorical shells Newton had described, for I hoped to give my friend joy in natural objects.

But translations of this sort do not give us the poem. Actually it is dependent, as so much of Yeats, on the opening stanza's imagery, here an imagery of birds that cross narrow Straits at evening "to light/ In the rich midnight of the garden trees/ Till the dawn break upon those mingled seas." The pun inherent in "light" (alight, brighten) reminds us that more than the seas are mingled: light itself is, for the time is evening—not midnight— when the birds are seen, and they will not be seen again until a second time of mingled light arrives to light the mingled seas.

It is evening itself also that causes Yeats to recall his boyhood walks by "Rosses' level shore," the memory that leads to the comment on Newton's metaphor. And that metaphor returns him to the present evening: "Greater glory in the sun,/ An evening chill upon the air." By this time, however, evening has expanded to the evening of life and Newton, the Great Questioner, has become the Great Questioner God. By this time also Yeats is free to let his imagination run on the sort of question "He" can ask and the sort of reply Yeats can "if questioned" make with "fitting confidence."

Though within "At Algeciras" neither question nor answer is given, a tentative answer seems to be offered in "The Choice," and from that answer something of the question can be determined. For in "The Choice" Yeats revises his youthful ambition to live a great life and accomplish great work. The perfect life necessarily excludes the perfect work, he now argues: if one chooses perfect work (as Yeats seems to suggest he has done) then perfect life must suffer. The artist, who chooses the world and its imperfection rather than "A heavenly mansion," must rage in earthly dark making poems rather than give himself up to saintly studies that will perfect his soul. He must, for the sake of his work, live life to the hilt.

The Great Questioner's question must then be something like

"What have you accomplished?" And the answer given in "The Choice" must be in the phrase: ". . . the toil has left its mark." Though the artist have nothing left but empty purse, vanity, and remorse, he has nevertheless been shaped by the toil itself, and —ironically—the perfection of what he *is* really achieved.

"Mohini Chatterjee," originally the second meditation on death, has a long history. Yeats had just turned twenty-one when he first met Babu Mohini Chatterjee, a Brahmin theosophist who assisted in the organizational work of founding the Dublin Theosophical Lodge. The meeting was an unforgettable one, and Yeats attempted to transcribe some of the Brahmin's ideas in verse (the since-discarded poem "Kanva on Himself"). In 1908, years later, Yeats set down the remembered important words in prose:

> Somebody asked him if we should pray, but even prayer was too full of home, of desire, of life, to have any part in that aquiescence that was his beginning of wisdom, and he answered that one should say, before sleeping: 'I have lived many lives, I have been a slave and a prince. Many a beloved has sat upon my knees, and I have sat upon the knees of many a beloved. Everything that has been shall be again.' Beautiful words that I spoilt once by turning them into clumsy verse.

Rectifying the early error of "Kanva on Himself," Yeats, in 1929, at last gave Mohini Chatterjee his due by versifying the prose passage and adding the "commentary" of the second stanza. In that commentary he associates the Brahminical doctrine with his own system of the soul's working out its destiny through a series of reincarnations that will ultimately give it its completed "final" form. Those things which through accident are denied in this life —Yeats's failure to win Maud Gonne, for instance—will, if fated, some time be satisfied, though grave be heaped on grave, unsatisfied lovers be reborn over and over until precisely the right combination of circumstances at last give them to each other.

"At Algeciras—A Meditation upon Death" suggests that it is necessary for the individual to shape his life to some design that a question may be answered. "The Choice" suggests the two ways that that life may be shaped and suggests the nature of the question. "Mohini Chatterjee" suggests the function of successive incarnations of the soul in ultimately satisfying the soul's primary need for communion with another soul. The only part of his central design not enunciated in these poems, the nature of the final escape from the round of reincarnation, is the subject of "Byzantium."

Yeats wrote "Byzantium" in Italy after his Malta Fever collapse. The first notes for the poem are recorded in his 1930 diary under the heading *"Subject for a Poem"* and are dated April 30:

> Describe Byzantium as it is in the system towards the end of the first Christian millennium. A walking mummy. Flames at the street corners where the soul is purified, birds of hammered gold singing in the golden trees, in the harbour, offering their backs to the wailing dead that they may carry them to paradise.

Yeats goes on to add that he has had the subject in his head "for some time."

In final form the much-revised poem is made carefully parallel to "Sailing to Byzantium." As in the earlier poem, the first stanza concerns itself with the flesh and blood world that is being left behind (the world of "unpurged images"). After that opening explicitly parallel stanza, the miraculous golden bird, the purgatorial flames, even the spirits crossing the sea are all recapitulated —but in reverse order to their appearance in "Sailing to Byzantium," for both setting and point of view have shifted radically. "Sailing to Byzantium" represents the voyage and is written from the point of view of the uninitiated outsider who leaves the material world for the immaterial. "Byzantium," on the other hand, is written from the point of view of the initiate who watches the uninitiated, unpurged spirits arriving from beyond the "gong-tormented sea" which separates Byzantium's reality from the flesh and blood reality of the twentieth-century world.

The poem is probably best apprehended dramatically. The first stanza sets the scene in Byzantium itself, its evening streets rapidly being cleared of late stragglers. The great cathedral's gong sends the last night-walkers singing out of sight. The city itself, architecturally coherent, "disdains/ All that man is"; for man is of necessity incoherent, trapped as he is within the structure of the two opposing gyres that determine his nature. Unlike architecture or art, shaped final things, man—as Yeats had pointed out in "Blood and the Moon"—is a creature swept by emotion, and conflicting emotion at that, "The fury and the mire of human veins."

The second stanza sets in the streets emptied of "night-walkers" the "walking mummy" Yeats had described in his first notes to the poem. This transparency floats into his sight already twice refined from flesh, "Shade more than man, more image than a shade." Only the idea of a ghost, equipped not even with a ghost's substantiality, "Hades' bobbin," the thing that had once been a man, the purified spirit which has already unwound the winding path of its human incarnations and has dreamed itself back to its elemental form, this "image" may breathlessly summon the breathless mouths of those spirits about to be freed from life's complexity and the round of reincarnations. Like the saints who step from the purifying flame in "Sailing to Byzantium," this superhuman form, this animating dead spirit ("death-in-life and life-in-death"), is the powerful force which will call to the Byzantine dancing place those unpurged spirits from beyond the gong-tormented sea.

Details of the dancing place constitute the third and fourth stanzas. The golden bird now is made of simple immutable stuff, "changeless metal," and scorns aloud things that change, natural things like the "common bird or petal" on the flowering perishable bough. (As Ursula Bridge notes, Yeats was almost certainly goaded into this stanza by Sturge Moore's April 16, 1930, letter which had attacked the golden bird of "Sailing to Byzantium" as an essentially natural thing: "Your *Sailing to Byzantium*, magnificent as the first three stanzas are, lets me down in the fourth, as such a goldsmith's bird is as much nature as a man's

body, especially if it only sings like Homer and Shakespeare of
what is past or passing or to come to Lords and Ladies." Making
his changeless bird now contemptuous of "all complexities of mire
or blood," Yeats insists that its song can be a derisive attack on
natural things.)

As the great cathedral gong strikes the witching hour of midnight (the "time" of the entire poem is, of course, confined to
those twelve crucial strokes), purgatorial immaterial flames appear on the Emperor's pavement, and the dancing "blood-be-
gotten" spirits who have been dolphin-ferried across the seas of
time and space begin the purgatorial dance so important to Yeats's
system. (It is anticipated by all the dancer images of his poetry
and particularly by the last line of "Mohini Chatterjee.") The
dance itself, as we know both from A *Vision* and from "Shepherd
and Goatherd" reverses mortal experience purifying it until "all
complexities of fury leave." All spirits, in Yeats's system, are of
course purified before being reborn; but in "Byzantium" Yeats is
offering the final purification by which the elemental patterns of
the dancing floor "break" the cycle of birth and rebirth, the bitter
compulsive necessity of the spirits to live their lives over and over,
begetting image after image.

The entire poem, richer than its parts, relies on the persistent
reader's accumulated knowledge of Yeats's symbols. Very carefully
put together (note, for instance, that stanzas I and III present the
disdaining scene, triumph of architect and artisan; that, interwoven in them, stanzas II and IV present the purged and about-
to-be-purged spirits; and that stanza V, in defining the function of
the dancing place, accounts for the ordering action of the arts of
stanzas I and III in releasing stanzas II and IV's spirits from the
reincarnation cycles), the poem is most remarkable perhaps for
the sheer bulk of its repeated terms. "Image," "gong," "complexities," "fury," and "mire" genuinely shape the poem; and supple-
mentary repetition weaves it into a cohesive whole. Thirty-five of
the forty-five words of the last stanza, for instance, appear at least
twice in the poem, and three of the remaining ten words are

closely related to others used in earlier stanzas (*dancing* echoing *dance, bitter* echoing *embittered, beget* echoing *begotten*).

Though the reader is not likely to see the link unless it is pointed out, the initiating image that suggested "The Mother of God" to Yeats is also a product of his interest in Byzantium. "In 'The Mother of God,'" Yeats explains, "the words 'a fallen flare through the hollow of an ear' are, I am told, obscure. I had in my memory Byzantine mosaic pictures of the Annunciation, which show a line drawn from a star to the ear of the Virgin. She conceived of the Word, and therefore through the ear a star fell and was born." Echoing themes from "Wisdom" and "Leda and the Swan" and anticipating those of "A Nativity" (where the star and ear image is used again), the poem correlates the initiating star, the star of Bethelehem, and the fallen star of the Christ child to Mary's terror in the direct communion with God.

Christianity fascinated Yeats. Accepting all its miracles, he found only its rejection of the personal ultimately distasteful. For if he were to reject the personal, he would, Yeats felt, be rejecting the way of the artist, the only way open to him. Though more vacillation than that between the Christian and non-Christian mystic is involved in "Vacillation," that theme runs behind it.

Compounded from opposites, the poem defines its problem in the opening lines. Man runs his course between extremities (the opposed ends of *A Vision*'s double cones, birth and death, day and night, etc.), and he normally defines the end of the pattern as "death" or "remorse." Yet if this definition is accurate, how can one account for the sort of joy some men (those mentioned at the end of Part III) experience as they come "Proud, open-eyed and laughing to the tomb"?

Men who can face the tomb with open eyes are symbolists, Yeats makes clear in the second section; and to illustrate their approach to the world he presents us with a favorite symbol, the mystic tree. Sources for it are scattered through all of Yeats's reading, yet the *Mabinogion*, Frazer, and *The Orations of Julian* should be singled out as particularly important. Its most conspicuous early use is in Yeats's poem "The Two Trees." It is this symbol he referred to in his 1921 letter to Sturge Moore which had listed as "main symbols" "Sun and Moon (in all phases), Tower, Mask, Tree (Tree with Mask hanging on the trunk), Well." And it is worth noting that before he finishes this poem he works in every one of these symbols but Well.

Letting his symbolist artist hang the Mask of Attis on the Mabinogion tree of opposites, Yeats points out that that artist may not comprehend the forces which he has put to work (he may "know not what he knows") but of one thing he is certain: "he knows not grief."

Partially autobiographical, the progress of the poem is from Yeats's youth (the double tree with its imagery drawn from his early Celtic and occult studies), through early manhood (the third section's references to money-making and a "fortieth winter"), middle age (incidents that take place after his "fiftieth year had come and gone" in parts IV and V) and finally to his last years and the mature wisdom that they brought him (parts VII and VIII).

The third section reminds the reader that man must live in both of the areas in which he vacillates. Even the poet must "Get all the gold" that he can, must "Satisfy ambition," must ram the trivial days he has animated "with the sun." Yet he must get not only gold but silver as well. He must get sunlight and moonlight. He must meditate on the maxim that women love the idle man (the poet, the man of moonlight, the man of silver) though "their children need a rich estate," so that though he pack his trivial days with the sun he must not forget the fruits of the moon.

And at forty, freed from the luxurious foliage of green tree, he must test his work by calculating its value to other artists, men who come "laughing to the tomb."

The fourth stanza is based on an incident Yeats recapitulated in the "Anima Mundi" section of his *Per Amica Silentia Lunae*. (That long essay itself is, in many ways, the primary vast footnote that should be appended to "Vacillation" examining, as it does, the "Condition of Fire" in terms of a "mask plucked from the oak tree," a Mask Yeats goes on to equate to his "imagination of rhythmic body.") He remarks in the essay that he sometimes becomes unaccountably happy:

> Perhaps I am sitting in some crowded restaurant . . . I look at the strangers near as if I had known them all my life, and it seems strange that I cannot speak to them: everything fills me with affection, I have no longer any fears or any needs; I do not even remember that this happy mood must come to an end.

In the poem the real experience is linked to the burning tree: like the tree, his body "of a sudden blazed," and he seems both blessed and capable of blessing others.

Yet such revelations cannot be sustained, and in section V an opposed mood, another vacillation, is expressed. Sometimes the entire figure of the tree—both its green aspect (when "summer sunlight" gilds "Cloudy leafage of the sky") and its barren "intricacy" that "wintry moonlight" makes visible—is blotted out by "Responsibility," memories of past actions or inactions, guilty memories that make creative activity impossible.

These memories lead in turn to the doctrine enunciated in the sixth section's refrain: " 'Let all things pass away.' " Since the art-initiating symbol (the tree, here abstracted to the "branches of the night and day/ Where the gaudy moon is hung"—a variant of his central tree symbol that Yeats had first discovered, probably in Lévi or Mathers, early in his occult investigations) is ultimately rooted in "man's blood-sodden heart," song itself is as mortal as its maker who must finally assert: Let all things—even song itself —pass away. (Yet to believe this need not, as Yeats indicates in "Lapis Lazuli," prevent the artist from facing the mutable world with gay eyes. The artist, seeing the pattern of mutability, has seen the design of all things.)

The seventh section gives us the debate that the poem has moved toward. For if all things pass away, soul may be right in insisting that the artist should attempt escape from things of this world, that he should aspire to a heaven from which there will be no return, the heaven of Christian dogma or the place where the spirit who passes through the purgative fires of "Byzantium" may find a final resting place. Burned out in Isaiah's coal (*Isaiah* 6: 6-7), that spirit will be purified of that "complexity" of life which Yeats's golden bird of "Byzantium" had mocked; transformed by "the simplicity of fire," he will find ultimate salvation.

Yet his is not the artist's salvation. And *The Heart* realizes what the consequence of accepting it would be for the poet. In such a heaven he would be "Struck dumb." Homer chose, all poets choose, a different fire: that of passion. "What theme had Homer but original sin?" The celebration of complexity, of life on earth, of vacillation—this alone is the poet's lot. "Predestined," as Yeats announces in the last section, he must reject the way of the Catholic scholar Baron Friedrich von Hügel who in *The Mystical Element of Religion* had argued the Christian vision as the artist's. Though Christian faith might free him from the necessary vacillation of the artist, and though all the miracles seem genuine, Homer must be Yeats's example "and his unchrisened heart." Choosing the path of the artist, the symbol of the sword and the green tree, Yeats makes his farewell in this poem to the temptations of Heaven. Reincarnation will be his "predestined" poet's part, life his theme.

The five lyrics that follow "Vacillation" are all written out of this conviction and, though based on intimate details of Yeats's personal life, all support the reworking of A *Vision's* material that that poem represents. "Quarrel in Old Age" focuses, in spite of its title, not on his present quarrel with Maud Gonne but rather on the fact that everything that now lives "has lived," that her essential self, the "lonely thing/ That shone" before his eyes had hit on her (targeted), still survives "beyond the curtain/ Of distorting days" in its elemental sweetness and that there it still treads "like Spring." In "The Results of Thought" Yeats assigns

Lady Gregory and Mrs. Shakespear to the same old age that has distorted Maud Gonne's "wholesome strength." The horrible "images" that they have become through the weight of time's "filthy load" bear no relationship to the secret self each carries within her. His system, Yeats contends, lets him "summon back" all that each of those fine ladies had been. It allows him to do this by letting him see the essential correlation of "All things." And in "Gratitude to the Unknown Instructors" Yeats pays his debt to those spirits, "authors" of A *Vision*, who had first guided his wife's hand and later spoken through her lips.

More complex than these poems, "Remorse for Intemperate Speech" offers once more a miniature history of Yeats's career. Like an actor seeking popularity he had once "ranted" to the crowd (written his early popular poetry) but then, determined to change "the part" he played, he found "Fit audience" among his "betters" (Lady Gregory and her friends). Nevertheless, Ireland had maimed him. And as in "Vacillation" he is predestined in his poet's path. "A fanatic heart," in spite of all his efforts to shape his own life, determines his progress. "Stream and Sun at Glendalough," the product of a brief stay on the Wicklow chicken farm of Francis and Iseult Gonne Stuart, illustrates the behavior of that heart. Stream and sun make his heart seem gay, but the memory of "Some stupid thing" that he had done (his one-time foolish proposal to now-happily-married Iseult) distracts him from his joy. Nevertheless memory of that joy—as memory of that radiant moment in the "crowded London shop" in part IV of "Vacillation"—gives him a sense of rightness, a sense of relationship to spirits "Self-born, born anew." In spite of the trap of man's fleshy mantle, moments of perception link him to eternal things.

Altogether different in tone, the twenty-five lyrics that comprise *Words for Music Perhaps* represent on Yeats's part a deliberate earthiness. If the grand design of *The Winding Stair* presents, as I think it does, a final commitment to life after the vacillation that followed the rejection of *The Tower's* pessimism, these poems are intended to mark in the reader's mind Yeats's final direction.

Yeats started work on them in Rapallo just as the winter snows of 1929 began to melt: "Now we are thawing," he wrote Mrs. Shakespear, "I am writing *Twelve poems for music*—have done three of them (and two other poems)—no[t] so much that they may be sung as that I may define their kind of emotion to myself. I want them to be all emotion and all impersonal . . . They are the opposite of my recent work and all praise of joyous life."

By the end of March he had finished six more—"unlike my past work—wilder and perhaps slighter." Though he felt several of them were "lucky," he was concerned that perhaps they had come too easily: "I am full of doubt. I am writing more easily than I ever wrote and I am happy, whereas I have always been unhappy when I wrote and worked with great difficulty. . . . If this new work do not seem as good as the old to my friends then I can take to some lesser task and live very contentedly." The poems continued to come easily all through the summer, and by September he was planning a series of thirty. Then Malta fever struck him, and when he recovered enough to write he set aside the series to work on *The Words upon the Window-Pane*. Not until fall of 1931 did he return to *Words for Music Perhaps*, but by then he was much more sure of himself. He especially liked the Crazy Jane group and he set about revising and adding to it. On November 23, he wrote Mrs. Shakespear to tell her that he had added another poem to that series. "Crazy Jane," he went on to explain, "is more or less founded upon an old woman who lives in a little cottage near Gort."

> She loves her flower-garden—she has just sent Lady Gregory some flowers in spite of the season—and [has] an amazing power of audacious speech. One of her great performances is a description of how the meanness of a Gort shopkeeper's wife over the price of a glass of porter made her so despair of the human race that she got drunk. The incidents of that drunkenness are of an epic magnificence. She is the local satirist and a really terrible one.

But long before, as early as 1904 in his notes to *Plays for an Irish Theatre,* Yeats had mentioned "an old woman known as Cracked Mary" and assigned her as the source for *The Pot of Broth's* song that refers to "poor Jack the journeyman." Whatever her origins, she came to assume increasing importance to Yeats, ultimately so monopolizing his interest that he declared, in a letter to his wife, "I want to exorcise that slut, Crazy Jane, whose language has become unendurable." But when the full text of *The Winding Stair* was in print she was still attractive ("I approve of her," he wrote Mrs. Shakespear) and he found the poems about her "exciting and strange." An old man's poems of passion, they became models for the remarkable sexuality he was to cram into his last verse: "Sexual abstinence fed their fire—I was ill yet full of desire," he wrote Mrs. Shakespear. "They sometimes came out of the greatest mental excitement I am capable of."

Certainly "Crazy Jane and the Bishop" relies for its strength on both imagery and subject matter which are explicitly phallic (Jack, before he had Crazy Jane's virginity, had stood like "a birch-tree"). But its greatest success is perhaps in the economy of its characterization. The hunchback Bishop (hunchbacks are among *A Vision's* "terrible" characters who, Yeats observes, are "multiple" men frequently fascinated with sin, themselves sterile, deformed, and malicious) has grown to be the coxcomb he had once accused Jack of being. Birch-tree Jack, on the other hand, though condemned and banished by the once-solid man now grown flabby, wanders a ghost (a remarkably potent one) in the night. And Crazy Jane, long since having abandoned the Bishop's hypocritical faith (his Bible, in her eyes, "an old book in his fist") calls down elemental curses beneath witchcraft's favorite tree, the blasted oak. (The blasted oak is, of course, an ironic comment on the fallen no-longer-"solid" Bishop; but we should bear in mind also that in its anti-Christian aspect it will shelter Jack and Crazy Jane.)

"Crazy Jane Reproved" seems to represent the arguments that the Bishop might have used back in those days when he was a young man, "Nor so much as parish priest," who told Crazy Jane that she and Jack lived "like beast and beast." If this reading is correct, Yeats probably saw the drama behind the poems in something of this light: Crazy Jane was loved by the young theological student who grew up to be the Bishop and by Jack the Journeyman. The Bishop-to-be saw to it that Jack was banished; but Jack, who had her body, had also her own true love. She consequently remained, in spirit at least, faithful to Jack. Whenever the Bishop arrives, she spits. "Crazy Jane Reproved" would, in this reading, represent the defense of the spiritual lover against the claims of things physical. All violence, for him, would be of no more significance than the yawns of Heaven. In accepting a bull (or a bull-like God) rather than a delicate lover, Europa played the fool. Offering the intellectual's pursuits (rounding the shell's elaborate whorl) rather than the physical passions of a bull-like "roaring, ranting journeyman," he manages in the refrain to seem only trivial: "Fol de rol, fol de rol."

"Crazy Jane on the Day of Judgment" continues this dialogue and might as easily be titled "The Bishop Reproved," for in it Crazy Jane points out, as Yeats's later lovers frequently do, that love must include both body and soul. Either body or soul by itself leaves love unsatisfied. With world enough and time, she seems to be saying in the last stanza, "true love"—love that encompasses body and soul—could really be shown. The day of judgment would prove her right.

"Crazy Jane and Jack the Journeyman" dips back to the passionate moments shared by the true lovers. Yeats tells a little of its genesis in a letter to Mrs. Shakespear. He had gone for a walk after dark and, in walking, began thinking of "the most lofty philosophical conception" he had found in working on A *Vision*. Suddenly he seemed to understand everything, "the nature of the timeless spirit." And as he walked and grew excited there arrived "that old glow so beautiful with its autumnal tint. The longing to touch it was almost unendurable. The next night I was walking in the same path and now the two excitements came together. The autumnal image, remote, incredibly spiritual, erect, delicate featured, and mixed with it the violent physical image, the black mass of Eden. Yesterday I put my thoughts into a poem which I enclose, but it seems to me a poor shadow of the intensity of the experience." That the poem represents some reflection of an experience shared by Yeats and Mrs. Shakespear seems obvious, but Yeats is not Jack the Journeyman, and Mrs. Shakespear is certainly not Crazy Jane, and we must steer clear of a strictly autobiographical interpretation.

A mixture of the experience of love and the perception of divine order, the poem—in context—represents Crazy Jane's realization that love's pattern is that of the gyre (here "a skein unwound" between dark and dawn). The "lonely ghost"—the one who does not experience love—can come to God. But lovers—Crazy Jane among them—experience the dreaming-back process Yeats outlined in *A Vision* and illustrated in "Shepherd and Goatherd." Dead, she will "leap into the light lost/ In [her] mother's womb." (After the dreaming-back process, according to Yeats, lovers' ghosts walk the earth seeking each other.) The tangle of tenses in the last stanza seems to say: Even if he were to leave me, the initial relationship formed when he first looked at me "that night" has so bound our destinies together ("The skein so bound us ghost to ghost") that my ghost must walk when I die (rather than go to God, to whom "single" ghosts ascend). We know, of course, from the first poem of the set that Jack's ghost is doomed to walk the earth.

"Crazy Jane on God" visualizes God as a repository of all archetypes (the *Anima Mundi* of Yeats's essays). Since He contains all forms and all events, He is timeless. Nothing, therefore, is ever really lost. The second stanza's battle (probably Thermopylae) never ends, though on earth it is long since finished. The third stanza ghostly manifestation that appears to Crazy Jane and wild Jack is admittedly unnatural and, therefore, Yeats would argue, a proof of the supernatural. The house that had one time been inhabited, still peopled by the ghosts that had lived in it, survives in *Anima Mundi* and can, when circumstances are right, be revitalized for a moment before human eyes. So in the last stanza, wild Jack is not lost even though dead. He is still her lover, though men use Crazy Jane's body as they use a road: "All things remain in God."

"Crazy Jane talks with the Bishop" returns once more to the theme of "Crazy Jane on the Day of Judgment," a theme Yeats will rework later in "The Three Bushes" and the related lyrics from *Last Poems*. The Bishop, still preaching soul rather than body, warns her that now she is old she should prepare for "a heavenly mansion" rather than a "foul sty." In good Shakespearean fashion, she responds that " 'Fair and foul are near of kin,/ And fair needs foul.' " Illustrating her thesis in the last stanza, she points out that no matter how proud the fair lady intent on love may be, " 'Love has pitched his mansion in/ The place of excrement.' " and consequently (and she puns on *soul* and *hole*) " 'nothing can be sole or whole/ That has not been rent.' " Only in experiencing *everything*, fair and foul, can the soul be made whole. Only by being torn can it ultimately be made "sole."

"Crazy Jane grown old looks at the Dancers," like much of Yeats's work, had its origins in a dream. "Last night," he wrote Mrs. Shakespear on March 2, 1929,

I saw in a dream strange ragged excited people singing in a crowd. The most visible were a man and woman who were I think dancing. The man was swinging round his head a weight at the end of a rope or leather thong, and I knew that he did not know whether he would strike her dead or not, and both had their eyes fixed on each other, and both sang their love for one another. I suppose it was Blake's old thought 'sexual love is founded upon spiritual hate' —I will probably find I have written it in a poem in a few days— though my remembering my dream may prevent that—by making my criticism work upon it.

Though his criticism seems to have operated on the last stanza, the theme of the first two seems identical to his dream-interpretation. The last stanza, examining the "reality" of such figures—the "ivory image" and her "chosen youth," ghostly dream-dancers—concludes that whether either, neither, or both of them died or seemed to die, the reality of the passion they symbolized is eternal: *"Love is like the lion's tooth."*

Yeats delighted in balance. Having devoted seven poems to Crazy Jane's earthy sensuality, he countered them with seven poems that celebrate the young idealistic love of a Romeo-and-Juliet pair of innocents. The girl and her starry-eyed lover dream of undying love in the face of a world of time and change which constantly intrudes on them. In "Girl's Song," the girl bursts into tears when, expecting to see her lover, she sees instead an old man who, presumably, reminds her that some day her lover will walk with a stick. Her question at the end of her song, however, is complicated. For she may have seen an old man young in heart or the oldness of a young man. Paralleling her horror vision, "Young Man's Song" presents her as someone who will change " 'Into a withered crone.' " Yet, as Yeats had asserted both in "Quarrel in Old Age" and "The Results of Thought," reality is not in appearance. In spite of flesh (the "fabric" of life, which fades), the essential self not only survives but antedates a mortal frame. Existing in its most beautiful state, " 'Before the world was made,' " the image in the lover's eyes—not the image on the photograph—represents reality. Though the lover's heart gives the lie to his initial assertion of the importance of flesh, "Her Anxiety" pleads for reaffirmation of love's truth. Offering an almost identical "lie" (that true love necessarily dies or at best alters into "some lesser thing"), she cries to her young man *"Prove that I lie"* (possibly punning on the last word).

"His Confidence," linked to "Her Anxiety" by rhyme (lie/buy), asserts as groundless her fears that "true love must die." The lover has (like Yeats himself) purchased "undying love" with a lifetime's devotion (the wrinkles at the corners of his eye). Returning once more for his image to "Quarrel in Old Age" in which he referred to his eyes that had "targeted" on Maud Gonne when he first saw her, Yeats shifts his arrow metaphor to that of a heart struck so hard it breaks in two. Rock, the "desolate source" of love, proves love to be undying.

"Love's Loneliness" returns to heartbreak and love's desolation. Rock looms to mountain, above it the moon's thin horn; the lovers, unlike those in A Man Young and Old, find not bliss but dread beneath the "ragged thorn." By all jagged things: mountain, the horn of the moon, the thorn—by love itself—their hearts are torn.

In spite of all their dread, however, dream comforts them. "Her Dream" associates her with the legend of Berenice whose hair, sacrificed for the safe return of her husband, had been immortalized in legend and astronomy as Coma Berenices. (Yeats had, of course, referred to it before in one of the two central images of "Veronica's Napkin.") "His Bargain" expands that image by linking it to "Plato's spindle," the unending cycles of Platonic years which spin like a gyroscope through eternity. In the complex image which Yeats finally constructs, Plato's spindle is the axle on which the gyre is wound. The whole ball (eternity) may dwindle as the thread (time) is unwound; but that, Yeats implies, is of little consequence. (The spindle-thread image is perhaps best visualized as a child's "yo-yo" which spins up and down a thread. As soon as it unwinds the thread, sheer inertia forces it to travel up the thread and so rewind it.) Ordinary men (Dan and Jerry Lout) exchange loves, seek out the variety that the shifting patterns of the gyres make possible to them both in their present lives and in their reincarnations. But the great lover —the "I" of the poem—has made an eternal commitment. Like the lover in Hafiz' Divan whose "bargain" ("I knew you before I was born, I made a bargain with this brown hair before the beginning of time and it shall not be broken through unending time") Yeats paraphrases, the girl's lover is unshakably fixed in his devotion. And if we take Plato's spindle to be the line extending through the axis of earth to the pole star round which Berenice's Hair and all the other constellations wind, what looks like a mixed metaphor at the end of the poem is discovered rather to be an elaborate one.

The seven Crazy Jane poems and the seven girl-and-lover poems represent extreme positions: songs of absolute experience and absolute innocence. The pair that follow them, "Three Things" and "Lullaby" represent "normal" love. "Three Things" assembles three kinds of pleasure that woman can get from love: the satisfaction she gets and gives in offering a child her breast (stanza I), the satisfaction she gets and gives in offering a lover her body (stanza II) and the satisfaction she gets from deceiving her husband, yawning in his face after a night with her lover (stanza III). "Lullaby" seems at first to be reworking the same material, with the lady in the first stanza noting that two radically different kinds of love can be satisfied by a woman's breast. But the strange appearance of Leda in the third stanza deepens the irony, and Yeats rearranges the scene he had constructed in "Leda and the Swan" to make that irony obvious to any careful reader. For Leda in the revised version experiences the double nature of love also, resting Zeus's swan head on her breast after their passion, as she will later rest the fruit of their passion, Helen, on her breast in maternal love. And Helen (the poem rounds carefully to its first stanza) will in turn cradle Paris' head on her breast as her mother had Zeus's. Though of small consequence in this poem, it is perhaps worth noting for those interested in Yeats's system, that Zeus in mating with Leda accomplishes "his predestined will." That he should will to mate with her is predestined (all things ultimately are determined by the system's pattern), but such predestination can only be accomplished through the free will of man who chooses the fate that is determined for him. Yeats worried about this problem for years, solving it tentatively by constructing the elaborate scheme of A *Vision's* True and False *Mask* and True and False *Creative Mind.*

Perhaps nothing can be said about the moving eloquence of "After Long Silence." Written for Mrs. Shakespear, the poem's precise statement of man's ironic anguish—impotent wisdom succeeding youth's ignorant passion—is an achievement that is both untranslatable and accurate.

Linked to "After Long Silence," which had drawn a curtain upon the "unfriendly night" of winter and old age, "Mad as the Mist and Snow" would bar the "foul winds" of such a winter out. But winds are a symbol of passion, and passion was a crucial experience not only for young Yeats but as well for all the classical authors who line his artifically-heated study. Like the "old friend" of the last stanza (probably Ezra Pound, since the poem was written in Rapallo) Yeats has aged into a time when wind makes him shudder, not with love's passion but the passion bred of impotence, the winter cold of age which looks back with tangled emotion on "mad" youth.

Quoting directly from Pound's *Cantos* ("the sun in a golden cup"), Yeats extends in "Those Dancing Days are Gone" the themes he has been working with in "After Long Silence" and "Mad as the Mist and Snow." Once more he draws on the opposed images of dancer and scarecrow, this time concluding that the one advantage of the aging poet is his freedom to tell truth. Yet truth, as Yeats knows, is a mysterious thing. And though he can speak directly to an unidentified "you" in the second stanza about the dead knave who had been her lover and the dead children they had begotten, the real truth he would sing, "whether to maid or hag," is that truth which can be contained in metaphor alone. The sun and moon he, as poet, carries in golden cup and silver bag are talismans against time. The symbolic truth they help him articulate frees him not only from time's tyranny but as well from otherwise ruinous unrequited love.

" 'I am of Ireland,' " compounded from Yeats's adaptation of a fourteenth-century lyric that he had once heard Frank O'Connor recite and a now-deleted passage from the third scene of the original *Countess Kathleen*, shows no traces of its mixed ancestry. The voice from Ireland's past—the voice of Cathleen ni Houlihan herself perhaps—calling to the "one man alone" of modern times who could hear it pleads for a dance. But "the Holy Land of

Ireland" is "a long way off" from modern Ireland, the night—as all of the poems of this part of *Words for Music Perhaps* insist —"grows rough," and modern musicians create no music for dancing. But the dance may still take place. For time (not only clock time but musical time as well) runs on. This is a fact that both the voice from the past and modern man can agree on; and so long as time is somehow kept, the dance is possible.

If "Those Dancing Days are Gone" and " 'I Am of Ireland' " seem to reject the dance while at the same time creating it, "The Dancer at Cruachan and Cro-Patrick" asserts the reality of both dance and dancer. In this poem the dancer is St. Cruchan. Yeats, forgetting his name in his *Essays, 1931 to 1936,* celebrated him in prose and verse as the saint who had sung hymns in praise of "Him" (presumably Christ) as a man who had achieved animal perfection.

The vision of perfection as the form behind all the transitory forms in a mutable world is anticipated in this poem and is the subject of the four poems which bring *Words for Music Perhaps* to an end.

Making the speaker of three of them "old Tom the Lunatic," Yeats rounds the entire group by returning to a masculine counterpart of Crazy Jane. For like Crazy Jane, "Tom the Lunatic," though momentarily blinded by age, though momentarily accepting imagery of death (seeing the title song's second stanza figures "in a shroud"), penetrates the deceptive flesh to see beyond it an imperishable reality. Everything, as he points out in the last stanza, whether fish, flesh, or foul, whether male or female, "Stands in God's unchanging eye/ In all the vigour of its blood." Time changes all things, but the essence of all things—the vital principle, the "power" of all things (the image is charged with sexuality) —"stands." Founded on both of the poems which precede it, "Tom at Cruachan" refers back to St. Cruchan's vision of animal perfection and draws its dominant image of mare and stallion from "Tom the Lunatic." St. Cruchan's song is now to be an immense metaphor for the conception both of Christ and of the world: " 'The stallion Eternity/ Mounted the mare of Time,/ 'Gat the foal of the world.' " And the metaphor will account for the double nature of man which has troubled old Tom in "Tom the Lunatic." For man is both perishable and imperishable, a creature compounded from Time and from Eternity, a dying indestructible thing. "Things," Yeats reasserts in "Old Tom Again," are not created in an earthly "building-yard" but rather "out of perfection sail." The "self-begotten" Platonic images which initiate form do not fail, in spite of the fact that "fantastic men" (materialists) assume that death ends man's career. Both an earthly beginning and an earthly end, Yeats's metaphor asserts, are illusory.

If "Old Tom Again" offers things sailing out of perfection into the seas of mortality, "The Delphic Oracle upon Plotinus" presents Plotinus, "Buffeted by such seas," attempting to catch a glimpse of the Golden Race where on the eternal shore they stand beckoning him on. Trapped as he is in mortal fluids (which in turn are trapped in him), "Salt blood blocks his eyes." But dimly, at least, he sees the immortal souls who—like him—had visualized perfection while still in flesh. Constructing his "plot" from a passage of the *Oracle* of Apollo which he had seen translated in Porphyry's "Life of Plotinus," a commentary on a different translation of that poem by G. R. S. Mead (at one time Secretary of the Theosophical Society) and probably—as T. R. Henn has noted —Henry More's "The Oracle," Yeats welds into ten compact lines ideas suggested to him by Porphery's essay "The Cave of the Nymphs" and a great deal of other occult and neo-Platonic reading. Optimistic, cheerful, as impersonal as Yeats wished the entire set to be, "The Delphic Oracle upon Plotinus" links the two different worlds symbolized and seen by Crazy Jane and the infatuated idealistic couple whose poems follow hers. Breasting mundane seas, Plotinus narrows the gap between the world's reality and the golden dimly-perceived supernatural reality that hovers for Yeats faintly, alluringly, at the distant limits of vision.

Though they were in date of composition among the earliest poems in *The Winding Stair*, Yeats placed at the end of that

volume the group titled A *Woman Young and Old*, probably in
an effort to make the refutation of *The Tower* and its parallel
series, A *Man Young and Old*, obvious to his reader.

The poems in A *Woman Young and Old* progress in strict
chronology from the woman's childhood in "Father and Child"
to her suggested death in "From the 'Antigone.'"

"Father and Child" presents her as innocent coquette. Based on
a remark of Yeats's daughter (paraphrased in the last two lines),
the poem is intended to report the child's first impression of masculine beauty. "Before the World was made," similar in title and
theme to material in "Young Man's Song" and "His Bargain,"
makes her a little older—say, late in her teens—and sets her experimenting with make-up before her mirror. Trying to construct
a Mask for her ideal self, she sees love as deception—an art—that
might lure her lover to fall in love with the woman she imagines
herself to be. "A First Confession," which Yeats described to Mrs.
Shakespear as "an innocent little song," ages the girl only slightly,
since it is set immediately after the affair for which the girl has
prepared herself in "Before the World was made." Though she
has successfully flirted, she is pleased not so much with the sexual
experience as with the lover's "attention." Seeking in the Zodiac
for the "truth" she cannot find on earth (an image developed in
poem VI of the series), she fears that "empty night" might reveal
something of her own emptiness. "Her Triumph" recapitulates
both that emptiness and defines the corruption inherent in her
casual approach to love. She has done "the dragon's will." But
now a true lover has appeared who, standing "among the dragon-
rings" like a Saint George or Perseus frees her from her own evil
nature. Though she mocks, he masters her mockery; and nature is
revealed in all its symbolic glory to the transformed pair. (They
stare "astonished at the sea" and hear "a miraculous strange bird"
shriek at them. The shriek of that bird links, of course, to the
woman who in A *Man Young and Old* shrieks with ecstasy when
she first experiences love and to the man in the same series who
does not shriek.)

"Consolation," echoing Sophocles, is the first of two poems which explore the kind of wisdom lovers alone can achieve. The last lines, which make the poem—as Yeats notes—"not so innocent," become an ironic commentary on the woman's realization that her experience of passion could never have been as intense as it was if she had not first been devout. (Conscious of parallels between Eve's original sin and her own, she assures the sages that the place in which mortality begins is the place where mortality —through lovers' ecstasies—can be forgotten.) "Chosen," more complex, presents the second of her insights into love's wisdom. Originally an experimental immitation both of the meter and the metaphoric structure of Donne's "Nocturnall upon St. Lucie's Day," the poem defines the "utmost pleasure" of love as that moment of stillness when for an instant—at Yeats's favorite moment of perception, daybreak—true interpenetration of personality seems really to take place, "his heart my heart did seem," and the universe becomes momentarily coherent, the Zodiac changed miraculously into the symbol of perfection, the sphere. This imagery seems, perhaps, more difficult than it really is. The lover moves like a sun through the figures of the Zodiac and at the same time like a naturalistic sun around the earth-mother beloved. (He touches her body with his fire, sinks in the west, rests on the "maternal midnight" of her breast, and rises at that daybreak which will once again separate them. Daybreak is therefore a thing of "horror," but it also gives the lovers the instant of stillness in which both together seem to float on the "miraculous stream" of the milky way at precisely that point of intersection with the Zodiac which, according to Macrobius, transforms the normal spiral pattern of reincarnating existence into the sphere of transcendental perfection.)

"Her Triumph" has brought the lovers together, "Consolation" has sent them to bed, "Chosen" has given the woman—through love's stillness—an instant of insight into the nature of the perfected soul and an experience of perfect communion. "Parting," as its title suggests, takes place immediately after the daybreak moment of illumination that had been the subject of the second stanza of "Chosen." The lovers are to part, and Yeats appropriately selects dialogue as the clearest indication to the reader that interpenetration has been replaced by isolation. Echoing *Romeo and Juliet,* Yeats drives daylight and man's daylight world between the lovers. In spite of all the attractions of the lady's "dark declivities," the lover—day's man—must rise to shining isolation.

"Her Vision in the Wood," the first of the three "old" poems, can best be understood if one bears in mind the last stanza's assertion that the visionary troop had in their invocation to the slain body of Adonis conjured up in the secret wood "no fabulous symbol" but rather both the lady herself and her "heart's victim." They had unintentionally called her to the sacred spot to be a witness to the symbolic death of torn Adonis; and she, by the symbolic wound she has given herself, is able to participate in the ritual. But the Adonis proves to be her own lover. As she, "Too old for a man's love," wounded by her own nails and so like the visionary lover "blood-bedabbled," stares into the drying "glazing eye" of "That thing all blood and mire, that beast-torn wreck," "love's bitter-sweet" floods back over both of their bodies. Each wounded yet loved by the other, each made impotent—she by the "dry timber" of age and he by the boar's wound—the ancient lovers are nevertheless momentarily revitalized by the blood which flows down their loins. (Yeats is careful in lines 8 and 9 that there can be no doubt about the place in which the lady wounds herself.) But the moment of interpenetrating eyes is all they have. The Adonis-lover dies. She falls, shrieking, to earth.

Yet Adonis is a fertility god. He will survive his wound to be reborn both on earth and in the supernatural world of the gods. He will survive the grave. Something of that survival is defined in "A Last Confession," the ninth song of the series, a song concerned—as is the ninth song of *A Man Young and Old*—with "The Secrets of the Old." After recapitulating the "plot" of the series, the "misery" caused by her true lover (the one she had loved with her soul and whom she had visualized as Adonis in "Her

Vision in the Wood") and the bodily pleasure she had found with the inconsequential lover of her youth, the old woman goes on to spell out one of Yeats's favorite doctrines. Once she and her true lover are out of the body, that true lover, the man who had given her misery, the man who had parted from her at dawn and whom she had loved with her soul, will return to her and the two love-making spirits will "Close and cling so tight,/ There's not a bird of day that dare/ Extinguish that delight." Using the "bird of day" that had divided the true lovers in "Parting" to remind his readers of the imagistic structure of the series, Yeats focuses their interest on the vision of flame-like supernatural passion. Disembodied spirits, he had remarked in *Per Amica Silentia Lunae*, ". . . are moved by emotions sweet for no imagined good but in themselves . . . and I do not doubt that they make love in that union which Swedenborg has said is of the whole body and seems from far off an incandescence." This reference to the passage from Swedenborg is to Yeats of obsessive importance. He returns to it again and again. In a late letter to Mrs. Shakespear, for instance, he speaks of "that saying of Swedenborg's that the sexual intercourse of the angels is a conflagration of the whole being," and it was exactly this sort of conflagration that he felt he had found in some of the Japanese Nōh plays and that he was in part attempting to symbolize in his play *Purgatory*. Here the true lovers achieve that phoenix-like flame, a flame brighter than day, a flame no bird of day would dare, or for that matter could, extinguish.

"Meeting" describes their last earthly confrontation, each hating the other's ugliness and his own. Spirits hidden by old age's "masker's cloak," they now wear Masks altogether different from that which the woman had tried on in "Before the World was Made." Like that of "Crazy Jane grown old . . ." their love has transformed to hatred. Yet beneath the "beggarly habiliment" of flesh is supernatural reality's "sweeter word."

As death of the tragic hero had brought to final focus *A Man Young and Old*, death of the tragic heroine brings to focus *A Woman Young and Old*, and the passage "From the 'Antigone' " ends appropriately in song and prayer. "Love's bitter-sweet" had been, as "Her Vision in the Wood" indicated, the single meaningful experience of the woman's life. But such is not just this woman's experience; it is the experience of all women and all men. It is the essential characteristic of life itself which death always tragically overcomes. Translating Sophocles, Yeats affirms, as he had in *The Tower*, life's bitterness; but, setting life against death, he reminds us, as had Sophocles, of its sweetness as well. "Overcome—O bitter sweetness," both poets begin and they end—as poets must—with prayer and song, their heroines descending "into the loveless dust."

12 * From 'A Full Moon in March'

Unlike those in *The Tower* and *The Winding Stair*, the poems collected in *From 'A Full Moon in March'* never satisfied Yeats as a totality. He liked particular poems, but he was unhappy with the book they shaped into. "I don't like it—" he wrote Dorothy Wellesley, "it is a fragment of the past I had to get rid of."

Not that he hadn't struggled with the poems. Each one of the ones that had been written before *Supernatural Songs* represented a painfully hard birth. After Lady Gregory's death he had felt "barren": "I had nothing in my head . . . Perhaps Coole Park where I had escaped from politics, from all that Dublin talked of, when it was shut, shut me out from my theme; or did the sub-conscious drama that was my imaginative life end with its owner? but it was more likely that I had grown too old for poetry." Deciding that he had to force himself to write, he turned notes he had used on an American lecture tour into "Parnell's Funeral"

and wrote the prose draft of *The King of the Great Clock Tower*
"that I might be forced to make lyrics for its imaginary people."
But he doubted the quality of his work and started a short tour
of literary friends in the hopes of getting helpful criticism. Unfortunately, Ezra Pound, the first man whom he consulted, volunteered nothing more than a one-word opinion: "Putrid." Yeats
nevertheless plodded ahead, reworking poems he was dissatisfied
with, searching through his plays for lyrics that could be improved,
trying earnestly to beat back the sterility which he felt had over-
taken him.

By the spring of 1934, however, Yeats, convinced that it was
literal sterility that accounted both for his physical ailments and
the drying up of his muse, submitted himself to the Steinach
operation. Whether thanks to monkey glands or more metaphysical promptings, he experienced a sudden burst of creativity that
barely flagged until the time of his death. He wrote the *Supernatural Songs* in great excitement, tacking them onto the random
collection that constituted his sister's Cuala Press edition of *The
King of the Great Clock Tower* after that edition was already in
the press. As soon as it was in print, he set about rearranging the
songs and turning the prose version of *The King of the Great
Clock Tower* into verse and then, still dissatisfied, started fresh
and reworked the material of that play into *A Full Moon in
March*, which he also promptly saw into print. Both of these editions contained groupings of the lyrics that survive as *From 'A
Full Moon in March.'*

In these years, 1934 and 1935, Yeats was conscious of a growing
desperation: there might not be time to create the great design.
He almost literally shoved the lyrics of the *Full Moon in March*
volume out of the way in order to get on with fresh material as
soon as, at the end of 1935, he saw a plan for the final phase of
his work taking shape. With luck, he must have felt, he could fit—
as he had always fitted in the past—the recalcitrant lyrics into
what would become a more coherent organization of material. He
almost, in fact, managed it. But time ran out on him. Or perhaps

he concluded, as he was going over the proof sheets for that Definitive Edition which would put his poems in final form—his death only days away—that the very fragmentation of *From 'A Full Moon in March'* was, after all, an essential part of the design—a disorder from which the last sweet song would rise triumphant.

Disorder, certainly, is its subject matter. The opening poem, "Parnell's Funeral," is founded on it. Yeats felt that Ireland had, perhaps more violently than the rest of the modern world, entered the final phases on his visionary wheel. Anarchy, the rule of mob, was riding high. Strangers—foreigners—had been responsible for the deaths of Emmet, Fitzgerald, and Tone; but an Irish mob, "popular rage," had dragged down Parnell. Repudiating at the end of the first part his whole association with democracy, Yeats attacks the "lie/Bred out of the contagion of the throng" that had become the modern Irish state.

Only Parnell, he maintains in the second part, had had the hero's strength of character to resist the mob. Had de Valéra "eaten Parnell's heart" and so gained his strength, a real leader rather than a "loose-lipped demagogue" would have been at the head of the state. (Yeats later qualified his opinion of de Valéra, seeing him as a man helpless against the destructive force of democracy.) Had Cosgrove really ruled, Yeats's friend O'Higgins might have escaped murder. Even General O'Duffy—the would-be fascist leader whose Blue Shirt movement Yeats briefly supported—might, granted Parnell's character—have made a good leader. But the isolated man, the hero, the man who accepts in his solitude the "bitter wisdom" mob-hating Jonathan Swift had articulated, is necessarily in our day destroyed.

Yeats symbolizes that destruction in the difficult image that begins the poem—the falling star that had, Maud Gonne told Yeats, flashed out of the sky in broad daylight as Parnell's body was being lowered into his grave near the "Great Comedian's Tomb" (O'Connell, whom Yeats contrasts to "tragedian Parnell" in the notes he had written for the first printing of the poem). Linking that falling star to the "archer" coins he had read about in S. W. Grose's *Catalogue of Greek Coins in the Fitzwilliam Museum, Cambridge,* Yeats does his best to establish the death of Parnell as an event of cosmic importance, a Heaven-ordained sacrifice similar to that of the other fallen star of his poetry, Christ; the death of Parnell therefore becomes the symbolic death that announces the transformation of an era, the moment when "An age is the reversal of an age." (The best commentary on that archer image, incidentally, is Yeats's own in the notes that are printed at the end of the *Autobiography*.)

"Three Songs to the Same Tune" was written as the result of his brief flirtation with General O'Duffy's Blue Shirt movement. Discouraged by his difficulties in founding the Irish Academy of Letters and by the Abbey Theatre's continuing difficulties of its own, Yeats had become convinced that the sacrifices that had brought the Free State into existence had been wasted. The kind of democracy that resulted had not achieved the "Unity of Culture" of which he had dreamed; instead, a mob which actively despised culture seemed to be in power, tying the hands of a helpless government. "The mob reigned," Yeats noted at the time. "If that reign is not broken our public life will move from violence to violence, or from violence to apathy, our Parliament disgrace and debauch those who enter it; our men of letters live like outlaws in their own country." Writing his "trivial songs" for the "marching men" who might come to overthrow the mob, Yeats, carried away with enthusiasm, volunteered as well "what remains to me of life."

But General O'Duffy's rebellion soon proved, Yeats felt, more comic than heroic. Six months later, by the time the second edition of his book was ready for the press, he had decided O'Duffy's cause was a lost one and he rewrote the songs: "I increased their fantasy, their extravagance, their obscurity, that no party might sing them." Reworked a third time, they stand in their final form in *Last Poems*. More interesting as technical experiments in the use of refrain than as finished poems, the versions in *From 'A Full Moon in March'* give the reader unacquainted with Yeats's extravagant revision an opportunity to compare drafts with those in the later collection.

Two of the three songs from plays that follow also demonstrate Yeats's interest in the contrapuntal effect of refrain, the "Alter native Song for the Severed Head in 'The King of the Great Clock Tower,'" for instance, tolling off to the tune of the Great Clock Tower's "slow low note" a roll call of the heroic Irish characters from Yeats's plays and poems: Cuchulain; Niamh, who had guided Oisin across the sea in *The Wanderings of Oisin*; Naoise and Deirdre in *Deirdre* who had played chess as they awaited Conchubar's fatal arrival; Aleel and his Countess from *Countess Cathleen*; Hanrahan, the wild hero from Yeats's early stories; and the feather-haired king who had been hero of one of Yeats's early stories and who was to be the God in Yeats's then-unwritten *The Herne's Egg*. Like Yeats, who could not in these years forget the ticking "infernal machine" of time itself, these characters march to the strokes of "an iron bell."

"A Prayer for Old Age," one of the first poems Yeats worked on after his operation, represents a reaffirmation of an old doctrine: "He that sings a lasting song/ Thinks in a marrow-bone." Returning to the Mask of the wise, wanton, fool, Yeats experiments once more with poetry of direct speech. But it is a Mask he constructs. He does not want to *be* "A foolish, passionate man" but rather to *"seem"* one.

"Church and State" is another "Matter for old age meet," and is a product of Yeats's final disillusionment with O'Duffy. Originally printing the song immediately after his note dissociating himself from the Blue Shirts, Yeats intended the poem to be taken as his final rejection of all political activity. Paraphrased, its theme is simple: I had dreamed of a glorious rebellion against the mobs with Church and State at last triumphant. But "That were a cowardly song," for the Church and the State might very well themselves be "the mob that howls at the door!" Rebellion would consequently be meaningless; all it would accomplish would be a change in mob.]

Closer to his heart, the *Supernatural Songs* consider once more the hoops, rings, circles, and coils by which "Natural and supernatural . . . are wed." Ribh, whom Yeats makes his speaker, is supposed to be an early Christian hermit who, "were it not for his ideas about the Trinity," would be, in Yeats's eyes, "an orthodox man." But what for Yeats is orthodox is not so for everybody, and Yeats later added a prefatory note explaining that "The hermit Ribh in 'Supernatural Songs' is an imaginary critic of St. Patrick. His Christianity, come perhaps from Egypt like much early Irish Christianity, echoes pre-Christian thought."

Yeats uses the first poem of the set, "Ribh at the Tomb of Baile and Aillinn" to set the scene, to establish time and place, and to link themes developed more fully in other poems to these. Ribh, 90 years old, his career as a hermit suggested by "this tonsured head," sits in the "pitch-dark night" reading an open book. The darkness is important, for the "pitch-dark atmosphere" is impenetrable only to the "you" of the first line, the normal man who has not amalgamated "water, herb and solitary prayer" into the magic formula which enables Ribh to read by supernatural light. That light itself, like the inextinguishable light already commented on in "A Last Confession," is created by the incandescent "intercourse of angels" which Yeats had read about in Swedenborg and which, for him, made meaningful human love. "Why not take Swedenborg literally," he wrote Mrs. Shakespear nearly a year before he had begun work on *Supernatural Songs*, "and think we attain, in a partial contact, what the spirits know throughout their being. He somewhere describes two spirits meeting, and as they touch they become a single conflagration. His vision may be true, Newton's cannot be." For the purpose of Yeats's poem, the spirits are those of Baile and Aillinn, about whom he had written a poem in 1903, who "on the anniversary of their death" which is itself "The anniversary of their first embrace" meet, purified, above the symbolic trees under which they are buried. There the passionate spirits, interfused, produce the circle of magical light in which the old hermit reads his "holy book."

Miracles such as these, Yeats felt, would have enabled his early Christian to discover connections between Christianity and an earlier Platonic tradition. Ribh, in some ways Yeats's ideal Christian, sees no incongruity, therefore, in reading his breviary in the light given off by the very un-Christian lovemaking "angels" of Irish legend. His holy book, the magic he has studied, the ghostly lovers themselves are all miraculously joined in the supernatural.

The "juncture of the apple and the yew" may, in Yeats's mind, have in part symbolized this combination of traditions, the Biblical apple intertwined with the pagan yew. But such interwoven trees are favorites in folk lore, representing almost always the communion in death of life-separated lovers (in the poems grouped with "The Three Bushes" Yeats offers another treatment of the same image), and Yeats is here deliberately drawing on a folklore tradition.

The circle of light in which Ribh reads, however, is of both occult and neo-Platonic significance and is linked to the correlations of above and below spelled out in "Ribh denounces Patrick." For in that poem all circles are interlocked. Natural and supernatural are wed with the self-same ring: things below (as Hermes Trismegistus' Emerald Tablet pointed out) are copies of things above. If the lovemaking angels produce ideal light-emitting passion, lovers on earth—less successfully but, because they must copy those above, inevitably—create a similar "conflagration." But below—on earth—all things are incomplete. Unlike angelic Baile and Aillinn, earthly lovers are not in their little passions "lost, consumed." Rather the brief conflagrations they create are "damped" by flesh or mind. The serpent coils of the physical— those same coils that so beset Adam and Eve—are intertwined in mundane lovers' embraces. Though copies of ideal passions (and therefore sharing God), human loves are incapable of complete self-consuming fire and so must lead to "multiplicity," reproduction. "The point of the poem," Yeats wrote Mrs. Shakespear, "is that we beget and bear because of the incompleteness of our love."

Ribh denounces Patrick, of course, because the "masculine Trinity" Patrick worships is compounded of Father, Son, and Holy Ghost. Such a Trinity, violating Hermes' principle of natural and supernatural correlation, is in Ribh's eyes "an abstract Greek absurdity" since all other natural and supernatural Trinities include woman as an essential ingredient.

"Ribh in Ecstasy" is a kind of apology. "You," either the startled man who in the first poem had found Ribh reading in the dark or the mystified reader of the first two poems of the set, find Ribh's language obscure, a thing of "broken sentences." But there is every reason for the sentences to be broken. Caught up in the mystical vision of the intercourse of angels, the contemplation of those "amorous cries" that penetrated the physical world from the world of supernatural "quiet" and that announced the moment when "Godhead on Godhead in sexual spasm begot/ Godhead," Ribh had himself become inarticulate until, the "shadow" of reality again cloaking it, his soul once more resumed "the common round of day."

"There" assembles all the crucial mythological circles—"barrel-hoops," serpents with tails in their mouths, "gyres," and planet paths—into Yeats's image for the ultimate form of things. This image is the sphere. Sun, converging gyres, knit barrel-hoops—no matter what we visualize—resolve finally into a design of eternal coherence—of God—which in the world above ("There") contains all in its organic unity, a unity which opposes yet reflects what on earth is fragmented into "multiplicity."

"Ribh considers Christian Love insufficient" marks one of the paths by which those in the world—in Hermes' territory labeled "below"—can come to a knowledge of God. Pure love, as Ribh has demonstrated in the first three poems of the group, is of God and therefore incomprehensible to man. But hatred, necessarily impure, is well within the province of man's action. Through hatred one can "clear the soul." (It was this sort of hatred that

Yeats had found attractive in Swift.) Having hated all the impuri-
ties that characterize humanity, one can then go on to postulate
man free of corruption—man in a sinless state. At this stage a
"darker knowledge" becomes available. For all human perception
of God—because born of corrupt flesh—is necessarily inaccurate.
One must consequently hate any notion of God born of human
thought, for hatred is the device by which we can return to that
ignorance essential to the final mystical vision. All thought—especially thought of God—must be resolutely rejected: "Thought
is a garment and the soul's a bride/ That cannot in that trash
and tinsel hide." "At stroke of midnight" (one remembers Byzantium's crucial hour when the dolphin borne souls arrive for final
freedom from the cycles of reincarnation) soul is at last cleansed
through hatred of flesh and hatred of all ideas of God for the moment of fulfillment, the mystical moment that had been referred
to in "Ribh in Ecstasy" when Godhead descends to man and in
soul's blood God lives.

"He and She" examines the same moment in the by-now-familiar imagery of A Vision. "She" is the soul at the fifteenth
phase; purified of flesh, soul is now in active pursuit of the "scared
moon" (He). The "sweet cry" that arises from both dancers as
they trip ecstatically through the heavens "shivers" all creation;
for like the lovemaking angels, or like Godhead begetting Godhead "in sexual spasm" to the tune of "amorous cries," they have
reached the moment anticipated at the end of "Ribh considers
Christian Love insufficient," the instant of interpenetration between God and the soul, the moment of mystical ecstasy. Yeats,
who classed the poem as one "of a personal metaphysical sort
. . . on the soul," was careful to tell Mrs. Shakespear that "It is
of course my centric myth."

"What Magic Drum?" is deliberately ambiguous. Focusing on
the instant of that "sexual spasm" which has been so much Yeats's
concern in all these poems, it reminds us that Yeats has been
working not with one but rather with several different kinds of
spasms. Possibly describing the moment in Eden when the serpent

spoke to Eve, it can quite as well be taken as that moment when "Godhead begets Godhead," or that moment when "the mirror-scalèd serpent" twines her coil through mortal lovers' embraces, or the moment when "the serpent-tails are bit" and God begets himself on himself. Though all of these interpretations satisfy—the last satisfying me best—ultimately the poem must be taken as an achieved symbol: an object which represents one of those rings with which "natural and supernatural . . . are wed."

More explicitly spelling out correspondences, "Whence Had They Come?" links girl and boy to the Dramatis Personae above who lead them to cry "Eternity is passion," links the "passion-driven" man to those forces which lead him to sing out "Sentences that he has never thought," and links the passionate mob which had beaten down "frigid Rome" to supernatural models. But the conception of Charlemagne in the last line is of a different order. For here, as so often in Yeats's work, the hero is seen as born of a supernatural agency. A "sacred drama" was performed when "world-transforming Charlemagne was conceived." The God, as he had to Leda and to Mary, once more descended to alter human destiny.

"The Four Ages of Man" records the series of defeats administered to man as he progresses through life. Hatred of God ("his wars on God") here, as in "Ribh considers Christian Love insufficient," brings him at last to God's triumph. (Note how carefully Yeats uses the last line of "Four Ages" to send the reader back to line 19 of the "Christian Love" poem.) Something of the intellectual manipulation that went into Yeats's poetry can be seen in the letters to Mrs. Shakespear that culminated in this little lyric. On July 24, 1934, in a letter commenting on a book both of them had read, Yeats drew her attention to a symbolic structure involved in it:

Yes that book is important. Notice this symbolism

Waters under the earth⎫
      The Earth   ⎬ The bowels etc. *Instinct*

The Water = The blood and the sex organ.   *Passion*
The Air   = The lungs, logical thought   *Thought*
The Fire =   *Soul*

They are my four quarters. The Earth before 8, the Waters before 15, the Air before 22, the Fire before 1. (See A *Vision*, page 86.) Note that on page 85 of A *Vision* the conflict on which we now enter is 'against the Soul,' as in the quarter we have just left it was 'against the intellect.' The conflict is to restore the body.

Later in the same letter he expands his diagram:

The Earth = Every early nature-dominated civilization
The Water = An armed sexual age, chivalry, Froissart's chronicles
The Air   = From the Renaissance to the end of the 19th Century
The Fire = The purging away of our civilization by our hatred.

A day later Yeats hurried off another letter:

My dear Olivia, I muddled the explanation and the quotation from my own book. It is from page 35 (not 85) and it is there written that in the last quarter of a civilization (the quarter we have just entered,) the fight is against body and body should win. You can define soul as 'that which has value in itself,' or you can say of it 'it [is] that which we can only know through analogies.'

By August 7, Yeats had versified these ideas and sent a first draft of the poem to Mrs. Shakespear, adding, as he often did, a note of explanation:

They are the four ages of individual man, but they are also the four ages of civilization. You will find them in that book you have been reading. First age, *earth*, vegetative functions. Second age, *water*, blood, sex. Third age, *air*, breath, intellect. Fourth age, *fire*, soul etc. In the first two the moon comes to the full—resurrection of Christ and Dionysus. Man becomes rational, no longer driven from below or above.

The last three poems of the cycle turn more and more directly toward the design of A *Vision*, applying it first to historical figures, then to the stream of history, and finally to the significance of that historical stream.

"Conjunctions" came directly out of a set of correlations Yeats had hoped to find in his children. His daughter was to illustrate democratic, Christian, "objective" experience and his son aristocratic, pagan, "subjective" experience. Their horoscopes had been included in the automatic writing that became A *Vision*, and Yeats watched them eagerly, hoping to see appropriate signs develop. As soon as clues began to appear, he wrote the poem, enclosing it with an explanation in a letter to Mrs. Shakespear:

> I was told, you may remember, that my two children would be Mars conjunctive Venus, Saturn conjunctive Jupiter respectively; and so they were—Anne the Mars-Venus personality. Then I was told that they would develop so that I could study in them the alternating dispensations, the Christian or objective, then the Antithetical or subjective. The Christian is the Mars-Venus—it is democratic. The Jupiter-Saturn civilization is born free among the most cultivated, out of tradition, out of rule. . . . George said it is very strange but whereas Michael is always thinking about life Anne always thinks of death. Then I remembered that the children were the two dispensations. Anne collects skeletons. . . . Then she loves tragedies, has read all Shakespeare's, and a couple of weeks ago was searching reference books to learn all about the poison that killed Hamlet's father. When she grows up she will either have some passionate love affair or have some close friend that has—the old association of love and death. . . . When George spoke of Michael's preoccupation with Life as Anne's with death she may have subconsciously remembered that her spirits once spoke of the centric movement of phase I as the kiss of Life and the centric movement of phase 15 (full moon) as the kiss of Death.

Less complex, "A Needle's Eye" returns to the stream of history and one of Yeats's favorite images, that needle's eye that had seemed so significant in "Veronica's Napkin."

But it is in "Meru" that Yeats hoops together not only civilization and the pattern of history, but as well this group of circling poems. Reality as we know it, the whole record of human events, is no more than "manifold illusion" that creates "the semblance" of rule and order. Doomed to error, as Ribh had pointed out in "Ribh considers Christian Love insufficient," man nevertheless is a thinking animal who "despite his terror, cannot cease/ Ravening through century after century," both studying history and living it, always in search of some kind of final reality, "Ravening, raging, and uprooting that he may come/ Into the desolation of reality."

But that reality itself can never be found in things of the world. For that reason, Yeats has his Christian hermit turn not only from that which in his denunciation of Patrick had been described as "An abstract Greek absurdity" but as well from Egypt, to which he had earlier displayed loyalty: "Egypt and Greece, good-bye, and good-bye, Rome!" For all Western thought has been on the wrong track, he now argues. Final perception can come alone to the naked Indian hermit "upon Mount Meru or Everest" who, beaten night-long by "winter's dreadful blast" of snow accepts a last vision of pure cyclical activity, all man's relentless pursuit both of things and of wisdom finally meaningless. Only such men "know/ That day brings round the night, that before dawn/ His glory and his monuments are gone."

"The last kiss," Yeats once wrote Sturge Moore, "is given to the void." And perhaps in his investigations of Indian thought for his introductory essay to his friend Shri Purohit Swami's translation of Bhagwan Shri Hamsa's *The Holy Mountain* (the record of "initiation on Mount Kailās in Tibet") Yeats found the new matter which he had been seeking, the new clues to the essential nature of things, clues that made the void visible.

Pattern itself had always been the answer. But now the pattern revealed more complex form than his early investigations had anticipated: "Perhaps some early Christian—Bardaisan had speculations about the sun and moon nobody seems to have investigated

—thought as I do, saw in the changes of the moon all the cycles," Yeats wrote in *Wheels and Butterflies:*

. . . the soul realizing its separate being in the full moon, then, as the moon seems to approach the sun and dwindle away, all but realizing its absorption in God, only to whirl away once more: the mind of a man, separating itself from the common matrix, through childish imaginations, through struggle—Vico's heroic age—to roundness, completeness, and then externalising, intellectualising, systematising, until at last it lies dead, a spider smothered in its own web: the choice offered by the sages, either with the soul from the myth to union with the source of all, the breaking of the circle, or from the myth to reflection and the circle renewed for better or worse. For better or worse according to one's life, but never progress as we understand it, never the straight line, always a necessity to break away and destroy, or to sink in and forget.

If pattern itself is the final order, Yeats is through Ribh saying good-bye to more than Egypt, Greece, and Rome. Not only is he abandoning them, and the civilizations they have artificially hooped together. He is abandoning as well logical thought—such systems as they had created. The final perception is illogical, he asserts in these poems, the mystic's perception. Isolated on the mountain, he will find God in chaos to which, he seems at last to say, all order, all pattern, reduces itself. Still seeking pattern, he has moved beyond his early search for the design of an ordered universe. Now his vision is to be the design of essential universal disorder.

13 * Last Poems

If the pattern of the poems in *From 'A Full Moon in March'* is chaotic and seems to accept elemental chaos as its central image, the pattern of *Last Poems* swings one final time toward order. All things may be meaningless, Yeats in these verses seems to be asserting, but the man who comprehends the meaningless designs has achieved the most that can be accomplished in life. Having lifted himself to the vantage point of age (poem after poem sets the central character climbing, his goal some high point: a pair of stilts, "middle air," a mountain top), Yeats is able to form a final attitude. Though in seventy years, he reports in the little lyric "Imitated from the Japanese," ". . . never have I danced for joy," now joy is at last to be his. Not the lover's joy, the young man's fragile delight in spiritual communion. But rather the reckless joy of a "Wild Old Wicked Man" who, looking on all things with a careless eye, is free to enjoy them for themselves. Seeing the form of "The Gyres" from the height of his hard-won freedom, he is able to "laugh in tragic joy." Like the poets and tragic heroes praised in "Lapis Lazuli," he is able to discover "Gaiety transfiguring all that dread" and at last, like his imagined climbing Chinamen in that poem, to look out "On all the tragic scene" with "ancient, glittering eyes" that, mid many wrinkles, "are gay." His song, rounding in "Under Ben Bulben," the poem that was intended to end this final book—to return him once again to Sligo where his work had begun and to point a direction for the cold, laughing song of the future—lifts to praise of "Porter-drinkers' randy laughter" and "lords and ladies gay" who though "beaten into the clay" survived through "seven heroic centuries."

Yeats himself, however, during these extremely productive last three years of life was a man conscious of shortness of breath, sleeplessness, failing energy. Sure of a final attitude toward life and art, stocked—thanks in part to his new friend Dorothy Wellesley's aggressive correspondence and conversation—with an ample supply of poetic subjects, Yeats found only physical exhaustion an insurmountable enemy. Plans for the final shaping of his life and art were constantly before him. He wrote and revised at a furious pace, assembling 1938's *New Poems* for his sister's press while at the same time planning with Dorothy Wellesley a series of *Broadsides*, ballads and songs to be printed with appropriate music. *Purgatory* and *The Death of Cuchulain*, his last two plays, were written, and he rushed to Dublin to see the Abbey production of *Purgatory* for which his daughter had designed sets. The promised "de Luxe" edition of his complete works seemed about to materialize, and he set himself to the painful work of writing prefaces for poems, plays, and essays. He prepared for the press the first issue of *On the Boiler*, an occasional publication in magazine format which he intended to use as an organ for getting into circulation new work as it was written, poems, plays, or dogmatic essays which would "lay aside the pleasant paths I have built up for years and seek the brutality, the ill breeding, the barbarism of truth."

Much of the flavor of this time is caught in **Last Poems**. The section has two very clear divisions, the first—the poems bounded by "The Gyres" and "Are You Content?"—is a reprint of 1938's *New Poems* and was carefully edited and organized by Yeats. The rest of the section represents his rather more loosely integrated last work and was published after his death. "Under Ben Bulben," however, was certainly visualized by Yeats as a "final" work and is appropriately printed, and I suspect he would have approved the order, as a matter of fact, of most of the final poems.

"The Gyres" announces what will be the dominant theme of all the major poems that follow it. Though "numb nightmare" now determines world history, though the end of a historical cycle draws in sight, nothing that happens is of real significance. Ultimately the now-unfashionable gyre of "workman, noble and saint" will return; history will reverse itself. "We that look on," artists and philosophers—not participants but wise spectators—"laugh in tragic joy."

That the artist finds delight in the world spectacle is, of course, not a new idea in Yeats. As early as 1910 in his essay "J. M. Synge and the Ireland of His Time" he had explicitly underscored it:

> There, is in the creative joy an acceptance of what life brings, because we have understood the beauty of what it brings, or a hatred of death for what it takes away, which arouses within us, through some sympathy perhaps with all other men, an energy so noble, so powerful, that we laugh aloud and mock, in the terror or the sweetness of our exaltation, at death and oblivion.

Details of the poem have made critics sweat. ("Old Rocky Face" has been variously identified, to list only the most likely contenders, as Shelley's Ahasuerus, Yeats's own opposed Mask, and the "Rocky Voice" that speaks from the "cleft that's christened Alt" in "The Man and the Echo." No one, so far as I know, has suggested that it might be the Rocky Face of the moon which controls the gyres and which peers from the cavern of night, so that theory had best be tacked on, too.) But the central themes are clear. Yeats had once wasted time and energy sighing for the "painted forms" of the past, "but not again." Now he will accept the artist's god-like role of spectator, a role that necessarily wears a Mask contorted into the grimace of tragic joy. Though all themes are tragic, though the gyres whirl the world over and over again through cycles of triumph and necessary defeat, the artist, granted insights into the gyres' vast design and granted as well the creative power to fashion in his work equivalent designs, is free—as are all creators—to respond to the voice from darkness which articulates the command no artist dare reject, "that one word 'Rejoice.'"

"Lapis Lazuli" involves not only this kind of rejoicing but as well a whole series of themes that have by now become for Yeats standard fare: the recurring rise and fall of civilizations ("old civilisations put to the sword"), the nearness of our own civilization to its end ("Aeroplane and Zeppelin will come out,/ Pitch like King Billy bomb-balls in/ Until the town lie beaten flat."), and the triumph of art and philosophy over the "tragedy" of mere events ("All things fall and are built again,/ And those that build them again are gay.").

Though the themes are not unusual, the poem is made complicated by its form, for it seems to break into unrelated sections. Yeats loved a structure of this sort, using it in essays, poems, and plays. He presents sections of a work, planes which—fitted together by the reader—form a coherent object. The "form" of "Lapis Lazuli" is, in this respect, a sort of do-it-yourself poem. We are given sections of poetry which we must ourselves bolt together into final shape.

The opening stanza focuses on modern times (times bad as those of 1690 when King Billy of Orange pitched in bomb-balls at the Battle of the Boyne—and which found a modern counterpart in another King Billy, Kaiser Wilhelm II whose zeppelin and aeroplane had harried the English in the first world war). Even worse than the impending destruction, however, are those hysterical women who reject music, painting, and poetry—all "gay" art —in favor of politics, women like Maud Gonne and Con Markievicz who had lost their beauty and their voices in street-corner oratory. The rest of the poem, as a matter of fact, is a defense of the sort of art which they reject—an art which lets the artist face death without hysteria, with—instead—gay, ancient, glittering eyes.

The second stanza investigates the way artists' characters—fictional heroes—have met tragedy and death: "Hamlet and Lear are gay." Tragedy is wrought to its uttermost in their gaiety as they find and lose all that men have aimed at; for as both scenes and heroes literally "Black out" (Yeats is careful to keep all the imagery of this section theatrical), heaven blazes into the heroic heads. Such final insight—gay awareness of irrevocable defeat—is "Tragedy wrought to its uttermost."

The "Old civilisations put to the sword" which parade by at the beginning of the third stanza represent history's record of perpetual defeat and renewal. The artist, who contributes most to each civilization, will be as defeated as everyone else; but like his characters he will be gay in his defeat. Callimachus, the Athenian sculptor who in the fifth century B.C. had made the Erechtheum's "bronze lamp, shaped like a palm" (A *Vision*, p. 270) and who invented the running drill that afterwards was regularly used to simulate the folds of drapery in marble, was so thoroughly defeated by time that now only one dubious example—a marble chair—remains of his work. But individual defeat is not important to the artist, for he is man's necessary builder. And though he recognizes that "All things fall" he is also supremely conscious that all things "are built again."

The short fourth stanza at last reaches the object celebrated in the title, a lapis lazuli medallion that had been given to Yeats by Harry Clifton. On it was carved the figure of an old man and a servant.

The final stanza expands the fourth in very much the same way Keats expands the little town in "Ode on a Grecian Urn." Like Keats, Yeats moves into his scene. Not only does he present what is on the object; he presents as well what isn't. For the Chinamen of the fourth stanza are art-products. They are caught in static action, as Keats's villagers are caught. But Yeats—as Keats before him—is not content to see them in frozen motion, and he speculates about their destination. Thus by the middle of the fifth stanza, the Chinamen have gone beyond their place on the stone, have reached a resting place, have stopped climbing, have entered a "little half-way house," have seated themselves, and have settled back to contemplation of the "tragic scene" that is spread below them. The carving is abandoned for a world constructed in pure imagination.

To emphasize the imaginative nature of his scene, Yeats deliberately offers the reader a choice. For he can interpret the discolorations, accidental cracks, and dents of the stone in various ways. They can be taken as "a water course or an avalanche,/ Or lofty slope where it still snows." For each accident of the stone "seems" to have meaning, but that meaning—Yeats insists—is in the observer. The "meaning" of the work of art exists not in the artist alone but as well in the interpreter. "Meaning" hinges finally on the interplay that takes place between artist and art object, and between art object and audience. Yeats almost goes out of his way to establish this point. Though it might be snowing on that "lofty slope," he points out, it is equally possible that "plum or cherry-branch/ Sweetens the little half-way house/ Those Chinamen climb towards." For while Yeats offers tentative "meanings," we, reading the poem, must give them their final shape.

The Chinamen, having been lifted beyond the lapis lazuli scene to an imagined one, stare on all the tragic scene; and one of them requests "mournful melodies." These mournful melodies, reminding us that Yeats has already examined in the second and third stanzas drama and sculpture, introduce the musician and complete the trio of arts (visual arts, music, and literature) outlined in the opening lines of the poem: "the palette and fiddle-bow" and the poets that the hysterical women are sick of.

By this time, the reader should begin to see the scheme of the poem as something like this: Stanza I lists the three areas of art which, doomed to destruction, nevertheless go down to destruction gaily. Stanza II shows the gaiety inherent in tragic literature. Stanza III shows the gaiety inherent in the visual arts. Stanzas IV and V show the gaiety inherent in mournful melodies. Yeats also uses stanza V to integrate all of the materials he has drawn on before, locating on his lapis lazuli carving the "tragic scene" of the world and a singer of "mournful melodies," both of which induce the calm observing old Chinamen's eyes to glitter gaily.

When Yeats planned the poem he first saw it as an illustration of Eastern-Western differences: "Ascetic, pupil, hard stone, eternal theme of the sensual east. The heroic cry in the midst of despair. But no, I am wrong, the east has its solutions always and therefore knows nothing of tragedy. It is we, not the east, that must raise the heroic cry." Though this East-West division was certainly in Yeats's mind when he started the poem, it seems to me that in the finished version his interest has shifted to a focus on the three arts facing tragedy rather than on East and West facing tragedy (or more accurately on West facing tragedy and East facing "nothing of tragedy"). As a finished work it finds its theme in the conflict between art and those people of the world—hysterical women, to use his example—who would prefer action to contemplation, politics to art.

The poem is interesting too in its shift of tone from the first stanza's slangy, off-hand, deliberately "modern" manner ("everybody knows or else should know/ That if nothing drastic is done/ Aeroplane and Zeppelin will come out,/ Pitch like King Billy bomb-balls in/ Until the town lie beaten flat.") to the last stanza's elevated, formal dignity: "I/ Delight to imagine them seated there . . ./ Accomplished fingers begin to play./ Their eyes mid many wrinkles, their eyes,/ Their ancient, glittering eyes, are gay." Nothing in Yeats better illustrates his great control of language than this poem. It was, he felt, "almost the best I have made of recent years," and he was right.

"Imitated from the Japanese," a poem Yeats had adapted from a prose translation of a Japanese Hokku, reiterates his old-age "as-

tonishing" discovery of tragic joy and returns once more to the
dance image which he associated with experiences of insight.
Yeats's dancers move always in a self-contained coherent universe.
They experience an incommunicable sense of order. "Sweet
Dancer," the following poem, illustrates this sort of dance experience. Though the dancing girl seems "crazy," out of touch with
reality (her "bitter youth," her "crowd," and the "black cloud" of
worldly cares), she has in fact, Yeats argues, come at last to sweetness, to the discovery of artistic form and through that discovery
to ecstasy. Such an experience, larger than mere happiness, puts
her in touch with the supernatural patterns echoed in her dance.
Probably based on Yeats's disconcerting before-breakfast interview
with Margot Ruddock in Majorca, the poem is closely linked to
"A Crazed Girl."

Though Yeats from the beginning of his career displayed a
fondness for refrain, it is only in the late poems that it becomes
a characteristic device. Yeats's project in much of this poetry is to
root his form in whatever is most traditional, most of the people,
and at the same time to preach the necessity of an intellectual
aristocracy. Though these thematic interests brought him, almost
to his surprise, once more to political poetry, his conviction that
art is based in the uneducated masses helped return him to a careful re-examination of folk poetry. Diligently educating Dorothy
Wellesley in his ideas about the peasant foundations of art, he
soon found himself writing ballads and being educated by her.
At this time, he told Edmund Dulac, he wanted "to get back to
simplicity" and he decided that the best way to do it was "by
writing for our Irish unaccompanied singing." This project led not
only to ballads but as well to the grafting of ballad characteristics
onto conventional lyrics. The "Sweet Dancer" poem is a good example of the product that resulted, a conventional lyric made
public and a little strange by its ballad refrain.

An even more complicated structure was that which evolved
from his work on "The Three Bushes" and the related lyrics that

follow it. Yeats started the ballad as a kind of literary game, he and Dorothy Wellesley concocting a plot of shared love which each of them agreed to develop privately into poems. About half-way through the correspondence that arose as they compared drafts, Yeats decided that their poems could go into the *Broadsides* he was preparing for his sister's press. Though snags developed when he attempted to revise Dorothy Wellesley's work, in the long run their correspondence proved useful to Yeats, for he had to define and defend his own practice. As poems shuttled back and forth, Yeats became enthusiastic about the idea of expanding his ballad into a set of closely-related poems somewhat on the order of his *A Woman Young and Old.* Quickly, he settled down to serious work. He wrote songs for his character of the Lady, took time out to reassure Dorothy Wellesley that "There is no reason why you should not write a separate poem on the Rose Bushes," promptly offended her by making a whole series of revisions of her poem, apologized for his changes, made plans to meet her so that, among other things, they could "decide upon the name of the fourteenth or fifteenth century fabulist who made the original story," and wrote first as an independent lyric and then, very slightly revised, as his "Lover's Song" a six-line lyric suggested to him in part by Fragonard's painting "Cup of Life," in part by one of Dorothy Wellesley's poems ("Matrix"), and in part by an experience shared with her—a discovery of a kind of intellectual sensuality he had, he felt, never experienced before. By mid-November, 1936, the work on the series had become obsessive. Yeats wrote very quickly the two Chambermaid songs and shipped them to Dorothy Wellesley with a note explaining that he had decided to describe "*The Three Bushes* as 'founded upon an incident from the *Historia mei Temporis* of the Abbé Michel de Bourdeilie.' " Five days later he mailed another letter which included a revision of the Chambermaid's second song and a new song for the Lady (now "The Lady's First Song"). By this time Dorothy Wellesley, having been subjected to a good deal of criticism, was ready to criticize Yeats's work, particularly the "worm" image he had used; and Yeats, with a good deal of heat, defended his image: "The 'worm' is right, its repulsiveness is right—so are the adjectives—'dull,' 'limp,' 'thin,' 'bare,' all suggested by the naked body of the man, and taken with the worm by that body abject and helpless. All suggest her detachment, her 'cold breast,' her motherlike prayer."

By mid-December Yeats had completely revised his ballad and sent it to his sister as a contribution to the *Broadside* series. He was pleased with it and anticipated its appearance in the same set with Dorothy Wellesley's poem: "Do let me have your new ballad of the lady, lover and chambermaid," he wrote her. "I have greatly improved mine."

Borrowing the "O my dear, O my dear" refrain from "a Gaelic ballad" he had once rewritten for the 1908 edition of *The Hour-Glass,* echoing phrases and ideas from such diverse earlier work as "Baile and Aillinn," his own comment on that legend "Ribh at the Tomb of Baile and Aillinn," and the lyric "Three Things," Yeats nevertheless works hard to make "The Three Bushes" a good replica of a folk song. The foreshortened plot, the sharply characterized speakers, the rapid exchange of dialogue are exactly the sort of thing he found in *The Oxford Book of Ballads* which, a gift of Dorothy Wellesley, he kept beside his bed.

Though his ballad itself provides plot for the series, its themes are most fully developed in the supporting lyrics. The conflict between soul and body is dramatized when the subjective "daylight lady" struggles against her consciousness of sin and the objective chambermaid accepts "Strange night" which brings the lover to her. In spite, however, of the two women's determination to "cram love's two divisions" by each offering the lover only her own specialty, each cannot help speculating what it must be like to be the other. Each, in a sense, is Mask for the other and envies that thing which she cannot be.

Between them, however, they satisfy the lover and successfully "keep his substance whole"; and it is perhaps appropriate that the lover's six-line poem binds in its double "sighs" the Lady's third song ("All the labouring heavens sigh") to the Chambermaid's first one ("What's left to sigh for?"). Experiencing simultaneously the love of soul (thought, which sighs for "I know not where") and the love of body ("For the womb the seed sighs"), he finds "rest." He is, of course, deceived. But that, Yeats implies, is not of great significance. Like the bird, a symbol of wholeness, man sighs for the airy region of the soul's reality yet accepts peace that descends on a physical nest. Making, as he had done in "Leda and the Swan," the center of the poem the instant of consummation, Yeats balances rest against passion's sighs.

The design of the first half of *Last Poems*, those that had in 1938 been printed as *New Poems*, is exceptionally clear. "Objective" philosophical poems—"The Gyres" and "Lapis Lazuli"— establish the theme of tragic joy, while the "objective" ballad and related lyrics of "The Three Bushes" illustrate it. Following these, a set of five intensely personal lyrics locates tragic joy in Yeats and his friends. "Public" poems—epigrams and the new ballads Yeats was experimenting with—follow the personal studies of tragic joy and are rounded at the end by the retrospective "Municipal Gallery Revisited" and "Are You Content?" which summarize and criticize his total achievement.

The first of the five personal lyrics, "An Acre of Grass," looks back toward the sort of philosophical detachment Yeats had celebrated in "Meru" and which he had seemed to praise both in "The Gyres" and "Lapis Lazuli." Proper as that attitude is, Yeats here asserts, it cannot be maintained by the practicing poet. Though Yeats's "temptation is quiet," an old man's rest, that kind of quiet cannot lead to work of enduring merit. In spite of the fact that quiet gives him truth, it provides no machinery for working that truth into poems. Neither "loose imagination" nor the mind's casual focus on flesh (the "rag and bone" that it consumes) is enough to "make the truth known." That can be achieved only through mystical insight, and mystical insight comes only with "frenzy." Consequently the poet must overthrow the quiet man he has become; he must remake himself into the stereotype of mad old prophet: Timon, Lear, or Blake. Inspired by frenzy, his quiet will give way to an "eagle mind" that can "Shake the dead in their shrouds" and so justify itself.

"What Then?" reworks similar material through a chronological "poet's progress." As his *Autobiography* makes clear, Yeats and his father—if not his "chosen comrades"—were in his childhood assured that he would grow famous, and Yeats certainly crammed his twenties with the painful toil of copying manuscripts, editing anthologies, and learning vast amounts of what turned out to be useful occult theory. He did achieve the goals he set for himself: money, good friends, "A small old house, wife, daughter, son," and an international reputation as "great man." He even, in terms of that youthful dream of Unity of Being, "Something to perfection brought." Yet he, too, like "Plato's ghost," was obsessed with the notion of something yet to come, the mysterious untranslatable feeling that at any moment might be discovered the clue that would make meaningful the whole process. "All life," he had written at the end of *Reveries over Childhood and Youth*, "weighed in the scales of my own life seems to me a preparation for some thing that never happens," and it is this feeling that he draws on in these autobiographical pieces.

If "What Then?" seems to suggest that all the "meaningful" planned events of life are ultimately inadequate, "Beautiful Lofty Things" reverses the proposition to conclude that events trivial in themselves prove ultimately significant. Not only are events trivial in themselves asserted to be significant, but the whole youthful notion which lay behind "What Then?"—that a self can be deliberately constructed—is rejected. For the beautiful lofty things that have made life meaningful have been gratuitous experiences of personality, great unforgettable actions which merely happened yet which gave Yeats crucial insight into the heroes ("All the Olympians") who shaped not only his career but, in the long run, who shaped him. And each of those events, unplanned, was, he now asserts, necessarily unique: "a thing never known again." Defining as it does an anguish shared by all men—the feeling of helpless pathos before time's fatal obliterating impact, the irrevocable blow which cancels out all persons and things—the poem locates in the experience of individuals—in the valuation of them—life's "meaning."

Discovering the beautiful, lofty thing—what Joyce called an "epiphany"—is for Yeats of supreme importance. The significant act, the defiant necessary gesture which marks the individual as unique, is precisely that thing which the artist must capture if he is to create work of real value.

"A Crazed Girl" is, as Yeats points out in his seventh line, concerned with just this matter. For the girl he describes is "A beautiful lofty thing, or a thing/ Heroically lost, heroically found." The event itself that had been the foundation for Yeats's epiphany became public property when Margot Ruddock's "suicide attempt" was widely reported. Yeats, who saw no point in further confusing an already confused story, persuaded her to write an account of her early-morning visit to him and her subsequent peregrinations. Her short essay, samples of her poetry, Yeats's "A Crazed Girl," and a brief introduction by him were assembled in her book *The Lemon Tree*.

The events were in themselves uncomplicated. Yeats had corresponded with her about her poetry when he was assembling the *Oxford Book of Modern Verse*. Though he felt she was talented, he felt also that her work was undisciplined; and he was a little put out to find himself deluged with bundles of manuscripts which she expected him to criticize. Then, without warning, she descended on him in Majorca, demanding that he justify both her work and her life. He managed fairly tactfully to ship her off to Barcelona, but soon afterwards he had a wire from the British Consul that she had broken her kneecap after having "fallen out of a window." Her own account of these events ("Almost I Tasted Ecstasy") was the foundation for Yeats's poem. In her essay she described the death-wish that had prompted her to leave London and come to Yeats. But when she reached him, her terror was still with her:

Yeats read some poem about the sea. I slipped out when nobody was looking. I went slowly down the shore through the rain; I thought 'if I am to die something will help me', I stood on the rocks and could not go into the sea because there was so much in life I loved, then I was so happy at not having to die I danced.

In Barcelona, after she had broken her kneecap, she was sent to a hospital; but she managed to escape from the hospital, get down to the docks, and hide in the hold of a boat where, she said, she sang a song that began "Sea-starved, hungry sea,/ In a stretched hand humility." Yeats, who once more rescued her, found her shaken but sane.

Incorporating both her experience and her song into his poem, Yeats sees in her instant of crazed vision the naked experience of poetry, the view of the world that accounts for art.

"To Dorothy Wellesley" considers also the role of the irrational forces that go into the making of both the poet and his poem. Though the poet must be "Rammed full" of experience, though he must consume both the "sensuous silence of the night" and the dreaming darkened landscape, he must also, holding for the moment all objects under his control, wait. In that interval, powers, "The Proud Furies," will rise to him. Yeats who had heard his poem praised as "terrific" felt the adjective appropriate, that the strength of the poem lay in the feeling of conflict it engendered. "We have all something within ourselves to batter down and get our power from this fighting," he wrote Dorothy Wellesley. Great drama, he went on to say, demands that the characters give one the feeling that they are "holding down violence or madness . . . All depends on the completeness of the holding down, on the stirring of the beast underneath." His own poem, he felt, "should give this impression. The moon, the moonless night, the dark velvet, the sensual silence, the silent room and the violent bright Furies. Without this conflict we have no passion only sentiment and thought." The conflict in the poem was, he said, unplanned; but that conflict is essential to the artist. "That conflict is deep in my subconsciousness, perhaps in everybody's."

One way of expressing this basic conflict is in the creation of "objective" works, poetic Masks which will shape into a public form the subjective material the artist necessarily works with. The ballads and epigrams that follow are for Yeats such a Mask, this time a beggarman's one. "I speak through the mouth of some wandering peasant poet in Ireland," he explained to Dorothy Wellesley when he sent her the first draft of "The Curse of Cromwell." "I am expressing my rage against the intellegentsia by writing about Oliver Cromwell who was the Lennin of his day." He liked the poem, feeling that once more he had returned to the folk themes he had tackled as a young man but that now he approached them as a master. "I have recovered a power of moving the common man I had in my youth. The poems I can write now will go into the general memory."

Whether or not "The Curse of Cromwell" goes into the general memory, part of it, at least, Yeats would have been quick to assert, comes out of it. For the thesis behind the poem is that which Yeats claimed to find in *Anima Mundi* and which he turned to in his play *Purgatory*: Spirits after their deaths live on; the deserted house still draws to its ruined door those men and women of the past who had loved or hated it. Thus things and people "both can and cannot be." The spirit survives, though not the flesh; and the poet is still the servant of dead aristocratic swordsmen and ladies "though all are underground."

The two ballads on Roger Casement were a direct result of Yeats's reading *The Forged Casement Diaries*. Not only did the poems illustrate the sort of modern degradation he had used for subject in "The Curse of Cromwell," they also gave him an opportunity once more to defend things Irish against English corruption. The first version of "Roger Casement" had recklessly joined the name of Alfred Noyes to that of Spring Rice as a whisperer of slander, which disturbed not only Alfred Noyes but Dorothy Wellesley as well: "Please don't insist on this savage attack . . . Let us find out the facts first. If you were God Almighty I would say the same to you." Yeats, however, stuck to his guns:

"I could not stop that ballad if I would, people have copies, and I don't want to." But after Noyes had written what Yeats described as a "noble letter" to the press in which he suggested that an official inquiry headed by Yeats be set up to investigate the truth behind the diary of the purported "pervert," Yeats recast his poem substituting "Tom and Dick" for Alfred Noyes.

Like "The Ghost of Roger Casement," "The O'Rahilly" and "Come Gather Round Me, Parnellites" attack the "learned historians" who, Yeats maintains, rewrote history to blacken Ireland's reputation and brighten England's. But truth, Yeats argues, survives in the legends of the people, such legends as those he draws on, the handsome young saffron-kilted boy writing his name in blood "Somewhere off Henry Street" during the terrible days of the Easter Week Rising, or Parnell loving the lass sold and betrayed by her husband, Parnell himself betrayed by "The Bishops and the Party."

These legends, "stories that live longest," survive because they have entered the popular imagination, have become genuine folk material, "sung above the glass." And Yeats, as ballad singer, poet of the people, composer of drinking songs, carves a few more wrinkles in his beggarman Mask to make it that of "The Wild Old Wicked Man." This bawdy song, written—according to Dr. Jeffares—"to Lady Elizabeth Pelham," presents Yeats in one of his favorite roles, that of the wandering minstrel grown old, eloquent in sensuality: "Words I have that can pierce the heart." Though the wild old wicked wanderer is certainly not Yeats, there is also no question that Yeats well understood the emotions of a man whose last prayer would be " 'Not to die on the straw at home.' " Irritated from being too much looked after in sickness, Yeats was in these years filled with restless energy. "O my dear," he wrote Mrs. Shakespear in the spring of 1936, "as age increases my chains, my need for freedom grows. I have no consciousness of age, no sense of declining energy, no conscious need of rest. I am unbroken. I repent of nothing but sickness." Making his old man, "His stout stick under his hand," almost as virile as the "warty lads" whose warts, he explained to Dorothy Wellesley, were indications of sexual potency, Yeats is careful once more to side with flesh rather than soul. "I choose the second-best," the "coarse old man" explains as he rejects the "old man in the skies" for "a woman's breast."

The four epigrams "The Great Day," "Parnell," "What Was Lost" and "The Spur" contribute to this Wild-Old-Wicked-Man Mask. There is, as a matter of fact, a good deal of evidence to support the contention that in these years Yeats had begun to see himself as exactly the man of "lust and rage" he celebrates in "The Spur." He wrote to Ethel Mannin, for instance, of "My rage and that of others like me," a rage which, he felt, lifted him above all political issues. "We may . . . be the first of the final destroying horde." Parnell, the "lost king" of "What Was Lost," will be his only hero; he will welcome "revolution and more cannon-shot" because revolution brings the nightmare cycle to an end.

In a world gone insane, drunkenness is the only proper state for Yeats's perceptive hero who is, unlike other men, able to see the impending disintegration of all things; and "A Drunken Man's Praise of Sobriety" and "The Pilgrim" turn the world topsy-turvy as the Wicked Wild Old Man whirls into a dance designed to let him drink his fill and yet "stay a sober man." A serious parody, Yeats's gyrating drunkard moves in the elemental circles of that dance which brings sober vision to a dead drunk world. Similarly, "The Pilgrim," with its horror-vision of the nonsense syllables of the dead, sends a former drunkard on a search for enlightenment. His destination is ancient Ireland's holy island of Lough Derg. But neither fellow pilgrim, ghost, nor ferryman make an answer comprehensible to his sober ears. Even though he had seen Maeldune's immortal eagle hurrying to the waters of life, he "never stopped to question." In the end, he returns to the public house bearing back as a prize only the nonsense syllables which, sober, he will never understand.

All of these ballads, intended as *Broadsides*, were made public as possible. Yeats's project in them was to find a language which would assure them the widest possible circulation ("The young will sing them now and after I am dead," he wrote Ethel Mannin) but which would still give him an opportunity to preach his favorite dogmas.

Not all of them, of course, preached. "Colonel Martin," for instance, seems to be little more than the entertaining Galway story which Yeats had as early as 1910 used as an illustration in a lecture on the value of personality in dramatic art. Yet both in that lecture and in the 1935 ballad that Yeats constructed from it, Colonel Martin triumphs as a man of unique character. Like the action of "A Crazed Girl" or that of Lady Gregory in "Beautiful Lofty Things," the colonel's action becomes one of those epiphanies that give the artist insight into man.

The two remaining ballads in this group, "A Model for the Laureate" and "The Old Stone Cross," are popular statements of *A Vision*'s central image of modern degradation. Ironically titled, "A Model for the Laureate" traces the decline of rule from the first stanza's good and great kings, through the second stanza's beggar-kings and dictatorial rascals who—in spite of being corrupt —still managed to rule, to the last stanza's indescribably bad "modern throne" on which sits a figurehead run by "office fools" and celebrated by the "bought" cheers of "public men." Though poets might keep their lovers waiting in order to make honorific lyrics in praise of either the first or second stanza's rulers, "The Muse is mute" before the indecent corruption of the modern king. The "model" for the laureate is, consequently, silence.

"The Old Stone Cross" continues this attack. "This age and the next age," the final ones in *A Vision*'s cycle, necessarily "Engender in the ditch." Statesmen and journalists are liars. Folly cannot be distinguished from Elegance. But worst of all, reports Yeats's *"man in the golden breastplate"* (the observant ghost from the buried heroic past who peers out from beneath the "old stone Cross") are modern actors, naturalists all, who playing heroic parts —playing, say, the character of the golden-breastplate man himself

—"shuffle, grunt and groan" in their ignorance of the high stuff of tragedy, the "unearthly stuff" that "Rounds a mighty scene." Yeats, who had seen his Cuchulain subjected to Stanislavsky's "method," speaks with conviction.

Though "The Spirit Medium" seems to banish poetry and music, substituting for them a mysterious activity with the spade (both gardening and grave digging), "Those Images" expresses Yeats's determination once more to "make the Muses sing." Addressing himself in the opening line, Yeats struggles to abandon both the poetry of abstract thought (the neo-Platonic speculation that takes place in "The cavern of the mind") and the sort of political poetry General O'Duffy had tempted him to write (the "drudgery" that lets the Muse wander off to Moscow's communistic dogma or Rome's fascistic one). The real material for poetry, Yeats now claims, is in neither of these areas, but rather in an imagery founded directly on nature, "the wild"—an imagery of lion, virgin, harlot, child, and eagle. Balancing violent experience (lion and harlot) against peaceful innocence (virgin and child), Yeats hopes for insight through "An eagle on the wing." It is these five (I assume he links them to the five senses) "That make the Muses sing," for in the powerful correspondence between "the wild" and the supernatural, poetry is born.

Yet the images of art can also lead to poetry. And in "The Municipal Gallery Revisited" Yeats turns once more to "the images of thirty years," paintings which sum up his life, paintings which present his "permanent or impermanent images," and which in turn lead him to recollections of literary images "out of Spenser and the common tongue."

His great poem was itself a by-product of the effort of a group of his admirers to provide him with enough money to live out the rest of his life in comparative ease. Yeats insisted on thanking them publicly, and in a speech before the Irish Academy of Letters on August 17, 1937, both anticipated and summarized his poem:

. . . I think, though I cannot yet be sure, that a good poem is forming in my head—a poem that I can send them. A poem about the Ireland that we have all served, and the movement of which I have been a part.

For a long time I had not visited the Municipal Gallery. I went there a week ago and was restored to many friends. I sat down, after a few minutes, overwhelmed with emotion. There were pictures painted by men, now dead, who were once my intimate friends. There were the portraits of my fellow-workers; there was that portrait of Lady Gregory, by Mancini, which John Synge thought the greatest portrait since Rembrandt; there was John Synge himself; there, too, were portraits of our Statesmen; the events of the last thirty years in fine pictures: a peasant ambush, the trial of Roger Casement, a pilgrimage to Lough Derg, event after event: Ireland not as she is displayed in guide book or history, but, Ireland seen because of the magnificent vitality of her painters, in the glory of her passions.

For the moment I could think of nothing but that Ireland: that great pictured song.

A few days after making his speech he started work on the poem itself. By September 5, when he wrote a letter about it to his friend Edith Shackleton Heald, it was finished: ". . . about ten days ago I began work on that poem on my visit to the Municipal Gallery I promised in my speech. I had first to make the prose notes and then write the verses at a little over a verse a day. It is finished now—seven verses of eight lines each—one of my best poems."

Praising first those political heroes—Roger Casement, Arthur Griffith, and Kevin O'Higgins—whose devotion of their lives to an ideal imagined Ireland had moved him, he goes on to his real subject: the persons who in their lives had constructed him—crucial women like Maud Gonne, "Beautiful and gentle in her Venetian way," and Augusta Gregory, whose life had been so rich in life itself that no artist could have captured "all that pride and that humility"; and crucial men like Hugh Lane, "onlie begetter" of the collection of paintings on which Yeats looks, and John

Synge, "that rooted man." Lady Gregory and John Synge, especially, he argues, had helped shape the aesthetic which guides his
work, the aesthetic which holds that a great art must be aristocratic
in spirit yet rooted in the life of the people, that it "Must come
from contact with the soil." This "dream," that "of the noble and
the beggar-man," is the common element in their work which
gives it a claim to greatness.

These ideas are, of course, deeply embedded in Yeats's work
and had, as a matter of fact, formed the core of the Swedish
Royal Academy lecture which he gave in connection with his acceptance of the Nobel Prize. Reconstructing his speech in *The
Bounty of Sweden,* Yeats remembered with surprise his own
fluency:

> I am speaking without notes and the image of old fellow-workers
> comes upon me as if they were present, above all of the embittered
> life and death of one, and of another's laborious, solitary age, and
> I say, 'When your King gave me medal and diploma, two forms
> should have stood, one at either side of me, an old woman sinking
> into the infirmity of age and a young man's ghost. I think when
> Lady Gregory's name and John Synge's name are spoken by future
> generations, my name, if remembered, will come up in the talk, and
> that if my name is spoken first their names will come in their turn
> because of the years we worked together. I think that both had
> been well pleased to have stood beside me at the great reception at
> your Palace, for their work and mine has delighted in history and
> tradition.' I think as I speak these words of how deep down we
> have gone, below all that is individual, modern and restless, seek-
> ing foundations for an Ireland that can only come into existence
> in a Europe that is still but a dream.

In "The Municipal Gallery Revisited," not only does Yeats, as in
many of his last poems, dip deep into the race, he also turns to
his own writing as a source for imagery and ideas. The fox and
badger material of the fifth and sixth stanzas, for instance, is a
loose reference to his 1902 essay "Edmund Spenser" in which he
had pointed out Spenser's devotion to the Earl of Leicester: "The

great Earl impressed his imagination very deeply also, for the lamentation over the Earl of Leicester's death is more than a conventional Ode to a dead patron . . . At the end of a long beautiful passage he laments that unworthy men should be in the dead Earl's place, and compares them to the fox—an unclean feeder—hiding in the lair 'the badger swept.' " Echoing both his own note on Spenser and Spenser himself, Yeats points up the implicit parallel between his own patroness Lady Gregory and Spenser's "great Earl."

Turning, as it does, history into pageantry and friendship into art, this rich poem does more than eloquently define Yeats's final view of his work transcending its subject: its plain beautiful speech lets Yeats for an instant seem to speak not to an imaginary audience but directly to us. "You that would judge me" is addressed not only to an unborn future but explicitly to you who read this page and to me.

If Yeats speaks directly to us in "The Municipal Gallery Revisited," to the men and women who survive him and who therefore are, in terms of his poem, his judges, in "Are You Content?" he speaks to the past, the men and women who shaped the heredity of what was to be William Butler Yeats and who also, peculiarly, must judge the product that evolved through their loins into a poet. Evoking them in his opening lines, he calls on them as he calls on us in the Municipal Gallery poem "To judge what I have done." For their eyes, "spiritualized by death," can judge what his mundane eyes cannot.

This poem, which had been used to bring to an end *New Poems*, the last collection he saw through the press, prepares his reader for a final collection that Yeats never had time to put in shape. For, as he reviews his life and speculates about the ways in which he might spend his old age, he drums home dissatisfaction: "I am not content." Unwilling to be either a lazy infirm old man "Smiling at the sea," even though he smiles "In some good company," or what Robert Browning in *Pauline* had defined as "an old hunter talking with Gods," Yeats prefers to face death pen—

if not sword—in hand. He will die writing, discontented till the whole design be shaped.

The remaining poems in *Last Poems* introduce no new material, no really new attitudes; but they do represent an astonishing variety of forms and themes. It is almost as if Yeats—conscious of his impending death—were calling up characters, ideas, and poetic subjects for a last farewell, a sort of final benediction to his art itself. Relatives who had figured in his *Autobiography*, men who had taken part in the 1916 Easter Rising, Maud Gonne—all reappear; favorite characters return from his earlier poetry: Cuchulain, Oisin, Crazy Jane; Sligo scenery rises again into sight; favorite images—bird, tree, tower, his arrow-like star—once more parade by. One after another, he drags them back to sight for a last look before dismissing them for a final time.

This, I realize, is a sentimental attitude; but Yeats, in this respect at least, was something of a sentimentalist, and it seems not altogether unlikely that some such thought was in his mind as he worked over his last poems.

"Three Songs to the One Burden," for instance, reaches far back to construct its refrain from a remembered conversation with Mary Battle, his uncle George Pollexfen's second-sighted servant. She had described some supernatural women and compared them to the equally grand supernatural men of the country: "They are fine and dashing-looking, like the men one sees riding their horses in twos and threes on the slope of the mountains with their swords swinging. There is no such race living now, none so finely proportioned." Yeats never forgot those horsemen on the mountain, but as he grew older they became associated in his mind with powers of final destruction. "I am a forerunner of that horde that will some day come down the mountains," he wrote Ethel Mannin late in 1936, and they reappear of course in "Under Ben Bulben."

Rooting his first song both in Irish mythology (Manannan, the founder of Mannion's family, is himself the son of the Irish sea god Lir, and consequently "rich on every shore") and his own personal mythology (Crazy Jane), Yeats makes his Roaring Tinker a defender of the aristocracy. The second song shifts abruptly from mythology to personality, using as its central character Yeats's cousin Henry Middleton who lived near Sligo in a house called "Elsinore." But theme remains much the same. As Manannan in the first song has declined to Mannion and the rest of the world farther still, here Henry Middleton recognizes "The wisdom of the people's gone" and locks his gate against the "devil's trade" of the young whom he, pitying, bars out. The last poem, political, reassembles the "players" who had acted out the great drama of Yeats's time, that of Easter, 1916. Unlike the earlier two, this poem makes an ambiguous forecast (". . . who knows what's yet to come?") and brings us closer to that time when the horsemen come down off the mountain to obliterate present chaos and introduce a new antithetical order. It is this poem toward which the others drive. But together—mythological, personal, and political—they integrate in a common refrain the three areas of Yeats's greatest interest.

The dramatic monologue "In Tara's Halls," like the first of the "Three Songs to the One Burden," returns to mythology for its subject. One of the few of Yeats's lyrics to employ the bare poetic diction he had devised for his late plays, it seems, preceding "The Statues," naked. Stripped of rhyme, confined to one ironic image ("adventure"), it relies for its power on characterization, brutally direct speech, and carefully controlled repetition. (Repetition, as a matter of fact, substitutes for rhyme.)

"The Statues," on the other hand, is as complex as "In Tara's Halls" is simple. Yeats, who was attempting to account for modern Ireland and at the same time to reconcile differences between Eastern and Western philosophy, uses three groups of statues to correlate West, East, and Dublin: Phidias' "plummet-measured" Greek figures, a fat Buddha, and the statue of Cuchulain in the Dublin post office. (That this last statue was in his mind is clear from an important letter to Edith Shackleton Heald in which he explains that "Cuchulain is in the last stanza because Pearse and some of his followers had a cult of him. The Government has put a statue of Cuchulain in the rebuilt post office to commemorate this.")

Since the poem has been subjected to a number of peculiar readings, it seems best to attempt a straightforward paraphrase. The first stanza creates no great difficulties once one has decided what the "it" is that Pythagoras had planned. Obviously one reading of that "it" is the notion of number that makes possible the "plummet-measured" faces of Greek sculpture. Beyond that, we may be justified in speculating that he planned as well the consequence of number, the whole evolution of Western society. (Pythagoras here is a rough equivalent of the man who invents any abstract system—such a system, say, as that Yeats uses in *A Vision*.) But as Yeats goes on to suggest in his first stanza, such an abstract system is likely to seem to lack "character." Abstraction, however, is always the framework on which character is built, and Yeats assures us that the Greek boys and girls could respond to plummet-measured faces by pressing against them live lips. Passion could bring character.

But, the second stanza asserts, it is not the boys and girls, not even Pythagoras who brings that passion to the statues in the first place and in whom final greatness therefore resides. That greatness is in the artists who with "mallet or a chisel modelled these/ Calculations that look but casual flesh." It is the men who give body to the abstract system, the creative workers, who make any system meaningful. (To continue the personal parallel, it is Yeats as artist, the man who uses the abstract theorizing of *A Vision* as framework for poems, who is capable of greatness.) In Greece, it was these artists, articulating the Greek ideal, who really defeated the Persian horde at Salamis. "The many-headed foam," symbol of disorder in general and Asiatic "formlessness" in particular, was defeated by Phidias when he gave "women dreams" (the first stanza's girls have grown older and will continue to age until in the third stanza they are metamorphosed to "Grimalkin," the she-cat ancient crone who "crawls"—too old for passion—to Buddha's emptiness) and gave dreams themselves shape in his statues, gave "dreams their looking-glass."

The most important thing to see in the third stanza is that the image that crosses "the many-headed" is headed from West to East, is going from Greece to Asia and not in the other direction. Yeats makes this very clear in his letter to Edith Shackleton Heald. "In reading the third stanza remember the influence on modern sculpture and on the great seated Buddha of the sculptors who followed Alexander." The image which crosses the seas sits down, consequently, in Asiatic "tropic shade" and, because in the East, necessarily takes on the characteristics of that place. It grows "round and slow"; its "empty eyeballs"—similar to the empty eyeballs Yeats had observed in some Greek and Byzantine sculpture —know an Eastern rather than a Western wisdom: "That knowledge increases unreality" and that consequently all experience is no more than a hall of mirrors (in Hermes' formula, below mirroring above which mirrors below which mirrors above, ad infinitum). When Eastern gong and Irish conch signal "the hour to bless," the end of our cycle on Yeats's lunar clock, the old woman will crawl to Buddha's vision of emptiness and give her love to it.

The last stanza attempts to account for the heroic possibilities of Ireland. For "When Pearse summoned Cuchulain to his side," he summoned the as-yet-uncreated statue and all the potency of form which goes with art. By this act of invocation, "The Irish" may have freed themselves, Yeats insists, from the wreckage of modern times. They may, as Greece and as India, have found their definitive image. Climbing to "their proper dark" they may be able to trace out the lineaments of the hero of that "ancient sect" into which they were born and, shaping his "plummet-measured face," they may be able to define an Irish future which is a unique synthesis of East and West in the same way that Phidias had defined the Western future and that Alexander's sculptors had helped define the East's.

Though in such a short account of the poem it is impossible
to indicate the function of darkness, dreams, mirrors, and images,
perhaps merely singling them out will lead the reader to a structural analysis of the poem. Nor can I hope here to demonstrate
how that "fat/ Dreamer of the Middle Ages" is compounded from
Yeats's image of the Buddha himself, his theories about the fat
fool of medieval literature, and a remembered photograph of William Morris. (Morris's eyes, Yeats said in *Four Years*, were "like
the eyes of some dreaming beast" and his broad body was reminiscent of the fat fool of legend who "half remembers Buddha's
motionless speculation." Morris himself, of course, dreamed of the
middle ages.)

Like "The Statues," "News for the Delphic Oracle" is founded
on a notion of the essential interrelationship of mythical figures.
The sculptured figures of Greek gods, Buddha, and Cuchulain are
made parallel in "The Statues"; in "News for the Delphic Oracle"
the "golden codgers" of all mythologies, and some from history
too, sprawl about on supernatural grass. Yeats brings the Delphic
Oracle "news" of several kinds. For one thing he can happily report that Plotinus, who in the Delphic Oracle's poem was having
a rough swim of it, finally finished his salty crossing. He can also
report that several individuals the Delphic Oracle would have been
surprised to find on the golden shore are in fact there. Not only
does Pan have a cavern from which intolerable music descends,
but "Man-picker Niamh" and the man she picked are well established with the chosen, their wanderings ended. In case we are
worried about the geography of the place, the second stanza locates it not far from Byzantium. For the dolphins still ferry in innocents who, true to *A Vision*'s system, dream back through their
lives until "They pitch their burdens off." Like all immortals discovering the blisses of immortality, they find themselves uttering
cries which are "sweet and strange" in the laughing, "ecstatic
waters."

The nature of the song sung by the choirs of love, those who
proffer "sacred laurel crowns" to the newly arrived, might also

startle the Delphic Oracle. For their song seems to be sung to the tune of Pan's "intolerable music"; and the dance of the immortals culminates in an orgy. The naïve naked lovers of the third section are bemused by the delicacy of flesh; "But Thetis' belly listens" to Pan's pipes, and we can have every expectation that in no time at all Peleus and Thetis will join those nymphs and satyrs who "Copulate in the foam." (Readers who remember the significant sighs of "The Three Bushes" and its lyrics are, of course, prepared for the extravagant physicality of the last section of this poem. The clue had been extended at the very beginning when "the great water sighed," "And the wind sighed too," and man-picker Niamh "leant and sighed/ By Oisin," and tall Pythagoras "sighed amid his choir of love" and Plotinus, after looking about, surmised what was about to happen, "stretched and yawned awhile," and finally "Lay sighing like the rest." Poussin's *The Marriage of Peleus and Thetis*, a painting with which Yeats was obviously familiar is, as T. R. Henn makes clear, a primary source for the poem.)

"Three Marching Songs," now interrelated by mountain pass and tambourine and made eloquent by haunting choruses, demonstrates Yeats's careful reworking of material; but, haunting as those choruses are, they can hardly compare to the strange power of the refrain of "Long-legged Fly." Constructing his poem from three silences and the minds which move upon them, Yeats finds once more in the spheres of politics, of mythology, and of the arts figures to illustrate the function of the person who discovers through Unity of Being a power to move other men. First-stanza's Caesar is—as are all great men in Yeats's work—isolated. Like the man in Yeats's tower, his eyes are "fixed upon nothing" in order that mind may move upon silence and so gather to itself the supernatural power by which it will rescue civilization. Helen of Troy, too, is isolated in a "lonely place"; and as her feet move through elemental secret dance patterns, "a tinker shuffle/ Picked up on a street," she assembles the power that defines her, that will force the topless towers to be burnt and succeeding ages to "recall that face." And so too Michelangelo, the artist, operates in isolation, his hand tracing out "with no more sound than the mice make" the images that parallel those images formed by his mind's silent action. (Michelangelo's ability to move ladies to passion is later drawn on in "Under Ben Bulben" where "globe-trotting Madam" finds that a glance at "half-awakened Adam" sets "her bowels . . . in heat.") Military leader, dancing girl, and artist are made through their communion with quietness half-human, half-divine. Seers, unconscious or only partly conscious of the sources of their power, they create the world.

Whether or not Iseult Gonne had been in Yeats's mind when he described the dancing girl in "Long-legged Fly," it is certain that her mother served as model for "A Bronze Head." This lovely, generous portrait combines two of Yeats's most persistent themes, those of contemporary degeneration and the ravages of time. Setting his first stanza in the Dublin Municipal Gallery where Laurence Campbell's bronze-painted plaster bust of Maud Gonne was on display, Yeats studies her old-age aspect which, except for "a bird's round eye," is "withered and mummy-dead." Yet the life in that round eye gives her the supernatural quality that he had observed in Byzantine ivories in which, as he noted in A *Vision*, "Even the drilled pupil of the eye . . . undergoes a somnambulistic change, for its deep shadow among the faint lines of the tablet, its mechanical circle, where all else is rhythmical and flowing, give to Saint or Angel a look of some great bird staring at miracle." Like that of a "great tomb-haunter," that eye seems to be terrorized of its own emptiness.

Setting against the darkness of her old age the "magnanimity of light" she had once been, Yeats speculates about the complex nature of flesh which, changing, houses an unchanging thing, a thing that may never accurately be mirrored in the body. The last two stanzas return to the second line of the poem, expanding the observation that the head is "Human, superhuman." For even when he had first known her he had seen the human, the natural, the "wildness" in her. She seemed to him to have suffered a soul-shattering "vision of terror" which in turn made him "wild." But she seemed too to be "supernatural," "As though a sterner eye looked through her eye." Both terrorized girl and omnipotent judge staring "On this foul world in its decline and fall," she was —like his great heroines Mary, Leda, and Helen of Troy—mortal and immortal, girl and prophetess.

Constructing his poem around an imagery of natural and supernatural vision, he manages—as had the sculptors of staring faces whom he had praised in "The Statues"—to cloak his abstractions in the passions of the artist, to embody quite literally his "sleek," "most-gentle," "withered," "mummy-dead" "composite" in great art.

Maud Gonne had been loved as a woman of flesh and soul, but soul—through no fault of Yeats's—got the lion's share of love. Both "A Stick of Incense" and "John Kinsella's Lament for Mrs. Mary Moore," though in very different ways, remind us that there is danger in purely abstract passion, that we must found feeling in reality. As Yeats had noted in *On the Boiler*, ". . . we must hold to what we have [so] that the next civilization may be born, not from a virgin's womb, nor a tomb without a body, but of our own rich experience." "A Stick of Incense" versifies this idea; "John Kinsella's Lament" dramatizes it. Yeats's last ballad, and in many ways his best, it had been started on a visit to Edith Shackleton Heald. As much of the poetry of this time, it came very easily to him. "I have just thought of a chorus for a ballad," he wrote Edith Heald from Dorothy Wellesley's estate, "A strong farmer is mourning over the shortness of life and changing times, and every stanza ends 'What shall I do for pretty girls now my old bawd is dead?' I think it might do for a new *Broadside*." Eight days later, he enclosed a copy in a letter to Dorothy Wellesley from *Steyning*, Edith Heald's home: "I got it all upon paper the day after I arrived but I have worked on details ever since."

Startlingly different in diction, "Hound Voice" speaks not through Yeats's peasant Mask but through that different one of Old Prophet which he sometimes put on for Dorothy Wellesley. And though praising all "the women" that he had in his lifetime "picked," the poem seems to single out for very high praise Dorothy Wellesley herself, a woman who for years had been "companioned by a hound," who loved "bare hills," and who carefully avoided "the settled ground." But, as Yeats notes, all his ladies had experienced "Those images that waken in the blood." Maud Gonne, Mrs. Shakespear, Mrs. Yeats, Dorothy Wellesley—all of them had felt the supernatural sliding through their veins; all of them, though soft-spoken women, "yet gave tongue" to unearthly voices. The last stanza's association of Yeats and his ladies with legendary Irish heroes is, though faintly, intended to be prophetic. Modern seers and ancient hunters will make a rendezvous in death. There, no longer "slumber-bound," they will join, "wide-awake," a chase that ends with "chants of victory."

"High Talk" turns again to the artist in a degenerate world. Using his metaphor to attack naturalistic literature, Yeats points out that unless the artist puts on "high stilts" there is nothing to catch the eye of an audience. He himself, he explains, is not capable of the extravagant fantasy of past and better ages. ("Great-granddad had a pair that were twenty foot high." His own were "but fifteen foot" and they had been stolen by "Some rogue of the world . . . to patch up a fence or a fire." But now, for children and women's sake, he will "take to chisel and plane.")

"Malachi Stilt-Jack am I," he asserts; yet almost in the instant of asserting it he defines it as metaphor: "All metaphor, Malachi, stilts and all." And then, incredibly, he extends in the astonishing last three lines, metaphor to the entire world. The high flying barnacle goose, night that "splits" to let dawn break loose, the "great sea-horses" that "bare their teeth and laugh at the dawn" all combine—symbols of animate earth, air, fire, and water—into the vast violent stage on which the artist, now stretched to an immense figure, struts: "I, through the terrible novelty of light, stalk on, stalk on." Associated with all things that "run wild," sea, bird, and "the terrible novelty" of light itself, he illustrates "High Talk," the extravagant stuff that literature is.

Though Yeats's Malachi may be an allusion to the patriotic author of the twelfth book of the Old Testament Minor Prophets who had rebuked the priests for their negligence and who, like Yeats, had prophesied a coming time of judgment and punishment, more likely he is tied to St. Malachy, the twelfth-century saint who assisted Yeats's favorite Irish saint, Cellach.

"The Apparitions" turns once more to a variation of the scarecrow image. Founded on a series of death dreams (seven, rather than fifteen, according to T. R. Henn) that plagued Yeats in his last years, its focus is on the discovery of tragic joy that he had celebrated in "Lapis Lazuli" and that seemed to give meaning to the life of an aging poet. The joy, he contends, is needed "Because of the increasing Night/ That opens her mystery and fright." The "worst" apparition is, of course, that of his own empty coat.

"A Nativity" carries almost to the extreme edge of self-parody Yeats's fondness for the question as a literary device. Constructing from the answers to his questions a theatrical nativity-scene, he draws on painter Delacroix, poet Landor, and actors Irving and Talma for theatrical technicians worthy of the play he visualizes. But the central incident which their arts must work on is not a writer's invention but is instead supernatural in origin. Like the flare that fell through Mary's ear in "The Mother of God," "Another star has shot an ear" in this poem, an annunciation has taken place that, as in "Leda and the Swan," "Wisdom," and "The Mother of God," leaves the new mother "terror struck" before the impact of divine intercourse. This poem is typical of a large group of Yeats's later poems which are directly founded on paintings. This one seems to have been associated in his mind with the work of his friend Charles Ricketts, for he was careful to note in *On the Boiler* (Yeats always used his prose to provide indirect explications for difficult poems) that "Ricketts made pictures that suggest Delacroix by their color and remind us by their theatrical composition that Talma once invoked the thunderbolt . . ."

Though Yeats managed in most of the work of his last years to present the Mask of tragic joy that smiles behind "The Apparitions," "Lapis Lazuli," and "Under Ben Bulben," sometimes a contorted anguished face is visible by itself alone. Certainly it is this Mask of pain that Yeats wears in "Why should not Old Men be Mad?" "No single story," he insists, can be found of "an unbroken happy mind." Rather, man's stories are of men of promise who become drunken journalists, women like Maud Gonne ("A Helen") who, having accepted a "social welfare dream," climb on a wagonette "to scream." Faced with this kind of personal histories, an old man "should be mad." Punning on that last word, Yeats makes clear that an old man both ought to be angry and has every right to be insane.

Such a mad old man becomes the speaker of "The Statesman's Holiday." Yeats had planned the poem to appear in *On the Boiler* and prefaced it with a note explaining its genesis: "Here in Monte Carlo, where I am writing, somebody talked of a man with a monkey and some sort of stringed instrument, and it has pleased me to imagine him a great politician. I will make him sing to the sort of tune that goes well with my early sentimental poems." Though his old man is, of course, a fiction, Yeats may have been remembering his own days as a statesman and his experiences in the "great houses." G. B. Saul suggests that the "Oscar" of the fifth line may be "Oscar [Tschirky] of the Waldorf," but Oscar Wilde seems equally likely, which would support a reading of the "troop of friends" as the members of the Rhymers' Club who, according to Yeats's *Autobiography*, did talk of "odds and ends" when Yeats felt they should have been discussing artists' problems. Made intricate and rich by the opposed diction of the "modern" stanzas and their romantic refrain, the poem whirls finally into a dance, its rhythm pounded out to the beat of those twelve *with*'s and the "old foul tune" that sends the "Tall dames" walking for a last time "in grass-green Avalon."

If I am right in seeing these as poems of farewell, "The Statesman's Holiday" is Yeats's last look at the diction of his youth and "Crazy Jane on the Mountain" is his last look at that fierce old girl. This poem—which has cursing Crazy Jane discover in her old age and Yeats's something even worse than Church and Bishop, the inhumanity of modern politics which allowed George V to stick without a protest to his throne while his "beautiful cousins" of the Russian royal family were "Battered to death in a cellar" —sets up against decadent modern times an image of real royalty, Cuchulain and his spectacular queen "Great-bladdered Emer." Explaining in *On the Boiler* that "Emer is chosen for the strength and volume of her bladder," Yeats goes on to account for the importance of this strength and volume by offering another example from Irish mythology: "A woman of divine origin was murdered by jealous rivals because she made the deepest hole in the snow with her urine." Dorothy Wellesley, always delighted by color, suggested that he might do a separate poem on this theme. "The snow," she assured him, "gave the theme its poetry," and she added in illustration: " 'She made a deeper golden hole in the snow.' " Yeats, though impressed, did not write that poem.

In the poem he did write, Crazy Jane—confronted with her vision of past violent glory—realizes the paltriness of modern times: "I lay stretched out in the dirt/ And I cried tears down."

Like these poems, "The Circus Animals' Desertion" looks back on Yeats's early work. As does Crazy Jane on the mountain, he recollects—but now in his own voice—Cuchulain's "burnished chariot." He remembers the "stilted boys"—the young lovers of his early work (though being stilted they bear a family likeness to old Malachi Stilt-Jack of "High Talk")—and "Lion and woman," the sphinx which stalks so ominously through his prophetic poems. But no new theme for poetry arrives, and at the beginning of part II he reconciles himself to the enumeration of old themes. The correlation between an author's fiction and his biography quickly becomes his subject as, explicating *The Wanderings of Oisin*, he identifies Maud Gonne with Niamh. Maud Gonne had been the model, as well, for *The Countess Cathleen*. And yet, as he makes clear, the workings of an artist's mind can never adequately be explained. Though love for Maud Gonne had initiated *The Countess Cathleen*, "this brought forth a dream"—the play itself—"and soon enough/ This dream . . . had all my thought and love."

But it is not even the theme of a work to which an artist gives his devotion. He gives it to something even more abstract. It was not Cuchulain's fight with "the ungovernable sea" (the climax of *On Baile's Strand*) nor the "Heart-mysteries" that moved behind that theme which enchanted him. Rather it was "the dream itself," the dramatic structure of the work which was revealed in "Character isolated by a deed/ To engross the present and dominate memory." What Yeats is really saying in this poem is that for the artist, the problem of construction often becomes more exciting than life itself. Though Yeats's fictive ladies had been invented as "emblems" of Maud Gonne, once he had begun to think about them, "Players and painted stage" took all his love, "And not those things that they were emblems of."

Yet not even this is the final truth of artistic creation, and in his last stanza Yeats turns once more to an examination of the "masterful images" that he had made. That they existed is obvious, but he searches now for their source. And he concludes, as had a character in his youthful story "Rosa Alchemica," "that all life proceeds out of corruption." "The foul rag-and-bone shop of the heart"—what in "A Dialogue of Self and Soul" had been "that most fecund ditch of all" or in "Byzantium" the rejected "fury" and "mire" of human veins—is at the foot of the ladder of artistic creation. One end of the ladder, one end of the stilts Malachi Stilt-Jack walks on, one term of the extravagant metaphor that lifts poetry to the skies roots always necessarily in the junk-shop-grave —a place where rags are sold, and bones—of man's heart. That heart's progress through the poem (the word *heart* itself strategically placed in each section) becomes, of course, the poem.

"Politics," the little lyric that follows "The Circus Animals' Desertion," seems to illustrate its thesis. Once called "The Theme" and written as an "answer" to an article about Yeats which had appeared in the *Yale Review* and which had praised his "public" language but implied that he should use it on political subjects, the poem, he assured Dorothy Wellesley, is not based on "a real incident, but a moment of meditation."

The last four poems in *Last Poems* turn toward death. Yeats knew in these last months of his life that he could not expect to live much longer, but his mind was clear and only in the last days did he really see his death as an imminent thing.

Like the greater poem "Under Ben Bulben," "The Man and the Echo" reviews Yeats's life before turning to speculations about the nature of death. Yeats sets the scene near Sligo. His Man has climbed to the magical "cleft that's christened Alt" to ask questions of its oracular "Rocky Voice" that echoes out of a dark stone cave. "All that I have said and done," the Man insists, "Turns into a question." But being man, trapped in flesh, he never gets "the answers right." As he asks his questions, we realize immediately that he is Yeats himself. Did *Cathleen ni Houlihan* lead men to rebellion and death? Did his criticism of Margot Ruddock's poetry cause her to go mad? Could he have prevented Coole Park's destruction? Recklessly forgetting the prophetic rocky echo, he ends his questions with an assertion of guilt that brings Echo's quick reply, "Lie down and die." Yet the time is not ripe for death. That will be for Yeats when he reaches what in his October 9, 1938, letter to Ethel Mannin he described as *"The Critical Moment"*—that instant when "we enter by free will pure unified experience." This "true death" he feels can only come to the rare person who through analysis of the crucial incidents of his life has been able to purify himself immediately before his death in the instant granted him at *The Critical Moment*. It is this point of view that leads Yeats in the poem to assert that neither "a bodkin or disease" can give "release"; only the sort of philosophical speculation that he pursues, speculation that is designed finally to bring "in one clear view" an arrangement of the significant incidents of his "dirty slate," can lead him to the moment when he will be able to stand "in judgment on his soul,/ And, all work done," dismiss "all" and so sink "at last into the night."

Once more Echo has trapped him into a gesture toward death and commands "Into the night." Yet he has not quite made the final arrangement of thought. One question remains: "Shall we in that great night rejoice?" Man can be sure only of earth. All he knows is that "we face/ One another in this place." And then Yeats's Man's thought is lost—significantly in a death—as "some hawk or owl" descends from "sky or rock" to pounce on a "stricken rabbit." The rabbit cry—anguish screaming against death—distracts thought, lets the man momentarily escape the third imperative echo that will answer his last question and so send him into his grave. Yeats ends his poem in silence. But he knew, of course, his own work. And I suspect he hoped his perceptive reader would remember that the answer to the question "Shall we in that great night rejoice?" is both contained in it (Echo *must* answer "Rejoice!") and in his poem "The Gyres" in which the voice from the cavern knows no other answer ("Out of cavern comes a voice,/ And all it knows is that one word 'Rejoice!' ").

"Cuchulain Comforted" also involves a cry, though a bird cry, as Yeats takes his great character beyond that death he had given him in *The Death of Cuchulain*, the play he had in draft at the time of the poem and which he was making corrections on immediately before his death. Certain incidents of the play are so closely related to the imagery of the poem that they had best be summarized. At the end of the play Cuchulain faces the Blind Man who had been a character in *On Baile's Strand* and who will here kill him. Cuchulain's last two speeches anticipate "The shape that I shall take when I am dead,/ My soul's first shape, a soft feathery shape,/ And is not that a strange shape for the soul/ Of a great fighting-man?" The Blind Man, bringing his knife to Cuchulain's waiting throat, is the last man to hear Cuchulain speak: "I say it is about to sing." After dimming down quickly, the lights rise again on a bare stage on which stands a crow-headed woman, supernatural, *The Morrigu*, who immediately describes the men who gave Cuchulain his "six mortal wounds." As she finishes her speech, she fixes a black parallelogram, symbolic of Cuchulain's head, before six other parallelograms. Emer enters to dance before that head, moving "as if in adoration or triumph," and then stops suddenly, listening. All action has now ceased, and the stage directions make clear Cuchulain's transformation: *"There is silence, and in the silence a few faint bird notes."*

While the relationship between play and poem is obvious, Yeats hesitated to write the poem, waiting finally until a significant dream offered him details of the imagery. This presumably took place shortly before 3 A.M. on the morning of January 7, 1939, when he dictated the prose draft of the poem to Mrs. Yeats. (She reported both time and date to T. R. Henn.) Though the significance of Cuchulain's being welcomed by singing cowards seems obscure (unless Yeats wanted to suggest that Cuchulain's first experience in the afterlife would be precisely antithetical to his heroic actions on earth), the imagery itself is familiar. Birds once more appear in the trees, but now both trees and birds have been made ghostly. Eyes stare from insubstantial branches, timid "bird-like things" arrive to teach Cuchulain the customs of the place. Their action also involves a familiar image, for they explain " 'We thread the needles' eyes,' " and needles' eyes are associated in Yeats with the machinery of reincarnation (see particularly the poems "A Needle's Eye" and "Veronica's Napkin"). At the end of the poem, Cuchulain has taken up his shroud, begun to sew, and joined the twittering bird song with "changed" throat.

Yeats's last poem, "The Black Tower," presents a different kind of ghost. Cuchulain had been transformed, had lost personality in accepting the bird-shroud. But the "men of the old black tower" are protected by the ghosts of those men who, buried, "stand . . . upright." And though those upright bones shake in the winds that roar up the mountain, the living guardians of the tower, "oath-bound men," stand faithful to their lost king and lost cause. Like Yeats in being defenders of a defeated aristocratic order, they necessarily stand on guard against the bribes, threats, and whispers of those who carry the banners of corrupt popular politics. Prophetic, the poem brings us closer and closer to the end of the lunar cycle. In the second chorus one thin crescent of moon sheds "faint moonlight" into the tomb, but by the last chorus the tomb has grown "blacker," dark of the moon is about to arrive, and with it the cataclysmic end of an era which will hurl the old bones triumphantly back into the world. The old cook of the last stanza is, of course, a "lying hound" when he swears that the "king's great horn" is already sounding; for that horn cannot sound till the moon blacks out completely and the elemental transformation takes place.

"Under Ben Bulben" does exactly what it should do. It ends Yeats's work.

Through all of his life Yeats had dreaded the final word, the "last" statement that would end his last book. The sort of dissatisfaction that had ended *New Poems* ("I am not content") is characteristic of a man who found the only meaningful design to be that of antithesis. Over and over he explained to the public and to his friends (as he did in the letter to Ethel Mannin written three months before he died) that "To me all things are made of the conflict of two states of consciousness, beings or persons which die each other's life, live each other's death. This is true of life and death itself." A man himself, therefore, is in Yeats's scheme equipped with a double consciousness: a life-wish and a death-wish, if we like Freudian terms. And as a man grows older, as death daily increases within him, his joy in life necessarily grows. Conversely, Yeats felt, the younger a man is the more his attention is focused on death. But some time everyone's death-gyre must reach its perimeter, life's ebbing cone of light black out. By the summer of 1938, Yeats knew he had to begin the last poem, that—though it might not be needed immediately—it should be at hand. He started just in time. He had, when he dated the last draft "September 4, 1938," less than five months to spare.

The poem is a technical triumph. Yeats brought to it the easy conversational diction he had perfected in such "personal" poems as the Major Gregory elegy and the elegiac "Municipal Gallery Revisited." But here the elegy is for himself, a "cold" eloquent statement defining his convictions and spelling out in the last three lines, word by word, the epitaph that was to mark his grave.

The first section commands allegiance to his faith and quickly defines its two sources: the occult tradition rooted in ancient prophecy ("What the sages spoke/ Round the Mareotic Lake" and what "the Witch of Atlas knew") and the folk belief of the Irish peasants that he and Lady Gregory had so carefully investigated (the supernatural horsemen that ride from mountain to mountain, thundering on silent hoofs across the Sligo landscape).

The second section explicates the "gist" of this faith. From first to last it asserts that every man is subject to a whole series of reincarnations. All grave-diggers can do is to "thrust their buried men" back into *Anima Mundi*, "Back in the human mind again."

The third section with its paraphrase from Mitchel's *Jail Journal* offers as a "proof" of supernatural realities those rare moments of insight when we grow "tense/ With some sort of violence" and so are enabled to "accomplish fate." The man with such supernatural insight is able to "accomplish fate" because through that sudden instant of perception he is able to "Know his work." But to know it is not necessarily to do it. Parts IV and V are therefore directed to sculptors, painters, and poets, the artists Yeats best understood and whose work he valued most highly. Speaking now as practicing artist about to abandon his career to the young, he commands that they "do the work." They must "Make" man fill his cradles right by providing the necessary heroic images in which man can believe. (This idea is, of course, an expansion of that he had earlier articulated in "The Statues.") Painters and sculptors must remain in the main path that begins with Pythagoras and his theory of number and which, Yeats felt, could be traced most directly through Egyptian and Greek sculpture. For Yeats this path leads to Michelangelo's "Profane perfection of mankind" and Quattrocento's vision of Heavenly perfection. Calvert, Wilson, Blake, and Claude represent artists still in the great tradition, but they are corrupted because gyres run on—"the greater dream" has gone. Modern art, product of a historical cycle near its end, is characterized, in Yeats's eyes, by "confusion." Modern poets, too, have become "All out of shape from toe to top." Because they have forgotten or never known the great tradition of poetry, their language has become awkward, their themes corrupted. Only by turning to themes of peasant and aristocrat, only by turning to the past, can Irish poets create work which will gain them a future in which they will be "Still the indomitable Irishry."

In section VI and in the italicized epitaph, Yeats rounds to a close the "interesting" life he had projected as a young man, the life that he hoped would make him a great poet. Turning to the Sligo earth that he felt had made him, that earth, that piece of dirt, which as a young man in London he had so longed for that the longing had brought tears to his eyes, Yeats brings his reader down from bare Ben Bulben's head (where in his first section the supernatural horsemen had ridden) to that Drumcliff church in which his great-grandfather John Yeats had been rector, to the churchyard, to the ancient celtic cross, and finally to the block of native limestone "quarried near the spot," and, closer still, to the words, "no conventional phrase," cut "By his command" to commemorate the body beneath them and to send on his way the high horseman of the future, descended finally from Ben Bulben to harry the world.

A Yeats Chronology

1863: John Butler Yeats marries Susan Pollexfen.
1865: June 13: William Butler Yeats born.
1866: Susan Mary (Lily) Yeats born.
1868: Elizabeth Corbet (Lolly) Yeats born.
1871: Jack Butler Yeats born.
1871-75: Yeats educated by father who teaches "personality" in terms of Scott and Shakespeare.
1875-80 Yeats at Godolphin School, Hammersmith, England. Holidays in Sligo. Family moves to Bedford Park house in London.
1880: Land war brings family to Howth to take care of County Kildare property. Yeats enrolls at Erasmus High School, Dublin.
1882: First poems composed.
1884: Registers at Metropolitan School of Art, Dublin. AE fellow student. Father disappointed when Yeats refuses to attend Trinity College.
1885: First lyrics published in March issue of *Dublin University Review*. Yeats chairs first meeting of Dublin Hermetic Society.
1886: Art studies abandoned in favor of career as professional writer.

1887: Family returns to London. Mother suffers stroke which leaves her feeble-minded. Yeats joins Blavatsky Lodge of Theosophical Society in London, publishes first poems in English magazines, becomes literary correspondent for American newspapers *Providence Sunday Journal* and *Boston Pilot*.

1888: Meets William Morris, G. B. Shaw, W. E. Henley, and Oscar Wilde, Compiles *Fairy and Folk Tales*.

1889: Publishes first book of poems, *The Wanderings of Oisin and other Poems*. Essays, poems, short stories, plays planned. Editorial work, copying at Oxford; Blake edition begun with Edwin Ellis as collaborator. John O'Leary introduces Yeats to Maud Gonne.

1890: Joins Hermetic Order of the Golden Dawn.

1891: Founding member of Rhymers' Club and Irish Literary Society (London). *John Sherman* published.

1892: Founding member, Irish Literary Society (Dublin). Death of grandfather and grandmother Pollexfen. *The Countess Kathleen and Various Legends and Lyrics* published.

1893: *The Celtic Twilight* and three-volume *Works of William Blake* published.

1894: Meets Mrs. Olivia Shakespear through her cousin Lionel Johnson. Begins revision of all early poetry for first collected volume. *The Land of Heart's Desire* written, *The Shadowy Waters* begun.

1895: Editor: *A Book of Irish Verse*. Collected *Poems* published.

1896: Edward Martyn introduces Yeats to Lady Gregory. Moves to 18 Woburn Buildings. Tours west of Ireland with Arthur Symons. Meets Synge in Paris.

1897: *The Secret Rose* published. First summer at Coole Park. Speaking tours of England with Maud Gonne to raise funds for Wolfe Tone memorial.

1898: Travel: Paris, London, Dublin, Coole, Sligo. Work on *The Shadowy Waters*.

1899: Rehearses plays for first performances of Irish Literary Theatre at Ancient Concert Rooms, Dublin. *The Wind Among the Reeds* wins *Academy* prize as best book of poetry of the year. Visits Maud Gonne in Paris.

1900: Death of mother. Yeats succeeds Mathers as head of London branch of Golden Dawn.

1901: *Diarmuid and Grania* by Yeats and George Moore produced by Benson at Gaiety Theatre, Dublin.

1902: Founding of Irish National Theatre Society: Yeats, president; Maud Gonne, Douglas Hyde, George Russell (AE), vice-presidents. *Cathleen ni Hoolihan* produced. Lectures with Arnold Dolmetsch and Florence Farr on "Speaking to the Psaltery."

1903: *In the Seven Woods, Ideas of Good and Evil* published. Macmillan begins American publication. *The King's Threshold* written. First American lecture tour (40 lectures) financial success. Founding of Dun Emer Press by Elizabeth Yeats. Maud Gonne marries Major John MacBride.

1904: Opening of The Abbey Theatre. *Deirdre* written at Coole.

1905: *The Shadowy Waters* produced in London, immediately rewritten.

1906: Named director of Abbey Theatre with Lady Gregory and Synge. *Poems, 1899-1905* published.

1907: Yeats defends Synge at *Playboy* riots. Tour of Italian cities with Lady Gregory and her son Robert. John Butler Yeats sails for America.

1908: Eight-volume *Collected Edition* finished, complete revision of early work. *The Player Queen* begun for Mrs. Pat Campbell. Visits Maud Gonne in Paris, studies French.

1909: Death of John Synge. Editor: Synge's *Poems and Translations*. Meets Ezra Pound.

1910: Civil List pension (£150 per year) awarded with proviso that Yeats is free to indulge in any Irish political activity. Lectures in London to earn money for Abbey Theatre. Death of George Pollexfen.

1911: *Plays For an Irish Theatre* published. Meets George Hyde-Lees through Mrs. Shakespear, visits Paris with Lady Gregory.

1912: Abbey American tour involves arrest of actors in Philadelphia for production of Synge's *Playboy;* Yeats lectures at Harvard on "The Theatre of Beauty." *The Cutting of an Agate* (essays) published in America. Yeats forms second Abbey company in Dublin. Ezra Pound with Yeats, reads aloud in evenings, teaches Yeats to fence.

1913: Pound acts as Yeats's secretary. *Poems Written in Discouragement* (Cuala) published.

1914: American lecture tour. Joins Maud Gonne in investigation of Mirebeau miracle, writes unpublished account of investigation. Ezra Pound marries Mrs. Shakespear's daughter Dorothy. *Responsibilities* published.

1915: Winter in Sussex with Ezra and Dorothy Pound. Death of Hugh Lane on *Lusitania;* pictures controversy revived when Irish claim is rejected. Interest in Nōh plays stimulated by Pound.

At the Hawk's Well written, produced in London with Masks by Dulac, dances by Michio Ito. Yeats refuses offer of knighthood.

1916: Easter Rising in Dublin. John MacBride (Maud Gonne's husband) executed. Yeats visits Maud Gonne in France, buys Ballylee tower from Congested Districts Board.

1917: Proposes to Maud Gonne's adopted daughter Iseult at Coleville; proposal rejected. Marries George Hyde-Lees. Mrs. Yeats automatic writing begins on honeymoon in Sussex. *The Wild Swans at Coole* published.

1918: *The Only Jealousy of Emer* written. Yeats and wife supervise restoration of Ballylee. John Butler Yeats ill with pneumonia in New York.

1919: February 24: Anne Butler Yeats born. Yeats and family move into Ballylee. Yeats reluctantly refuses invitation to lecture in Japan.

1920: American tour with Mrs. Yeats. Sees father in New York for last time. Reading history and philosophy as background for *A Vision*. At work on *Four Years*. *Michael Robartes and the Dancer* published.

1921: August 22: William Michael Yeats born.

1922: Irish Civil War precipitated by Free State Constitution. February 2: Death of John Butler Yeats. *The Trembling of the Veil* published. Yeats invited to become member of Irish Senate, attends faithfully. D.Litt. conferred by Trinity College. Proofs corrected for Macmillan's Collected Edition; *A Vision* underway.

1923: November: Nobel Prize for literature awarded. Accepts in person, writes *The Bounty of Sweden*.

1924: Tour of Sicily, Capri and Rome with Mrs. Yeats.

1925: Visit to Milan. Lectures in Switzerland. Irish Senate speech on divorce. First version of *A Vision* printed.

1926: *Oedipus the King* adapted for Abbey. *The Plough and the Stars* riots at Abbey.

1927: *Oedipus at Colonus* completed. Major speeches in Senate. Lung congestion and influenza lead to collapse, order to take complete rest.

1928: Moves to Rapallo with family. Term as Senator ends; because of poor health, refuses to stand for re-election. Begins *A Packet for Ezra Pound*. *The Tower* published.

1929: Last visit to Ballylee. *Fighting the Waves* produced in Dublin with Ninette de Valois dancing. December 21: collapse in Rapallo from Malta fever.

1930: *The Words on the Window-Pane* written.

1931: First winter in Ireland since illnesses begin. May: D.Litt. degree from Oxford. August: last summer visit with Lady Gregory at Coole.

1932: May: Death of Lady Gregory. Yeats organizes Irish Academy of Letters. Last American lecture tour, profits for Irish Academy.

1933: Cambridge degree awarded. *The King of the Great Clock Tower* written. *The Winding Stair* (Macmillan) published.

1934: Steinach rejuvenation operation performed, Yeats regarding it as successful. May: trip to Rapallo to bring back furniture. *Wheels and Butterflies* published.

1935: Lung congestion returns. *Oxford Book of Modern Verse* underway. *A Full Moon in March* published. Seventieth birthday banquet. Meets Dorothy Wellesley, goes to Majorca with Swami Shri Purohit for winter, assists him in translation of *The Upanishads*. *The Herne's Egg* begun. First *Broadsides* published.

1936: Ill with "breathlessness." Margot Ruddock's suicide attempt. BBC lecture on Modern Poetry.

1937: Four BBC broadcasts. Revision of *A Vision* published. *Essays 1931-1936* published.

1938: Moves to south of France. *On the Boiler written.* May: Begins *Purgatory.* August: Last speech at Abbey Theatre on opening of *Purgatory.* October: Death of Olivia Shakespear. December: *Death of Cuchulain* begun.

1939: Sudden illness, Thursday, January 26. Death, Saturday, January 28. Burial: Roquebrune, France.

1948: September: Yeats's body returned to Ireland on Irish corvette *Macha.* Body piped ashore at Galway. Mrs. Yeats, Yeats's children, and Jack Yeats accompany funeral procession to Sligo. Military guard of honor at Sligo: government representative, Mr. Sean MacBride, Minister for External Affairs (Maud Gonne's son). Burial at Drumcliffe "under bare Ben Bulben's head" with stone inscribed as directed in "Under Ben Bulben."

Obviously the most important books for the person interested in Yeats are Yeats's own works: particularly the *Autobiography* (in early editions titled, more accurately, *Autobiographies*), *A Vision*, Yeats's essays, the *Collected Plays*, and Allan Wade's brilliant edition of Yeats's letters. All of these are published by Macmillan, the *Autobiography* being also available in a paperback edition published by Anchor Books.

Of the numerous studies of Yeats's poetry that have been attempted since Yeats's death, those which are likely to be of most use to the general reader are Richard Ellmann's two volumes, *Yeats, The Man and the Masks* and *The Identity of Yeats* (both published by Macmillan, *Masks* being also published in an Everyman paperback edition), Donald A. Stauffer's *The Golden Nightingale* (Macmillan), and T. R. Henn's *The Lonely Tower* (Methuen). Joseph Hone's *W. B. Yeats* (Macmillan) is the only biography that has yet been published, though A. Norman Jeffares *W. B. Yeats, Man and Poet* (Yale University Press) contains considerable biographical information not elsewhere in print.

For the Yeats scholar, three books are of particular value. Allan Wade's *A Bibliography of the Writings of W. B. Yeats* (one of the *Soho Bibliographies* published by Hart-Davis in London), carefully revised in its second edition, is both comprehensive and accurate in cataloguing Yeats's publications. A great bibliography, it is supplemented in part by George Brandon Saul's *Prolegomena to the Study of Yeats's Poems* (University of Pennsylvania Press) which locates the principal critical studies of each of Yeats's poems and which contains the best list of books and articles about Yeats that has to date been compiled. Allt and Alspach's *The Variorum Edition of the Poems of W. B. Yeats* (Macmillan) is an indispensable volume for the Yeats scholar who does not have access to a complete collection of first editions of the poems with all of their variant readings.

Index